Shakespeare and Postcolonial Theory

ARDEN SHAKESPEARE AND THEORY

Series Editor: Evelyn Gajowski

AVAILABLE TITLES

Shakespeare and Cultural Materialist Theory
Christopher Marlow
Shakespeare and Economic Theory David Hawkes
Shakespeare and Ecocritical Theory Gabriel Egan
Shakespeare and Ecofeminist Theory Rebecca Laroche and
Jennifer Munroe
Shakespeare and Feminist Theory Marianne Novy
Shakespeare and New Historicist Theory Neema Parvini
Shakespeare and Posthumanist Theory Karen Raber
Shakespeare and Psychoanalytic Theory Carolyn Brown
Shakespeare and Queer Theory Melissa E. Sanchez

FORTHCOMING TITLES

Shakespeare and Adaptation Theory Sujata Iyengar
Shakespeare and Performance Theory David McCandless
Shakespeare and Presentist Theory Evelyn Gajowski
Shakespeare and Race Theory Arthur L. Little, Jr.
Shakespeare and Reception Theory Nigel Wood
Shakespeare and Textual Theory Suzanne Gossett

Shakespeare and Postcolonial Theory

Jyotsna G. Singh

THE ARDEN SHAKESPEARE
LONDON • NEW YORK • OXFORD • NEW DELHI • SYDNEY

THE ARDEN SHAKESPEARE
Bloomsbury Publishing Plc
50 Bedford Square, London, WC1B 3DP, UK
1385 Broadway, New York, NY 10018, USA

BLOOMSBURY, THE ARDEN SHAKESPEARE and the Arden Shakespeare logo
are trademarks of Bloomsbury Publishing Plc

First published in Great Britain 2019
This paperback edition published 2020

Copyright © Jyotsna G. Singh, 2019, 2020

Jyotsna G. Singh has asserted her right under the Copyright, Designs and
Patents Act, 1988, to be identified as the author of this work.

For legal purposes the Acknowledgements on pp. x–xi constitute an extension
of this copyright page.

Series design by Sutchinda Rangsi Thompson
Cover image © Alexander Sviridovt/Shutterstock

All rights reserved. No part of this publication may be reproduced or transmitted
in any form or by any means, electronic or mechanical, including photocopying,
recording, or any information storage or retrieval system, without prior
permission in writing from the publishers.

Bloomsbury Publishing Plc does not have any control over, or responsibility for,
any third-party websites referred to or in this book. All internet addresses given
in this book were correct at the time of going to press. The author and publisher
regret any inconvenience caused if addresses have changed or sites have
ceased to exist, but can accept no responsibility for any such changes.

A catalogue record for this book is available from the British Library.

Library of Congress Cataloging-in-Publication Data
Names: Singh, Jyotsna G., 1951- author.
Title: Shakespeare and postcolonial theory / Jyotsna G. Singh.
Description: London, UK ; New York, NY : The Arden Shakespeare, 2019. |
Series: Arden Shakespeare and theory | Includes
bibliographical references and index.
Identifiers: LCCN 2018055713 (print) | LCCN 2018058714
(ebook) | ISBN 9781408185261 (ePub) | ISBN 9781408186053
(ePDF) | ISBN 9781408185742(hardback)
Subjects: LCSH: Shakespeare, William, 1564-1616–Criticism and interpretation. |
Shakespeare, William, 1564-1616–Influence. | Postcolonialism in literature.
Classification: LCC PR2976 (ebook) | LCC PR2976 .S475 2019
(print) | DDC 822.3/3–dc23
LC record available at https://lccn.loc.gov/2018055713

ISBN:	HB:	978-1-4081-8574-2
	PB:	978-1-4081-8554-4
	ePDF:	978-1-4081-8605-3
	eBook:	978-1-4081-8526-1

Series: Shakespeare and Theory

Typeset by Integra Software Services Pvt. Ltd.

To find out more about our authors and books visit www.bloomsbury.com and
sign up for our newsletters.

For Rhea and Shreya

CONTENTS

List of Figures ix
Acknowledgements x
Abbreviations xii
Series Editor's Preface xiii

Introduction: 'An Inventory of Traces' 1

PART ONE Shakespeare and Early Colonial History 21

1 Historical Contexts 1: Shakespeare and the Colonial Imaginary 23

2 Historical Contexts 2: Shakespeare's World and Productions of Difference 57

PART TWO Shakespeare, Decolonization, Postcolonial Theory 79

3 Past and Present: Shakespeare–Postcoloniality 81

4 Intersectionalities: Postcoloniality and Difference 101

PART THREE Shakespeare, Postcoloniality, and Reception Histories: Performance and Film 125

5 Global, Inter-cultural Shakespeares 127

6 Boundary Crossings on the British Shakespearean Stage 149

7 Shakespeare in Postcolonial Cinema: A Meditation on *Haider/Hamlet* 177

Appendix 195
Notes 197
References 217
Index 237

LIST OF FIGURES

1. *Antony and Cleopatra*, 2017. Josette Simon as Cleopatra. Directed by Iqbal Khan. Photo by Helen Maybanks © RSC   111

2. *Othello*, 2015. An enraged Othello with Iago. Directed by Iqbal Khan. Photo by Keith Pattison © RSC   156

3. A scene from Dash Arts' *A Midsummer Night's Dream* (2007), The Roundhouse, London. Directed by Tim Supple. Photo by Tristram Kenton   161

4. *A Midsummer Night's Dream*, The Globe, London, 2015. The Fairies and Bottom, with the Sitar Player. Directed by Emma Rice. Photo by Steve Tanner   167

5. *Much Ado About Nothing*, 2012. Beatrice and Benedick. Directed by Iqbal Khan. Photo by Ellie Kurttz © RSC   172

6. *Much Ado About Nothing*, 2012. Leonato and Hero at the Wedding. Directed by Iqbal Khan. Photo by Ellie Kurttz © RSC   173

ACKNOWLEDGEMENTS

A big thanks to Evelyn Gajowski for making this book possible, and for her support and comments as the project progressed. For me, it has been a rich journey into a field with which my academic explorations began, while also allowing me a chance to look ahead at promising, unforeseen directions of postcoloniality, so aptly evoked by Shakespeare: 'To unpath'd waters, undream'd shores' (*The Winter's Tale*, 4.4).

It has been a pleasure working with The Arden Shakespeare, and a special thanks to Margaret Bartley, Mark Dudgeon, and Lara Bateman, especially for your profound patience in terms of my need for more time. I am honoured to be part of this series.

For providing astute and productive comments on partial drafts as my project evolved, my special thanks to Abdulhamit Arvas, Dennis Britton, Nandini Das, Margaret Litvin, Neema Parvini, Amrita Sen, Gitanjali Shahani, and Emily Yates.

Farther afield, in the interlocking worlds of Shakespeare, postcolonial, and race studies, I am indebted to the work of several scholars and theatre practitioners, who have engaged and inspired me. Some contributions from them figure in this volume: Bernadette Andrea, Mark Thornton Burnett, Christy Desmet, Craig Dionne, Matthew Dimmock, Kim Hall, Alexa Huang, now known as Alexa Alice Joubin, Sujata Iyengar, David Johnson, Parmita Kapadia, Arthur Little, Michael Neill, Martin Orkin, Francesca Royster, Rob Roznowski, Ian Smith, Tim Supple, Ayanna Thompson, Shormishta Panja, Imtiaz Habib, Delia Jarrett-Macauley, and Virginia Mason Vaughan.

Finally, thanks to Iqbal Khan for sharing his work and ideas. His Shakespearean productions opened up new and exciting worlds for me.

Greg McClure, my student assistant, offered valuable research help throughout the process. Thanks to Sandra Beals who helped me enormously in getting the manuscript ready for submission.

Finally, on lighter touch, gratitude to my friends running the Chapelure café – often my scene of writing – for their excellent libations. And also, thanks to my friends, Gordon Stewart, and Reshma Sambare and Stuart McCracken for stimulating conversations, and always timely hospitality.

ABBREVIATIONS

ANC	African National Congress (South Africa)
MIT	Massachusetts Institute of Technology
The National	National Theatre, London
RSC	Royal Shakespeare Company, Stratford-Upon-Avon
TLS	*Times Literary Supplement*
West End	A common term for mainstream professional theatre, staged in large theatres in or near the West End of London

SERIES EDITOR'S PREFACE

'Asking questions about literary texts – that's literary criticism. Asking "Which questions shall we ask about literary texts?"– that's literary theory'. So goes my explanation of the current state of English studies and Shakespeare studies, in my never-ending attempt to demystify and simplify theory for students in my classrooms. Another way to put it is that theory is a systematic account of the nature of literature, the act of writing and the act of reading.

One of the primary responsibilities of any academic discipline – whether in the natural sciences, the social sciences or the humanities – is to examine its methodologies and tools of analysis. Particularly at a time of great theoretical ferment, such as that which has characterized English studies and Shakespeare studies, in recent years, it is incumbent upon scholars in a given discipline to provide such reflection and analysis. We all construct meanings in Shakespeare's texts and culture. Shouldering responsibility for our active role in constructing meanings in literary texts, moreover, constitutes a theoretical stance. To the extent that we examine our own critical premises and operations, that theoretical stance requires reflection on our part. It requires honesty, as well. It is thereby a fundamentally radical act. All critical analysis puts into practice a particular set of theoretical premises. Theory occurs from a particular standpoint. There is no critical practice that is somehow devoid of theory. There is no critical practice that is not implicated in theory. A commonsense, transparent encounter with any text is thereby impossible. Indeed, to the extent that theory requires us to question anew that with which we thought we were familiar, that which we thought we understood, theory constitutes a critique of common sense.

Since the advent of postmodernism, the discipline of English studies has undergone a seismic shift. The discipline of Shakespeare studies has been at the epicentre of this shift. Indeed, it has been Shakespeare scholars who have played a major role in several of the theoretical and critical developments (e.g. new historicism, cultural materialism, presentism) that have shaped the discipline of English studies in recent years. Yet a comprehensive scholarly analysis of these crucial developments has yet to be done and is long overdue. As the first series to foreground analysis of contemporary theoretical developments in the discipline of Shakespeare studies, *Arden Shakespeare and Theory* aims to fill a yawning gap.

To the delight of some and the chagrin of others, since 1980 or so, theory has dominated Shakespeare studies. *Arden Shakespeare and Theory* focuses on the state of the art at the outset of the twenty-first century. For the first time, it provides a comprehensive analysis of the theoretical developments that are emerging at the present moment, as well as those that are dominant or residual in Shakespeare studies.

Each volume in the series aims to offer the reader the following components: to provide a clear definition of a particular theory; to explain its key concepts; to trace its major developments, theorists and critics; to perform a reading of a Shakespeare text; to elucidate a specific theory's intersection with or relationship to other theories; to situate it in the context of contemporary political, social, and economic developments; to analyse its significance in Shakespeare studies; and to suggest resources for further investigation. Authors of individual volumes thereby attempt to strike a balance, bringing their unique expertise, experience, and perspectives to bear upon particular theories while simultaneously fulfilling the common purpose of the series. Individual volumes in the series are devoted to elucidating particular theoretical perspectives, such as adaptation, cultural materialism, ecocriticism, ecofeminism, economic theory, feminism, film theory, new historicism, postcolonialism, posthumanism, presentism, psychoanalysis, queer theory, and race theory.

Arden Shakespeare and Theory aims to enable scholars, teachers and students alike to define their own theoretical strategies and refine their own critical practices. And students have as much at stake in these theoretical and critical enterprises – in the reading and the writing practices that characterize our discipline – as do scholars and teachers. Janus-like, the series looks forward as well as backward, serving as an inspiration and a guide for new work in Shakespeare studies at the outset of the twenty-first century, on the one hand, and providing a retrospective analysis of the intellectual labour that has been accomplished in recent years, on the other.

To return to the beginning: What is at stake in our reading of literary texts? Once we come to understand the various ways in which theory resonates with not only Shakespeare's texts and literary texts, but also the so-called 'real' world – the world outside the world of the mind, the world outside the world of academia – then we come to understand that theory is capable of powerfully enriching not only our reading of Shakespeare's texts, and literary texts, but also our lives.

* * *

I am indebted to David Avital, publisher at Bloomsbury Academic, who was instrumental in developing the idea of the *Arden Shakespeare and Theory* series. I am also grateful to Margaret Bartley and Mark Dudgeon, publishers for the Arden Shakespeare, for their guidance and support throughout the development of this series.

Evelyn Gajowski
Series Editor
University of Nevada, Las Vegas

Introduction:
'An Inventory of Traces'

Why did Shakespeare choose Othello, a Moor, a racialized 'other', as the protagonist of one of his classic tragedies? Did Shakespeare and his contemporaries have any direct contact with peoples from Africa, with New World 'Indians', with Jews, and with Asian East Indians? Did Prospero's relationship with Caliban invoke a colonial allegory of Western 'discoveries' of the New World? Why did Shakespeare insert the figures of the 'Indian boy' and the Indian 'votaress' with evocative associations of 'India' in *A Midsummer Night's Dream*? Such questions lead us to consider whether the Shakespearean era was a period of an emergent, Western global colonialism (which some define as proto-colonialism).[1] Individually, some of these references may seem fleeting and innocuous – mere 'traces' – but they also function as signposts for the imaginative

---

The title of the 'Introduction' is taken from Edward Said's (1979) formulation below:

> In *The Prison Notebooks*, Gramsci says, 'The starting-point of critical elaboration is the consciousness of what one really is, and [of] "knowing thyself" as a product of the historical process to date, which has deposited in you an infinity of traces, without leaving an inventory ... therefore it is imperative at the outset to compile such an inventory'. (25)

All quotations from Edward Said's *Orientalism* (1979) are taken from this edition (New York: Vintage Books). However, it was first published in 1978 (New York: Pantheon Books).

'travels' of the plays across varied racial, religious, geopolitical, cultural and sexual boundaries, as well as markers for shifting modalities of difference and alterity represented in them. It is from such questions that we can trace the genesis of postcolonial Shakespeare studies.

These concerns raised in relation to Shakespeare's plays have only increased in relevance and urgency since the 1980s to our contemporary global era, given the growing ideological struggles for racial, gender, and social equality – as well as the need for understanding across nations and religions. And in today's world, I believe, Prospero's iconic line in *The Tempest* (5.1), pointing to Caliban: 'This Thing of Darkness/I acknowledge mine', continues to reverberate suggestively; it calls upon wide-ranging audiences to recognize marginalized communities and accept 'otherness', even if under duress. Even in its most beneficent implications, Prospero's acknowledgement of Caliban prevents any sense of moral closure to his magical interventions. As the all-powerful Magus, he breaks the illusion of the stage, providing an aesthetically satisfying bond with the audience in the epilogue; and as Prospero's magic is stilled, we, the audience, have to leave the island. And yet, Prospero seems to seek validation and forgiveness from the audience, while Caliban sues for 'Grace' and repudiates Stefano and Trinculo as the wrongly chosen masters.

For some audiences, Caliban's enslavement by Prospero's magic may not be completely forgotten. Issues of legitimacy and authority – of the rightful ownership of the island – it seems, are simply deferred in the (desired) applause of the spectators. These very issues continue to concern us as the forces of globalization spawn new mutations of postcoloniality – of differences, inequities, hierarchies, and exploitations – that mark our own times and continue to haunt our readings of Shakespeare's play, as well as his other works representing the global early modern. While Shakespeare's emergent colonial engagement with New World 'discoveries' in *The Tempest* may seem distant, its evocation of threatening and denigrated 'others' – 'Thing[s] of darkness' – of our neo-liberal globalization continue to lurk in the shadows in the twenty-first century, a period that, 'post 9/11', one critic defines as 'our colonial present' (Gregory 2004: 1–5).

Thus, in recognizing colonialism – and its continuing effects – as a viable, ongoing historical category, while launching postcolonial explorations into Shakespeare's works, we are led to ask: 'What is postcolonial theory?' Put simply, it is an academic study of the cultural legacy of European colonialism, showing how the literature of former colonial powers represented and often distorted colonial history and the experiences of the native subjects and, how, in turn, colonized peoples articulated and reclaimed their identity and history by interrogating European culture and history. Thus, postcolonial criticism is interested in the shaping power of European discourse about the 'East', identified by Edward Said (1979) as 'Orientalism', as well as in non-European responses to and interventions in these dominant constructions. It is worth noting here, however, that initially, Shakespearean postcolonial studies took shape in making observations about emerging colonial paradigms in English literature and culture *during* the early modern period. In this approach, its early emphasis was on the marginalized/colonized figures in the Shakespearean world – 'Moors,' 'Turks', 'Indians', 'Jews' and others. The field, however, has *not* exhausted itself around these issues. In fact, in its mutations, it has often moved beyond the earlier colonial paradigms involving oppositions between colonial/postcolonial and self/other, while increasingly attending to a polyphony of voices beyond the binary of colonizer/colonized. Overall, we should also appreciate that a postcolonial perspective on Shakespeare's works performs a proleptic historical function in revealing England's expansionist role, while also providing a critical vocabulary whereby we can work through the past in the present and vice versa (Singh and Shahani 2010: 127–30). And in this endeavour, in postcolonial (as in race) studies in the early modern period, the task of disarticulating associations between the playwright's works and 'whiteness' continues apace. I use 'whiteness' as a term that conflates assumptions about an immutable human nature and a timeless English Shakespearean canon by and about 'white' people. Furthermore, some key terms in the postcolonial vocabulary – 'otherness', 'resistance', 'subversion', 'appropriation', 'decolonization' and 'cultural translation' – are now more widely re-deployed in the new inter-cultural Shakespearean disseminations world-wide. Conceptually, these categories illuminate the trajectories of the varied modes of resistance to colonial discourse.[2] Overall, these inter-cultural responses to Shakespeare – on stage, in film, and in other media – cover an interesting range of artistic representations and adaptations giving voice to the formerly colonized.

As I write in 2018, postcoloniality, I argue, is a state and condition – a mode of apprehending alterity, difference, and inequities – more than simply a politically inflected theoretical approach. The distinctive markers of this condition are evident in the burgeoning postcolonially inflected scholarship that has expanded the Shakespearean archive to varied spaces, places, and historical moments, especially evident in the critical responses and stage and film reviews of the past decade or so. Thus, in tracking Shakespeare's interactions with local knowledges, native cultures, and east–west geo-politics, the thrust of this scholarship has moved beyond Western, institutional parameters, and Shakespeare's works are increasingly used to tell stories about diverse lives and experiences. Besides theatre companies, these include settings such as refugee camps and school rooms, and native idioms and languages ranging from Bengali to Arabic, Singhala, Japanese, Mandarin, and others. Animating these new stories are the ideological struggles of our times concerning, for example, racial, intercultural, and religious differences, the purity of the state/nation, gender stereotypes and hierarchies, and class and property conflicts. An increasing number of Shakespearean scholars recognize the boundary-crossing drives of recent appropriations and re-interpretations, following the imperatives of the historical moment, while blurring any divide between the 'global' and 'local'. Volumes and collections such as *Native Shakespeares*,

Bollywood Shakespeares, *Shakespeare and World Cinema*, *Chinese Shakespeares*, and *The Arab Shakespeare Trilogy*, among several others, testify to this trend.[3]

In this vein, I posit a postcolonial Shakespeare at a far remove from the implicitly white 'Renaissance man' of the Western canon. While mining the works of the playwright for traces of colonial and postcolonial histories and cultures, ranging from the early modern period to the present, my approach is *not* teleological or all-encompassing in its scope. Instead, I map evolving discursive and performative milieus – in a series of 'turns' or foci – covering Shakespeare's world and the twentieth- and twenty-first-century reception and responses to his plays. Quite simply, this book follows a trajectory of 'travelling' Shakespeares through intersecting itineraries of exploration and discovery in the early modern period as well as in contemporary appropriations within diverse multicultural, native, and global settings. In an organization of three sections, *Shakespeare and Postcolonial Theory*, Part I focuses on Shakespeare's world, illuminating 'traces' of England's global, colonizing imaginary at the intersections of dramatic works and travel narratives in the early modern period. It also offers a glimpse of early modern London and its stage and society as they were shaped by the era of commercial and cultural expansion. Part II examines the impact of postcolonial theory and criticism beyond the early modern period, exploring the shifting reception and appropriation of Shakespeare's works within 'non-metropolitan', marginal locations, whether in the West or *beyond*. I use variants of the above term throughout book to signal 'local knowledge' as distinct from the 'metropolitan centres of Shakespeare study'.[4] Charting responses to Shakespeare during the 1960s decolonization, through Edward Said's *Orientalism* (1979), and to the politically inflected theories from the mid-1980s onwards, this section tracks postcolonial Shakespeare studies as a *disciplinary formation*. Finally, Part III delves into postcolonial Shakespearean 'afterlives' in the varied, more recent reception histories of the works on stage and screen in the West and beyond.

Critical engagements with selected interpretations and reviews, rather than close readings of Shakespeare's plays, are interwoven within different chapters throughout the volume. The plays included are: *The Tempest, Othello, The Merchant of Venice, King Lear, Antony and Cleopatra, Cymbeline, A Midsummer Night's Dream, Much Ado About Nothing, Richard III,* and *Hamlet*. In the sections on performance, I focus on the discourse emanating from the critical and theatrical reviews of stage productions, rather than on the live performances. Finally, critical responses to the plays are interspersed with references to historically relevant cultural texts of the early modern period and of our own times.

Chapter 1, 'Shakespeare and the Colonial Imaginary', represents the mid-sixteenth to seventeenth centuries as an era of 'discovery' and commercial 'traffic', though not as a strictly colonial period as such. Within this context, I reappraise the relevance of Shakespeare's 'obvious' postcolonial plays, *The Tempest, The Merchant of Venice*, and *Othello*, in relation to travel and encounter narratives, a popular genre of the print culture that produced the colonizing imagination of the period. By contextualizing Shakespeare's plays within English (European) narratives of trade and 'discovery', such as in travel anthologies by Richard Hakluyt (1589, 1598–1600) and Samuel Purchas (1625), a postcolonial inquiry casts a different light on them; it makes visible characters previously located on the margins of the European consciousness – from worlds 'elsewhere' – for instance, Moors, Jews, Indians, and others. Thus, when we include the travel and 'discovery' texts in the contextual archaeologies of these three works, they illuminate the complexities of Western racial, ethnic and religious categories in ways that, in turn, deepen the historical and affective resonance of the plays themselves.

Chapter 2, 'Shakespeare's World and Productions of Difference', follows England's global, colonizing imaginary and its material and affective impact on London's society and the stage. Though many historians recognize Shakespearean London as a city of demographic and class realignments with an influx of strangers, the 'foreign', alien, and non-English elements of the city typically have *not* been central to their perceptions and assumptions. Viewing early modern London through a postcolonial lens, this chapter highlights England's global reach in cross-cultural contacts and imperial ambitions. Intertwined mercantile and political alliances with Ottoman and Moroccan kingdoms coupled with a growing trade in East India and forays into the New World marked a remarkable shift in the English world view and tastes, especially for foreign commodities, and often accompanied by an anxiety about aliens and 'others'.

Next, this chapter recapitulates London's popular stages within this new global milieu, thus, re-examining English encounters with cultural 'others' seen on stage. While postcolonial scholars typically focus on 'Turks' and 'Moors', I ask how Shakespearean audiences may also have been intrigued by 'Indians', and by the idea of 'India' itself. A series of innovative essays on the role of the changeling 'Indian boy' and his mother the 'Indian votaress' in *A Midsummer Night's Dream* illuminate the play's colonial, 'Indian' themes, beginning with Margo Hendricks's article in 1996. While the changeling boy often puzzles audiences, or is reduced to a prop, this scholarship explores the Indian contexts of the play in relation to discourses of trade, travel, and colonialism – to the East Indies spice trade, for instance. Other Indian-themed readings draw further attention to 'India' through the Oberon/Indian boy/Titania triad that reconfigures 'India' in terms of a global homo-erotic imaginary, while also relating the play to the abduction of young boys in the context of Anglo-Ottoman power struggles. Thus, a play popularly viewed as quintessentially 'English' yields new historical insights about the period and its impact on Shakespeare's work.

Opening Part II, Chapter 3, 'Past and Present: Shakespeare–Postcoloniality', moves from a proleptic, postcolonial gaze on the early modern global and imperialist imaginings – especially on the London stage – to anti-colonial responses to Shakespeare's work from the 1950s onwards (which underpinned later postcolonial theory under Edward Said and others). Charting the decolonizing movements in Africa, the Caribbean, and Latin America, I show how non-Western intellectuals, all former colonial subjects, resisted the 'civilizing mission' of the British Empire and Shakespeare's role in it. Thus, Shakespeare's iconic status is greatly tempered in their appropriations and re-configurations of a key text such as *The Tempest*. Viewing Prospero as a colonizer while identifying with Caliban, impelled these anti-colonial revisions of *The Tempest*, a vital text during the liberation movements of the 1950s, 1960s, and 1970s that were exploring political and psychic possibilities beyond colonialism. Drawing on a brief reading of Aimé Césaire's iconic *Une Tempête* (1969), and an overview of George Lamming's *Pleasures of Exile* (1992), Roberto Fernandez Retamar's essay, *Caliban* (1969), E.P. Kamau Brathwaite's poem 'Caliban' from the collection *Islands* (1969), and Ngũgĩ wa Thiong'o's *A Grain of Wheat* (1975), this chapter moves through varied settings in former colonies in Africa, the Caribbean, and Latin America, while evoking, through *The Tempest*, a polyphony of voices in varied anti-colonial histories.

Next in this chapter, I further examine the ground-breaking legacy of Edward Said's *Orientalism* (1979) (introduced in Chapter 1), showing how Shakespeare studies took a postcolonial 'turn' in the late 1970s through the early 1990s. After Said made the assertion that the 'serious study of imperialism and its culture was [no longer] off limits for the literary cultural establishment as a whole' (13), Shakespearean literary scholarship in the 1980s and 1990s expanded its historical scope to include colonial and postcolonial sources. This critical shift was represented, for instance, by studies of *The Tempest* in relation to colonialism by Paul Brown, Peter Hulme and others (Chapter 1), and more distinctly postcolonial work by Ania Loomba, Jyotsna Singh, and Martin Orkin, to name a few, that coalesced around the role of Shakespeare in the British empire and its aftermath.

Chapter 4, 'Intersectionalities: Postcoloniality and Difference', turns to Western theoretical and political re-orientations *after* Edward Said's *Orientalism*, from the early 1980s through the 1990s to the present. Once the liberal humanist consensus about a timeless and 'universal' Shakespeare was disrupted, politically inflected criticism from the 1980s onwards began to recognize intersectional connections, for instance, between colonialism, race, and gender. This chapter begins with a 'real time' description of a conference entitled 'Shakespeare–Postcoloniality', held in Johannesburg, South Africa in July 1996, at the University of Witwatersrand, two years after the first democratic elections in 1994, when South Africa was under an ANC (African National Congress) government. As a participant, I witnessed how Shakespearean postcolonial studies took shape 'on the ground', so to speak. Thus, not surprisingly, interrogations of colonization, empire, and their postcolonial aftermath in South Africa and other former British colonies shaped the agenda of the conference, whereby Shakespeare's plays were *intersectionally* linked to continuing material and discursive struggles for racial, economic, social, and gender equity in the global north and south.[5]

Taking a cue from these intersectional orientations in Johannesburg, this chapter takes a seemingly digressive path, showing how Shakespearean works can further pluralize and complicate these global struggles. What I attempt here are three diachronic readings, providing insights into the rise of private property, class, and implicitly racial struggles in *King Lear*; into feminist interrogations of racialist and Orientalist sexual discourses in Western cultural representations of Cleopatra, especially on the stage; and into engagements with imperial patriarchy, and gendered nation formation in Shakespeare's *Cymbeline* in the early modern period – as well as during historical 'reconciliations' in postcolonial South Africa and in Israel. In offering these postcolonial perspectives on the above three plays – not typically viewed as such – I bring together critical interpretations and reviews of productions into productive conversations with colonial and postcolonial histories – including past and present representations of race and gender difference – but without eliding postcolonial theory with other critical orientations.[6]

Opening Part III, Chapter 5, 'Global, Inter-cultural Shakespeares', turns to the more recent global repertoire of non-Western, 'native' appropriations. Following the paradigm shift of the 1980s and 1990s, Shakespearean studies have become more cross-cultural and cosmopolitan, moving *beyond* Western, institutional parameters as they chart diverse non-Western, 'native' adaptations and revisions in text and performance. On stage, film, and other media in disparate locations, the works (mostly plays) have been appearing in forms that are multifarious, while taking on regional manifestations: Chinese Shakespeares, Bollywood Shakespeares, Japanese Shakespeares, Arab Shakespeares, and Black and Asian Shakespeares in Britain, among others.

Following the trajectories of these movements of 'appropriation' and 'adaptation' – often implying a resistance or veneration (or both) of the original work – this chapter demonstrates how these inter-cultural encounters constitute a *legacy* of postcoloniality, though often in new variants; the old colonizer–colonized binary relationship is now refracted through our world of migrations, diasporas, exile, and East–West inter-culturalisms. Appropriation itself is often viewed as a 'multi-lateral reception' through what Margaret Litvin describes as a 'global kaleidoscope of intertexts', in recognition of a polyphony of voices that may lurk behind any Shakespearean adaptation.[7] How do these inter-textual, inter-cultural trends expand and complicate our perspective on non-Western revisions of Shakespeare? I explore the implications of this question in the production reviews of Ong Keng Sen's pan-Asian, multilingual production of *King Lear* (*LEAR*, 1997); of an Indian performance of *Hamlet* in an indigenous *Jatra* (folk theatre) form by Salim Ghouse (Bombay 1992); and of an Arab *Richard III*, one of the three plays comprising *The Arab Shakespeare Trilogy* (2014) by Sulayman Al-Bassam, a key figure from the Arab world within the recent Global Shakespeare movement. As a context to my discussion of Al-Bassam, I briefly chart the complex phenomenon recognized as 'Arab Shakespeares', offering a selective perspective on the role of Arab Shakespeare translation, production, adaptation, and criticism through the twentieth and twenty-first centuries. This survey is followed by a brief discussion of Al-Bassam's Royal Shakespeare Company (RSC) Arabic *Richard III*, mainly through his articulations of his own inter-cultural, creative philosophy and practice.

Chapter 6, 'Boundary Crossings on the British Shakespearean Stage', moves the scene to inter-cultural Shakespeare in contemporary, multiracial, multiethnic Britain. If traditionally Shakespeare has been considered as the universal Bard, as well as a cultural signifier for a reified 'Britishness', today such categorizations seem outdated in new considerations of 'race' and performance. In *Shakespeare, Race and Performance: The Diverse Bard* (2017), Delia Jarrett-Macauley astutely charts some aspects of the Black and Asian participation in Shakespearean performance and, in fact, the very conditions of postcoloniality are reflected in her description of the contributors to this volume:

> [They] are of 'divers kind' [in Middle English], born on different continents, aware of the discontinuous histories that have shaped colonial and postcolonial worlds ... feeding off Shakespeare ... [they] have crossed boundaries, from one continent to another, from margin to center, or from ethnically led training to mainstream invention, troubling and unsettling their 'roots'. (4)

By recounting the early black and Asian entries into the previously closed cultural territory of Shakespearean drama, by companies such as Talawa Theatre Company (1986) and Tara Arts (1977), I evaluate their contributions as they expanded British cultural life, making people with different origins visible to the society and culture at large. These early racial and ethnically inflected offerings represent a period when Britain was just coming to terms with its diversity. In recent years, it seems, the British stage is further divesting itself from its singular 'white' English identity in multiple adaptations and interpretations. A distinctive aspect of these changes at the intersections of race, gender, and performance involves non-traditional casting. Confronting earlier gendered and racialized exclusions, British theatre practitioners are exploring bold policies of inclusive casting, extending boundaries far in 'excess' of traditional affiliations between specific roles, genders, races, and cultures (among others).

As a key instance in this new 'turn' in non-traditional casting on the British Shakespearean stage, I draw on the RSC's *Othello* (2015) directed by Iqbal Khan. In a surprising 'twist' on the idea of colourblind casting, Lucian Msamati, a British actor raised in Tanzania and Zimbabwe, made theatrical history by being the first black actor ever to play Iago at the RSC. The casting choice raised some important issues about whether we can move beyond black-and-white ideas of racism as a motivator for Iago, and where the play stands on issues of 'race' today. Next, I analyse reviews and directors' responses to three postcolonially themed productions that represent different intercultural renditions of 'India' on the Shakespearean stage: Tim Supple's RSC-sponsored production of a multilingual, multiethnic British-Sri Lankan collaborative performance of *A Midsummer Night's Dream* (staged RSC 2004, Roundhouse Theatre 2007); Emma Rice's culturally diverse *A Midsummer Night's Dream* at the Globe (2016), in which 'India' serves as a sensory backdrop, while her casting reflects a multiracial Britain, with black and Asian actors; and finally, Iqbal Khan's *Much Ado about Nothing* (2015) for the RSC, set in contemporary Delhi. All three productions in different ways demonstrate the continuing relevance of postcolonial vocabularies as they conceptualize 'India' both as an imagined/imaginary place depicted in the early modern play, as well as a site that exposes the cultural, racial, and social fault-lines of our own times in the 'real' India.

Chapter 7, 'Shakespeare in Postcolonial Cinema: A Meditation on *Haider/Hamlet*', ends the journey of this book by moving from the stage to the screen. In this chapter, my interest lies is the tradition of non-Anglophone Shakespeares, found in what is defined today as 'world cinema' (Burnett 2013), or a 'mode of filmmaking that takes place outside the Hollywood mainstream'. While eschewing English as the dominant language, Burnett focuses on Shakespearean productions from South and East Asia, Latin America, and Africa (5). Other critics and directors have also expressed enthusiasm for mining the plays for new meanings in non-Western contexts, and approaching the works 'in excess of their canonical, western uses'.[8]

Issues constellating around Shakespearean world cinema are diverse, complicating our understandings of national and regional cultures, as well as of the individual artists or 'auteurs' or individual craftsperson possessed of a distinctive vision' (Burnett 2013: 5). A figure in this 'world' cinema (or Global Shakespearean Cinema), who represents an auteur for a growing community of intercultural Shakespeare scholars, is Vishal Bhardwaj, mentioned earlier, whose 'Bollywood' appropriations of Shakespeare, *Maqbool/Macbeth, Omkara/Othello*, and most recently, *Haider/Hamlet*, mediate between the elite, Western intellectual associations with the plays and the local, non-metropolitan cultures and knowledges of the Indian Sub-continent. The term 'Bollywood' broadly denotes Hindi cinema made in North India, though its offerings are very varied in terms of artistic value (more later). My chapter offers a meditation on *Haider/Hamlet*, as a way of stretching the parameters of what constitutes 'appropriation', being cognizant of the tensions between veneration or resistance toward the original work. Setting the film in Kashmir during the Kashmiri militancy and the brutal occupation by the Indian armed forces in the mid 1990s, Bhardwaj presents it in terms of a suggestive analogy: 'In my film, in a way, Kashmir becomes Hamlet' (Bhardwaj 2014). I further re-configure this mutually constitutive relationship between 'Kashmir' and 'Hamlet' by mapping the journey of the play into South Asian cultural and political contexts that affectively/ imaginatively put together the fragments of Kashmir – from the mid 1990s to the present. These local, non-metropolitan 'sources' or contexts for the film include the memoir *Curfewed Night* by Basharat Peer, the co-written documentary film *Paradise on a River of Hell* (dir. Abir Bazaz and Meenu Gaur), the poems of Kashmiri poet Agha Shahid Ali, and of the Pakistani poet Faiz Ahmed Faiz, among others.

II

In exploring postcolonial Shakespeare studies as a disciplinary formation (as outlined above), it is also important to recognize my *personal* impetus in pursuing some kinds of critical inquiries over others. My own engagement with Shakespeare, I believe, is deeply enriched by exploring his historical function in various lives and histories, individual, national, and global. As Edward Said reminds us in *Orientalism*, his own background as an Arab and Palestinian became interwoven within his engagements with Western colonialism. With these reflections, I thought it behooves me to 'know myself': first as a product of an education in India, with its 'traces' of an earlier, colonial educational agenda; and then as a scholar in the Anglo-American academy. Here, I draw on Edward's Said's call to compile an inventory of 'traces' marking my personal and intellectual journey that in part at least reflects the trajectory of Shakespeare's 'travels' and appropriations within diverse locations of 'multi-cultural', 'native', and 'global' Shakespeares.[9]

I initially came to Shakespeare as a scholar of English literature in India, via a largely Anglicized canonical curriculum from my early schooling onwards. My undergraduate education in India (Punjab University) was shaped by a coverage model that ranged from biblical and classical literatures, through major periods, genres, and literary figures like Chaucer, Shakespeare, Donne, Jane Austen, T.S. Eliot, the

Brontes, Tom Stoppard, Harold Pinter and the numerous other names that one would conventionally expect in a traditional English literature programme. These curricular representations were woven together via a conventional periodization in which different genres and periods were made to 'cohere' within traditional English and mostly nationalistic literary histories. Thus, in terms of my formal English literary education, I was, perhaps, not far removed from Macaulay's desired Anglicized subjects in nineteenth-century India, who ideally imbibed British cultural values through English literature as a project of supposedly moral edification. But that is only part of the story.

Overall, however, my early encounters with English literary works, and specifically Shakespeare in India, were not singularly reverential, nor were the works deemed as totally alien to Indian culture and society. In independent India, especially from the late 1970s and early 1980s onwards, English literature was also domesticated and English-educated Indians may have felt it to be 'our own', given that an increasing 'Indianness' suffused the identity formations even of English-speaking elites. For a long time there has also been, as many would recognize, a 'vernacular' of Indian English. Thus, even though we recognized Shakespearean characters as Western, and as 'white people', paradoxically, we also frequently inserted, within these works, Indian themes concerning love, marriage, family and class hierarchies, among others. Furthermore, it is also worth noting that in India the revered 'Bard' often escaped the singular constraints of formal literary studies via performance and film to become 'native' in richly diverse forms. Since independence, for instance, Shakespearean re-incarnations on the Indian stage have displayed a remarkable confidence in cultural appropriation via politically and affectively charged translations and adaptations by directors like Utpal Dutt, Ebrahim Alkazi and B.V. Karanth, among numerous others (Singh 1989). More recently, as I discuss in this volume, India has also witnessed a profusion of brilliant engagements with Shakespeare, especially in the Bollywood films of Vishal Bharadwaj in the past decade, and others from regional cinema, such as Jayaraj's *Veeram* (*Macbeth*) (2017). The prolific range of these current trends of 'going native', as I have argued elsewhere, open up affective possibilities of a global Shakespeare, not only becoming 'native' to and harnessing affective histories from other cultures, but also showing how these non-Western contexts – 'local knowledge' and experiences from non-metropolitan locations – produce new interpretive possibilities within Shakespearean language, meaning, and context (Orkin 2005: 3–4; Singh and Arvas 2016).

English literature as a field of academic study in India (especially in the past decade) has also expanded to cover Indian writing in English, including translations from the vernacular, as well as postcolonial and other theoretical perspectives. For example, syllabi from Calcutta University and Presidency University (Kolkata) have markedly global dimensions, covering canonical British and American literature, Indian literature in English, as well as postcolonial literature from Africa, Canada, the Caribbean and so forth.[10] My story of Shakespearean dissemination in India is not unique to the subcontinent and has its analogues in varying forms all over the former commonwealth countries in Africa and the Caribbean, as well as in settler colonies such as Australia and Canada. Shakespeare everywhere was an intrinsic part of colonial and partially at least, of postcolonial education. Earlier generations of colonial subjects such as Aimé Césaire, E.P. Brathwaite, Ngũgĩ Wa Thiong'o, and George Lamming called for decolonizing English education. In the 1980s India, however, English-speaking students saw Shakespeare in more benign and domesticated terms, though not without some dissonances.

III

Thus, embarking on an MA and PhD in American academia in the 1980s, I brought with me 'traces' of a familiarization with English literature – a comfort and ease that is typically the experience of many other English-speaking Indians. However, the perceptions I encountered in the United States assumed my study of English literature in India had *not* provided me with a strong Anglo-European 'background' for Renaissance studies in the West (as the early modern field was defined at the time). This was one challenge that often popped up in my professional endeavours, such as job interviews, during my early years. My intellectual journey here in the US began with explorations of new historicism through the mid-1980s, which was also a period of transition. On the one hand, earlier investments in a Western, canonical Shakespeare, including evocations of the 'Renaissance Man' and associations between the playwright's works and a uniform 'whiteness', were still staples of Shakespeare studies. On the other hand, fissures in these foundational assumptions and Western cultural boundaries *also* began to appear, via the influences of feminism, new historicism, cultural materialism, critical race studies and of critical theorists like Jacques Derrida, Jacques Lacan, Michel Foucault, Helene Cixous, Toril Moi, Catherine Belsey and Kate McKluskie, to name but a few.[11] I drew on these critical strains, especially on feminist theory, but my scholarship was (and continues to be) *centrally* shaped by Edward Said's landmark book, *Orientalism*, to chart a radically different inquiry. I began by exploring postcolonial configurations of a Global Renaissance (rather than a purely European one) – one that included trade, travel, and cross-cultural encounters, while also refiguring the Bard's works in terms of a global currency both in the colonial and postcolonial eras. In a Saidian mode, this enabled me to view the relationship between Shakespeare and the makings of the British Empire, which I later began to see as part of an era of expansion (Singh 2013: 1–15).

Today, the discourses of postcolonial theory, race studies, queer theory, and gender and sexuality studies have added many layers of intellectual and political complexity to the field of Shakespeare (and early modern) studies. These intellectual shifts both interact with and are enriched by innovations on the stage, especially in the British Shakespearean world. Varied and sometimes interlocking sub-fields have emerged as we learn more about early modern England (and Europe) in terms of an expanding, global world; these include cross-cultural encounters, with an emphasis on Anglo-Muslim interactions, early representations of racialized, non-Western 'others', as well as Shakespeare's 'travels' within varied histories, ideologies, and theatrical conventions.[12]

However, English departments typically do *not* reflect this global 'turn' and intellectual diversity in the racial and ethnic make-up of their early modern faculty hires and students. In part, this persistent 'whiteness' in terms of the colour of the membership in our field can only be remedied 'if [Shakespeare studies] were to support the inclusion of race studies more systematically and consistently. [Then] our ranks may diversify more rapidly and thoroughly' (Thompson 2013: 180). African-American scholars in the US are often expected to teach 'race' in disciplinary formations such as African-American studies; South Asians in the West are often slotted for postcolonial studies; and others, who identify themselves in terms of varied ethnicities, Latinx, Arab-American, Native American, among others, are encouraged to teach according to their ethnic identities, shaping the institutional structure of English departments along lines of experiential, and essentialist identity politics. This structure shows how good intentions of equity and representation can sometimes have unintended consequences. In these demarcations in which race and ethnicity are bracketed off, 'whiteness' I believe gets re-inscribed as the majority embodiment of English departments and scholars of colour in general are 'encased in the personal', evident in 'visible facts of our visible selves, whereby [scholars of colour become] walking exemplars of ethnicity and of race' (Karamcheti 1995: 138). In a related vein, Arthur Little elucidates complex burdens of the 'personal' faced by scholars of colour, while mapping how their struggles may lead to re-inscriptions of 'whiteness' (2017). Within this environment, despite the critical diversification, early modern studies still remains closely bound to the European template. Relatively few scholars of colour (though slowly and productively increasing) are found among the large numbers of Shakespeareans. (This past year has seen some more movement toward diversity in organizations such as the Shakespeare Association of America and the Folger Shakespeare Library.)

A recent, and public, spat at Cambridge University about 'decolonizing' and 'broadening' continues to remind us that in some centres of cultural power such as Oxbridge, Shakespeare's place continues to be within a largely 'traditional' and 'canonical' curriculum that privileges 'white male authors', as a form of 'institutional racism'. This controversy seemed like a throwback to another era, though there was a recognition of a requirement to spend 'at least a week on an essay that looks at Shakespeare in a postcolonial context'.[13] This imperative was accepted for selected works, but binaries persisted in these recent discussions. While there was some recognition of the postcolonial contexts of plays such as *The Tempest* and *Othello*, race and colonial history were *not* 'considered part of the usual canon'.[14] Not surprisingly, then, my impression (based on a general perception) is that faculty who teach Shakespeare and those who are postcolonial scholars continued to be hired on different tracks.

Caught up in these complex and often contradictory developments shaping English literary studies – and early modern studies in particular – my own journey has been rich in personal self-discovery, but also more complicated and intellectually fraught in the institutional settings of English departments within the west as outlined above. As a scholar of colour and of Indian ethnicity who studied Shakespeare's works in their global, non-Western texts, I initially felt like an outlier at professional conferences and job interviews. In my years as a graduate student, members of the American and British scholarly community often drew attention to me with some bemusement as an 'Indian Shakespearean', as if using a 'phenomenological fit to match [my] race with subject'.[15] I would encounter a frequent curiosity toward my presence in Renaissance studies in the US: why would I be doing graduate work in Shakespeare studies, and why not a more 'Indian' subject matter? Such social interrogations led me to productively question: Why had I studied Shakespeare in India and how had his works arrived in India in mid-nineteenth-century colonial Calcutta?[16]

Thus, my personal 'otherness' within an Anglo-centric Shakespearean world became the impetus for my early interventions in associations between the literature and culture of Renaissance England. It led me to journey *back* to Indian Shakespeares and to reflect on how and why we should consider these works as 'universal', while being disseminated among former colonial subjects. Navigating the possibilities within these dialogues and dissonances between my own identity formations and the worlds of Shakespearean drama, I have been deeply enriched. I have learned, above all, that my experiences of Shakespeare shaped by my Anglicized Indian family background as well as by an Anglo-American culture in the US (and to a large extent in Britain), have been and continue to be *hybrid* and provisional, rather than bound within fixed categories of race and nation, as, I believe, are the Bard's works themselves.[17] In recent years, I have also been heartened by British Shakespeare productions with their representations of fluid identities of race and gender, as well as their bold embrace of radical cultural appropriations and mismatches. It is from these hybrid visions that I launch the journey of exploration in *Shakespeare and Postcolonial Theory*.

PART ONE

Shakespeare and Early Colonial History

CALIBAN
   For I am all the subjects that you have,
   Which first was mine own king;

   – *The Tempest* (1.2.342–43)

1

Historical Contexts 1

Shakespeare and the Colonial Imaginary

Colonial Encounters

The postcolonial terrain mapped in *Shakespeare and Postcolonial Theory* offers many byways and vistas for exploration, as I outline in the Introduction. My aim in the following chapters is to remain attentive to constantly changing scenes of diverse and contrasting aesthetic and political modalities in Shakespeare's plays, their contextual archaeologies, and varying reception histories. I begin *Shakespeare and Postcolonial Theory* by acknowledging the problematic or even futile task of locating any originary moment of colonialism. Historians typically agree that English (and European) imperial power was only consolidated in the late eighteenth/early nineteenth centuries. But from a postcolonial perspective, the cultural and literary texts and events representing interactions with non-Europeans from the early sixteenth century onwards also bear the marks of a 'colonizing imagination'. Thus, we can find a diverse body of works – plays, travel narratives, and entertainments, among others – representing the cultural and affective milieu of England's global expansion in commercial, cultural, and religious dimensions. I am interested in these creative and imaginative processes, particularly in how they evoke an emergent colonial imaginary constituting distinct values, institutions, laws, and symbols. Drawing on this historical overview, I want to recapitulate and reappraise the relevance of *The Tempest*, *The Merchant of Venice*, and *Othello* – the most common choices for postcolonial interpretation – in engaging with England's expansionist role, and especially as these plays relate to early modern travel narratives, a popular genre of the developing print culture. Key critical responses to these works in terms of their colonial contexts tell a clear story of the evolution of postcolonial Shakespeare studies, as well as of its intellectual and political stakes.

Shakespeare's *The Tempest*, first performed in 1611, has a complicated and varied reception history. But from the 1960s onwards, the colonial implications of the play became increasingly evident to generations of readers and viewers.[1] Following these interventions into earlier, (at least overtly) mostly apolitical, 'universal' readings of the play, as Peter Hulme (1986) suggests, the play is now considered by many as 'emblematic of the founding years of England's colonialism' (90). Moving onwards from the 1960s we can map evolving critical and literary representations of links between *The Tempest*, the New World ventures, Mediterranean/North African histories and geographies, and England's colonizing forays into border territories, such as Ireland. This critical turn led scholars to consider the broader implications of this play for a full understanding of the 'complex requirements of British colonialism in its initial phase' (Brown 1985: 48). Furthermore, this analogy can also apply to other similarly themed literary works of the early modern period, some examples being Shakespeare's *The Merchant of Venice*, *Othello*, *Titus Andronicus*, the 'Turk' plays such as *The Renegado* by Philip Massinger, *The Battle of Alcazar* by George Peele, and *Tamburlaine*, *Dido, Queen of Carthage*, and *The Jew of Malta* by Christopher Marlowe, among numerous others. Thematic resonances do not imply a strict empirical congruence among these texts and/or other non-European historical contexts. Instead, I believe, a more productive approach would be to explore the ways in which these works are imbricated in early modern ideological struggles about race, nation, religion, sexuality, and identity – especially as they play out in incipient colonial writings such as travel narratives.

What we find in both dramatic and cultural texts such as travel accounts is not a distinct ideological agenda of England's imperial role. We can nonetheless discern an early modern colonizing imagination at work – one that is global in scope, permeating tropes, fantasies, rhetorical structures, and visual images – often defining cultural 'others' in terms of binaries: civilization versus barbarism, white versus black, pious restraint versus uncontrolled eroticism, Christianity (the true religion) versus (blasphemous) Islam, among numerous others (Kamps and Singh, 2001: 2–3). Such stark frames of reference later justify and consolidate full-blown colonialism, and continue to animate productions of 'otherness' even today. As a familiar analogy, at the centre of these imaginings is the recurrent and ubiquitous trope of the early *colonial encounter*, which is also the pivot on which the plot of *The Tempest* rests.

Some nuance and qualification are needed here. While recognizing the long, retrospective reach of this colonial imaginary – whether we consider the period between the sixteenth century and late eighteenth century as *early colonial* or *proto-colonial* – the literary and cultural productions of this period, in the genres listed above, do not offer unified expressions of cultural dominance or Eurocentric attitudes.[2] In fact, critics are not entirely wrong, especially those covering the West and Islam, when they express scepticism about the parameters of English power and dominance over the newly 'discovered' lands; some also consider Edward Said's definition of 'Orientalism' as a colonial discourse to be somewhat irrelevant in this early modern period.[3] I would argue, however, that it is not unreasonable to apply Said's argument to the early modern period, though with some qualification perhaps, given that the material impact of Western power over the East was limited or minimal at that time. And here I would particularly like to push back at those critics who, in questioning the relevance of Said's ideas to the early modern period (prior to the eighteenth century), tend to flatten and simplify the premises of *Orientalism*, especially its emphasis on the systemic power of representational practices. In fact, some do acknowledge, as Jonathan Burton states, that the 'representative practices of high imperialism [can] be sometimes found germinating in earlier periods'.[4] In sum, the key task before us, I believe, is how to map early English (European) expansion – its colonial imaginings – though its emergent stages. *Orientalism* provides a useful critical vocabulary for doing so (as I discuss further in Chapter 3).

Overall, in this volume, I remain cognisant of the fact that cross-cultural encounters, exchanges, and power struggles were (and are) often uneven and hybrid – and that the tropes of 'otherness' have neither been uniform nor consistent. The complexities of these interactions are certainly evident in Shakespeare's plays and their critical reception, as well as in other cultural works that engage with colonial themes, as I demonstrate. What they reveal and illuminate are not so much the ideological agendas of the particular works, as the psychic and epistemological struggles shaping English (and European) engagements with non-European 'others'.[5] Working within the historical, conceptual frame outlined above, the postcolonial approach I take in this chapter investigates how the selected Shakespeare plays listed above relate to early English colonial (or proto-colonial) endeavours, represented in cross-cultural encounters between non-Western peoples and races and English travellers – explorers, merchants, Chaplains, official emissaries, and others.

It is generally accepted that *The Tempest* is the primary text on which postcolonial Shakespeare studies took root. When Anglo-American scholars from the early 1980s onwards began to emphasize a relationship between Shakespeare's *The Tempest* and its colonial contexts – from the New World Bermuda pamphlets about an English shipwreck in the Caribbean, to Caliban's anagrammatic transformation from Columbus' 'cannibal', and further, to Britain's internal hegemony over the Welsh and Irish – they, quite strikingly, signalled a postcolonial 'turn' and, in effect, a critical paradigm shift by inserting the play within early English colonial history and its imperial imaginings. The decolonization movements in former European empires earlier, through the 1960s and 1970s, had already exposed the play's allegorical identifications with European colonialism in the cultural works of Aimé Césaire, Ngũgĩ Wa Thiong'o, and Roberto Fernandez Retamar, among others (see Chapter 3). But postcolonial Shakespeare criticism of *The Tempest* in the Anglo-American contexts more radically accelerated these reappraisals of the play, from the 1980s onwards, when colonialism was no longer a subject 'off-limits' within the field of literary studies (Said 1979: 1–5). This new awareness led critics to explore how the West imagined the genesis, growth, and subsequent effects of its colonial empires

Once these were acknowledged, Shakespeare's *The Tempest* provided a fertile ground for tracking an emerging British colonialist discourse in the early modern period, encompassing the 'core', the 'semiperiphery', and the 'periphery' of Britain's domination. Such a discourse was eloquently articulated by Paul Brown in his ground-breaking essay, '"This thing of darkness I acknowledge mine": *The Tempest* and the discourse of colonialism' (1985):

> A brief survey of British colonial operations will help us to establish a network of relations or discursive matrix *within and against which* an analysis of *The Tempest* becomes possible. (51; emphasis in original)

In explaining his formulation, Brown provides some historical context:

> Geographically, the discourse operated upon the various domains of British world influence, which may be discerned roughly in the terms of Immanuel Wallerstein, as the 'core', 'semiperiphery' and 'periphery'. Colonialism therefore

comprises the expansion of royal hegemony in the English-Welsh mainland (the internal colonialism of the core), the extension of British influence in the semiperiphery of Ireland, and the diffuse range of British interests in the extreme periphery of the New World. (51–52)

Further, drawing on Edward Said's concept of an orientalist discourse, Brown offers a discursive template, which, as he argues, structures Prospero's seeming benevolent domination on the island. 'Colonial discourse voices a demand for both order and disorder, producing a disruptive other in order to assert this superiority of the colonizer' (58). And Prospero's power drives, according to Brown, are structured similarly:

> From Prospero's initial appearance it becomes clear that disruption was produced to create a series of problems precisely in order to effect their resolution ... [In this process] Prospero interpellates the various listeners – calls to them, as it were, and invites them to recognize themselves as subjects of his discourse ... Thus for Miranda he is a strong father who educates and protects her; for Ariel he is rescuer and taskmaster; for Caliban he is a colonizer whose refused offer of civilization forces him to strict discipline [and enslavement]. (58–59)

Prospero's colonizing activities are validated by his naturalized patriarchal authority, central to which is the control over Miranda's sexuality. According to Kim Hall (1995), 'the pressures of imperialism insist on the control and regulation of female sexuality, particularly when concerns over paternity are complicated by problems of racial and cultural purity' (148). At issue, then, is Prospero's justification of his colonizing activities and arbitrary rule, including sexual control, over the island's inhabitants. According to Prospero, Caliban's mother was the 'damned witch Sycorax', who 'For mischiefs manifold, and sorceries terrible / To enter human hearing, from Algiers ... was banished' (1.2.264–66).[6]

She was the 'blue-eyed hag' 'hither brought with child', whose enslavement he justifies (1.2.269). Caliban, in turn, responds to Prospero's history by claiming the island as his own legitimate inheritance:

CALIBAN
   This island's mine by Sycorax, my mother,
   Which thou tak'st from me ...
   For I am all the subjects that you have,
   Which first was mine own king; and here you sty me,
   In this hard rock, whiles you do keep from me
   The rest o'th' island. (1.2.333–44)

Prospero's earlier occlusion of the history of his arrival, narrated here by Caliban, as well as his usurpation of the island, also figure prominently in other early postcolonial readings, such as the influential essay by Francis Barker and Peter Hulme, '"Nymphs and reapers heavily vanish": the Discursive Contexts of *The Tempest*' (1985). They demonstrate that Prospero's denial of his 'dispossession [of Caliban], with retrospective justification for it, is the characteristic trope by which European colonial regimes articulated their authority over land to which they could have no conceivable legitimate claim' (Barker and Hulme 1985: 200). The success of this trope, of course, depends on our (audiences' and scholars') 'uncritical willingness to identify Prospero's voice as a direct and reliable authorial statement', which underpins interpretations of 'European and North American critics, who have tended to listen exclusively to Prospero's voice: *after all he speaks their language*' (Barker and Hulme 1985: 199, 204; emphasis mine). Here I primarily draw on the scholarship by Paul Brown, Peter Hulme, and Francis Barker, as a few key examples of the workings of colonial discourse in the play, though also recognizing the important contributions of Stephen Greenblatt and the new historicist movement in re-contextualizing Caliban and Prospero's story within the history and ideology of European conquests in the 'New World,' most notably in 'Learning to Curse'.[7] Thus, one can see how postcoloniality in the 1980s marked the pivotal moment when Prospero's audiences – and readers of Shakespeare – became more transnational, transcultural, as well as multilingual, and in effect, they *stopped* listening uncritically to Prospero, and instead, began to challenge the legitimacy of his colonizing activities. Those critics who, like Brown, Hulme, Greenblatt, and others were attentive to Caliban's claims and his efforts at resistance were closely reading the poetic language afforded to Caliban in Shakespeare's play, rather than simply accepting Prospero's justifications for *his* magically induced plots in his role as a surrogate playwright.

It is worth taking pause here, as Charles Frey reminds us in his article, '*The Tempest* and the New World' (1979), that even prior to these postcolonial interventions in the 1980s – since the eighteenth century at least – critics have been asking: 'What has *The Tempest*, if anything, to do with the New World?' (29). In 1808, for instance, Edmond Malone first argued that Shakespeare derived the title and some of the play's incidents from the Bermuda materials. Answers have been varied as were the points of view of the critics, and Frey cites from *both* those who sought to discredit New World sources for the Caliban–Prospero relationship as well as those scholars who emphasized the historical links between the New World materials and the play-text.[8] Overall, however, Frey's essay (like many of the critics he cites) is still invested more within a formalist approach rather than an historical one, as he sees the play's meaning in a 'linguistic and narrative force-field' rather than a single history, though he does concede its form to be a 'peculiar merger of history and romance' (33, 41). Strong formalist strains, as in Frey's reading, persisted in approaches to the play. Even after the legacy of decolonization, Western critics often saw the play generically, 'as a pastoral tragicomedy, [romance], with the themes of nature and art at its center, fully and confidently Mediterranean, as its title would suggest, a play moving majestically to its reconciliatory climax with hardly a ripple to disturb its surface' (Hulme 1986: 105). It is also important to remember here that critics such as Brown and Hulme also recognize other contextual geographies underpinning the play, such as references to Caliban's 'African' pedigree, which makes him distinctly Mediterranean, within the framework of 'dual topographies', and on which I elaborate in the next section.

Animating many standard Western readings, we can recognize a reconciliatory thrust to the play – often an unquestioned identification of Prospero with Shakespeare, the benevolent creator of theatrical plots and effects, as well as an analogue for a God-like figure with Providence on his side (Hulme 1986: 105). Not surprisingly, this naturalized acceptance of Prospero's fatherly benevolence was the staple for several generations of Anglo-American scholars. Such an ahistorical deification of Prospero's role shrinks the play's historicity. We lose the resonances of all the New World materials: about England's forays into the Americas, such as the early, though failed, Virginia colony, the first English permanent settlement in the founding of Jamestown in 1607, or Walter Raleigh's 'discovery' of Guiana and his failure to find gold in the mythical El Dorado.

Today, postcolonial reappraisals of Prospero's role and motives seem widely accepted as at least *one* valid interpretation of the play, though such readings, frequently labelled as 'colonialist', have continued to be interrogated and challenged. That said, such dismissals of the play's colonial themes imply a resistance to historical specificity, based on a relativistic assumption that one historical frame can be unproblematically replaced by another. Douglas Bruster is among several critics who have argued for a 'corrective' to 'colonialist' or postcolonial readings, as he states in his book chapter, 'Quoting the Playhouse in *The Tempest*' (2000). Here, Bruster expands on the possible sources of the play by making two claims:

> First, that *The Tempest* ... looks to the Globe and Blackfriars playhouses – and to the realities of working in those structures – for its most salient sources. Its

portrait of playhouse labor and experience includes not only Prospero as a playwright/director, but also Miranda as a figure of an idealized spectatorship and Ariel as boy actor. My second major claim, one that builds on this playhouse allegory, is that Caliban derived from Shakespeare's experiences with Will Kemp, celebrated Elizabethan clown known for his physical, even priapic comedy, his independent spirit, folk ethos, and intrusive ad-libs. (118)

Bruster wants to prove that 'much of *The Tempest's* politics are thoroughly "local", and that it "uses colonialism to talk about the theatre"' (117), which for him is equally as important a theme as the play's colonial contexts. He further buttresses his own argument by drawing on other literary critics that contextualize the play in English or European locations (as opposed to the New World):

Since the rise of a colonialist *Tempest*, a number of voices have challenged the foundations on which such an interpretation rests. Meredith Skura, Frances Dolan, David Kastan, and Jerry Brotton, among others, have offered reasons to be wary of reading the play as a straightforward allegory of European domination of the New World. Skura points out that the play remains a 'notoriously slippery' document and contains much that an intensively postcolonialist hermeneutics cannot account for …. Similarly, Dolan has changed the way we see the drama by arguing for an inherently small *Tempest,* one in which the crime of petty treason steers a counterplot in this 'shrunken, enclosed world … in which Prospero's household is the commonwealth' … In contrast David Kastan, suggesting that 'the Americanization of *The Tempest* may be itself an act of cultural imperialism', reads the play in terms of 'European dynastic concerns rather than European colonial activities', placing focus on James' negotiations with the Palatine in the years preceding *The Tempest.* (118–19)

Overall, while these readings, including Bruster's own, certainly add new layers to the genealogical archaeology of *The Tempest*, they all imply a need to elide or ignore colonial contexts.[9] In fact, he views interpretations he lists as a necessary 'corrective', cautioning us 'to be wary of reading it as a straightforward allegory of European domination of the New World' (118). But to call for a 'corrective' to a postcolonial inquiry into New World historical analogues implies that such an argument is 'wrong' and invalid, when this can be refuted by the well-worn acceptance of New World historical sources such as Strachey's *True Repertory*, Jourdain's *Discovery of the Bermudas,* and 'other extensive literature of European exploration' which Bruster himself lists (118–19).[10] Furthermore, critics like Brown, Hulme, Vaughan, Callaghan and others view the play's links to colonialism not simply in terms of New World encounters, but also within wider geographical circuits in the Mediterranean as well as to marginal regions such as Ireland. True, the play is capacious in representing the workings of power in varied contexts and locations, but a value-laden resistance, a 'corrective' to colonial history, only demonstrates a *continuing* need for postcolonial pedagogies and scholarship. Finally, I believe, Bruster's essay typifies a recurring trend to 'flatten' the complex operations of colonial discourse laid out by critics mentioned above, and does so by simply bracketing the play within English and European contexts.

Bruster's implicit resistance to colonial history becomes explicit in Meredith Skura's revisionist attempt to erase such a history. Arguing that there was no stable colonialist discourse that Shakespeare could be said to draw upon (1989: 52–57), Skura instead draws on a psychoanalytical paradigm, whereby she makes problematic assertions about 'man's timeless tendency to demonize strangers', 'the universality of racial prejudice', and of 'psychological needs' (45, 56). Skura describes postcolonial and new historicist critics as 'revisionists' and directs her critique at their insertion of the play into European colonial history of the New World:

> Revisionists argue that when the English talked about these New World inhabitants, they did not just innocently apply stereotypes ... [but] they did so to a particular effect ... [According to them], the various distortions were discursive strategies ... that the play shares with all colonial discourse, and the ways in which *The Tempest* itself not only displays prejudice but fosters and even 'enacts' colonialism by mystifying or justifying Prospero's power over Caliban ... The new point is that *The Tempest* is a political act ... The recent criticism ... flattens the text into the mold of colonialist discourse and eliminates what is characteristically 'Shakespearean' in order to foreground what is 'colonialist'. (45–47)

Her resistance is directed at postcolonial criticism's attempts at historical *specificity* and, not unlike some earlier critics, I believe she seems to be *only* listening to Prospero's account, while *occluding* the trope of the colonial encounter within European colonialism in the New World and elsewhere, as evidenced by her use of scare quotes. The singular voice, as Kim Hall (1995) aptly notes, is the critic herself: Skura's assertions 'rely on the notion of a unified and universal white subject – in other words, herself' (152). Of course, literary criticism must deploy varied lenses on viewing a particular text. And postcolonial readings offer only one of several valid interpretation or foci. But literary criticism, far from being an innocuous, blithely apolitical activity, can also re-inscribe unexamined habits of thought, whereby, as in Skura's case, the usurper's colonizing activities, which include the enslavement of Caliban and control of Miranda's sexuality, remain unquestioned or elided within domestic or universalizing contexts. Her surprise that the 'new readings' are making the play a 'political act' – and that literature can be used for political effect – is quite ironic in that her downplaying of the colonial sources of the play is in *itself* political.

Narratives of Travel, Trade, and 'Discoveries'

With its insistence on historicizing, a postcolonial approach often illuminates early modern English (and European) travels, 'discoveries', and mercantile ventures, especially beyond the boundaries of the West, thus offering a productive context for reading several of Shakespeare's works. How did the global imaginings of an expansionist nation shape the cultural landscapes of early modern England? The voyages of 'discovery' and trade produced a nationalist ethos – at the centre of which were the colonial encounters with non-European, racial 'others', generating complicated notions of identity, race, religion, nationalism and of human nature itself. In fact, the period traditionally designated as the European Renaissance is now increasingly re-configured as the Global Renaissance, characterized by various modes of boundary crossings, rather than being conceived of as taking place within particular national demarcations of Western countries such as Italy, England, and so forth (Singh 2013). The popularity of the travel genre as an important cultural form in England going back to the middle ages, but increasing in popularity from the late sixteenth century onwards, emerged from the expansionist climate of mercantile London and the rising prominence of the genre of travel compilations in many European countries (Carey and Jowitt 2012: 9). Following William Caxton's deployment of printing in England, 'voyage travels' under the auspices of trading companies, for instance, were not considered as 'after-the-fact accounts but ... as an integral part of the activities they documented' (Fuller 1995: 2). And postcolonial theory from Said's *Orientalism* (1978) onwards has also questioned the Eurocentric premise of 'discovering' lands, people, and valuable commodities – a process that is recounted in the earliest travel narratives through those of the sixteenth and seventeenth centuries. Here it is useful to remember that the cultural forms of the early modern period such as travel writing bore the marks of an increasingly global, colonizing imagination; thus, as Kim Hall observes, in English contexts, 'the geographic movement was also an imaginative and ideological expansion: pilgrims, merchants, pirates, and adventurers explored and reinvented the world often in their own image' (2007: 229). Among the recurring ideas around which the burgeoning English travel archive often coalesced was the special dispensation of England among nations and of Christianity as the true religion privileged by God.

To understand the range of the prolific production of travel writing in the period, two monumental anthologies of the travel genre serve as exemplary works: Richard Hakluyt's (c. 1552–1616) compilation of varied travel texts and related documents, *The principall Navigations, Voyages and Discoveries of the English nation* (1589, expanded in 1598, 1599, and 1600) and Samuel Purchas' *Hakluytus Posthumous, or Purchas his Pilgrims* (1625), which mostly consisted of travel accounts, including manuscripts inherited from Hakluyt.

While the two editors seem to have somewhat different agendas of promoting a mercantile nationalism and Protestant Christianity respectively, the numerous and varied travel accounts in *both* compilations highlight cross-cultural interactions that manifest themselves in economic, military, religious and social terms. Rhetorically and epistemologically, these exchanges are often structured in terms of struggles. Many narrators, for instance, claim to be 'eye-witnesses' – seeing, witnessing, knowing are familiar tropes in the travel genre – but the interactions between Western travellers/writers and natives they encounter also often involve varying forms of 'misrecognition', as Westerners struggle to maintain a coherent subjectivity in opposition or contrast to varying forms of 'otherness'.

A clergyman, geographer, consultant for various trading companies and advisor to Queen Elizabeth I, Richard Hakluyt was also the editor, translator, purveyor of travel accounts and 'a leading promoter of English commercial and colonial expansion in the late Tudor and early Stuart period', as defined by Carey and Jowitt (2012: 1–2). Helfers (1997) further offers an astute definition of Hakluyt's role: he is often seen as a 'potent catalyst for the exploration movement ... instrumental in colonization and trading efforts and so [becoming] one of the conduits for much of the ephemeral information then circulating, both in pamphlet and oral form' (163). While the materials included were disparate and heterogeneous, Hakluyt's overarching aim was to assert England's providential place among nations, which he explains in his *Epistle Dedicatory* to Francis Walsingham in his first (1589) edition, aiming to promote the commercial and moral superiority of the English nation:

> To speake a word of that just commendation which our nation doe indeed deserve: it cannot be denied, but as in all former ages, they have bene men full of activity, stirrers abroad, and searchers of the remote parts of the world, so in this most famous and peerless government of her most excellent Majesty, her subjects through the special assistance and blessing of God, in searching the most opposite corners and quarters of the world, and to speake plainly, in compassing the vast globe of the earth more than once, have excelled all nations and people of the earth. (3)

When Hakluyt views the English as 'stirrers abroad', he wants them to competitively pursue trading advantages, including the slave trade. In the *Preface to the Reader* to the second volume of the 1599 edition of the *Principal Navigations*, he is explicit in these objectives:

> Now it is high time for us [England] to weigh our anchor ... and with all speed to direct our course for the ... lightsome, temperate, and warm Atlantic Ocean, over which the Spaniards and Portuguese have made so many pleasant, prosperous, and golden voyages ... And had they not continual and yearly trade in some one part or other of

Africa, for the getting of slaves, for sugar, for Elephants' teeth, grains, silver, gold, and other precious wares, which served as allurements to draw them on ... and as proposed to stay them from giving over their attempts.[11]

Victorian critic J.A. Froude called *Principal Navigations* 'the prose epic of the English nation' (qtd in Carey and Jowitt 2012: 139). More recently Helgerson (1992) also asserts that '*Principal Navigations* played an important role in the emergence of ideas about an English "nation" by articulating a sense of overseas achievement proleptically, and by stressing the significance of mercantile, as well as aristocratic actors in the theatre of empire' (qtd in Carey and Jowitt 2012: 3). Samuel Purchas in *Hakluytus Posthumous, or Purchas his Pilgrims* (1625) (and his earlier editions) took on the mantle of Hakluyt, but his Christian religion informed his editorial process and his volume represents the development of a Christian cosmography, in a religious and proto-ethnological vein. His materials are overwhelmingly narrative in form and do not include documents such the lists, legal records, treaties, and letters found in Hakluyt. His primary aim is to explore the religious significance of travel, closely following traditions of 'late Medieval pilgrimage narratives' (Helfers 1997: 167–68). Notwithstanding their somewhat different foci, Hakluyt's and Purchas' prolific compilations of travel documents and narratives together represent a distinctive moment in English history.

Collectively, these writings bring to life a many-layered 'World of Travelers' for 'domestic entertainment', for encouraging patriotic, commercial/colonizing forays, as well as Christian (Protestant) proselytization beyond England. Not surprisingly, their depictions of the complexities of interactions with 'others' – and the ensuing power dynamics – in different settings and situations, evoke analogies in many of Shakespeare's works that engage with colonial or proto-colonial themes (even tangentially) and, perhaps, in less obvious ways, with varied permutations of stereotyped exoticism and alterity. For instance, the discursive milieu of these popular travel materials can easily accommodate and *add* historical complexity to a play like Shakespeare's *The Tempest* – which mirrors a travel account in its motifs of a sea-voyage, discovery, and encounters with a 'native'. This analogy is evident in varied critical responses to the play's geographical and topographical links to travel writing in the 'age of discovery' and to England's 'incipient empire', which Virginia Mason Vaughan and Alden T. Vaughan (2011) elaborate as follows:

> The voluminous literature of European exploration was rife with tempests, wrecks, miracles, monsters, devils, and wondrous natives ... *The Tempest* may ... be his oblique dramatization of Europe's age of discovery. Shakespeare's borrowings from several sixteenth-century travel narratives are overshadowed by his almost certain familiarity with William Strachey's 'A True Repertory of the Wracke, and Redemption of Sir Thomas Gates' on Bermuda in July 1609, Strachey had been aboard ... a relief expedition enroute to the English outpost in Virginia, when a hurricane scattered the fleet, sank one ship, and drove *Sea Venture* on to Bermuda's rocky coast. All passengers and crew reached shore safely. [Here] the survivors flourished for nine months ... before sailing to Virginia ... In early September 1610, Sir Thomas Gates arrived back in England with Strachey's epistolary 'True Repertory,' written during and immediately after the events ... [and] was probably read [as a manuscript] by many of London's cultural and political leaders. (41)

While the Strachey letter was an important item among other New World travel texts (though it was not published until 1625 in *Purchas His Pilgrims*) from which may have come the storm scenes, the island setting, the infighting among factions and beleaguered natives, critics also point to other geopolitical contexts and their literary implications that may have influenced Shakespeare in the writing of *The Tempest*. Like several of Shakespeare's plays, *The Tempest* points to many geographical details, but it is also marked by distinctive ambiguities, which Peter Hulme (1986) describes as the play's 'dual topography: Naples, Tunis, and Algiers, but also the still vexed Bermoothes' (107). This anachronism, as he elaborates, creates a geographical impasse:

> The island is the meeting place of the play's topographical dualism, Mediterranean and Atlantic, ground of the mutually incompatible reference systems whose co-presence serves to frustrate any attempt to locate the island on a map. Caliban is similarly the ground of these two discourses. As 'wild man' or 'wodehouse', with an African mother [Sycorax] whose pedigree leads back to the *Odyssey*, he is distinctly Mediterranean. And yet, at the same time, he is, as his name suggests, a 'cannibal' as ... [the] figure ... in colonial discourse – ugly, devilish, ignorant, gullible and treacherous – according to the Europeans' descriptions of him. (108)

The precise location of the island is unspecified – 'an un-inhabited island' says the *First Folio* (1623) edition of Shakespeare's collected works. But the topicality of a south Mediterranean setting and characters of African origin would have been familiar to early modern English audiences: an 'exiled Sycorax, and an embryonic Caliban from Algiers, as well as a widow Dido (anciently) and a Claribel (recently) from Tunis' (Vaughan and Vaughan 2011: 49). The colonial analogy, other critics argue, does not restrict itself to the Mediterranean and the New World, but also extends to England's colonial rule over Ireland, while pointing to the demonization of the Irish in writings of Edmund Spenser, Barnabe Rich, and others. Paul Brown articulates this analogy persuasively:

> We should note a general analogy between text and context: specifically, between Ireland and Prospero's island. They are both marginally situated in semiperipheral areas (Ireland is geographically semiperipheral, its subjects both truant

civilians and savages, as Prospero's island is ambiguously placed between American and European discourse). Both places are described as 'uninhabited', (connoting the absence of civility) yet are peopled with a strange admixture of the savage and masterless other. (Brown 1985: 57)

Other scholars have returned to this analogy: 'Ireland may well have served Shakespeare as a topical example of the complex issues of overseas settlement, political legitimacy, revenge and repentance' (Vaughan and Vaughan 2011: 52). Caliban's suitability for English perceptions of Irish men as uncouth, rebellious, and intoxicated – the wild Irish man – is also readily apparent in an illustration in John Speed's *Theatre of the Empire of Great Britain* (1611).[12] Recognizing these multiple topographies and competing frames of reference does not invalidate the trope of the 'colonial encounter', but rather, as Kim Hall (1995) astutely observes, 'opens up the possibility for Caliban to occupy multiple sites of difference' (151).

A postcolonial perspective on early modern European 'discoveries' and commercial ventures can also afford new contexts for reading other plays of Shakespeare, another example being *The Merchant of Venice*. The competing interests and cultural and racial conflicts imbricated within pervasive anti-Semitism, between the merchants and the money lender – the Christians and the Jew – can be better understood in the context of a new dependence on capital in a growing, though unpredictable mercantile economy, and attendant shifts in relationships between the two communities. The loss of Antonio's ships filled with silks and spices at the outset of the play signal an important reminder of growing English (and European) trade with the East Indies, among other regions. Expansion for purposes of trade and discovery led to a growing awareness among Europeans of changing geographical, racial, religious, and cultural/national boundaries; and not unlike in *The Tempest*, encounters with non-European and non-Christian 'others', in this case with the Jews, produce new categories of difference and hierarchy, specific to this period.

From this perspective, Shylock's historicized role evokes our empathy in the context of Christian Europe's prejudice against Jews at the time, based on the historical memory of the expulsion of the Jews in 1290.[13]

Like *Othello*, *The Merchant of Venice* is strategically set in Venice, a liminal geographical location that also became a potent symbolic site for Europe's boundary with the non-Christian world of the Islamic Ottoman Empire, as well as the location of the first ghetto for Jewry. In fact, in the sixteenth and seventeenth centuries, as Clare Carroll observes, the ghetto of Venice was well-known throughout Europe, representing both the Christian marginalization of the Jews and their economic and cultural drives toward power and independence:

> Venice was a place where Jews flourished, both in spite of and because of one of the worst forms of discrimination against early modern Jews: the ghetto ... Despite the difficulties the Jews continued to encounter, within the ghetto they developed a vibrant economy and culture ..., [building] a stronger community in the midst of continuing discrimination. [And while] the contradictions of the conditions of the Jews in early modern Venice crop up in every aspect of their lives – economic, religious, and cultural ... the Jews [nonetheless] became absolutely indispensable to the Republic: it was the heavy tax levied on them that paid for Venice's costly wars, and it was the Jewish moneylenders who most directly dealt with the needs of the poor. (Carroll 2004: 73–74)

Travel knowledge was also an integral aspect of Renaissance Venice's mercantile society and cultural interests. The 'horizons of Venetian travel' in the early modern period, as Deborah Howard (2005) describes, were clearly expanding through this prolific writing culture:

> Travel lore in its widest sense was an integral part of Venetian culture ... Within Venice this body of [travel] knowledge circulated freely, orally, and in manuscript form,

but during the sixteenth century its dissemination was to be transformed by ambitious printing initiatives. [And] a new genre, the printed anthology of travel narratives, gave added authority to geographical information and helped to shape the ways in which travelers were perceived. (29)

The Merchant of Venice vividly depicts a city on the cusp of this expansive 'travel horizon', enabling great mercantile wealth, while also open to the encroachments of foreigners and a dependence on their money for trade. A postcolonial reading is attentive to such changing geo-political and mercantile landscapes with their accompanying identity fault lines. Thus, the seemingly simple question of *The Merchant of Venice*: 'Who is the Christian? Who is the Jew?' (4.1.169) resonates with early modern European anxieties about fixing racial and religious boundaries in the face of growing travel, trade, expansion, and intermingling of peoples. A striking description of the play in *The Stationer's Register* highlights these ambiguities of place and identity: 'a booke of the Merchant of Venice, or otherwise called the Jew of Venice' (qtd in Neill 2000: 271). The mass displacement and exile of Jews through European history – caught in conditions of liminality of Venice's location – problematizes any easy alignment of geography and history. Jews – as a race, a nation, mostly cast in binary opposition to Christians – figure frequently in narratives of English (and European) travellers across lands within Europe and beyond. In fact, the 'landlessness and scatteredness of the Jews were topoi of long duration and repeated in various contexts ... [and] the expulsion of Jews from many European countries and cities ... could be represented in many ways, from brief marginalia in sixteenth century English chronicles to more lengthy lists of expulsions and returns' (Holmberg 2011: 15–17).

Their role in the colonial imaginary was marked by a distinctive ambiguity. Michael Neill, in *Putting History to the Question* (2000), tellingly notes why the figure of the Jew was even more troubling to European Christians than 'Moors' and 'Turks' in an era of expansion:

Of course the particular fear that attaches to the demon-Jew in early modern European culture has to do with his insidious role as the hidden stranger, the alien whose otherness is more threatening for its guise of semblance. This was a culture whose own expansionism, ironically enough, generated fears of a highly absorptive otherness ... in its fictions the Jew represents the deepest threat of all – that of a *secret* difference, masquerading as likeness, whose presence threatens the surreptitious erosion of identity from within ... [and] the great advantage of Moors over Jews – or so it might seem to early modern Europeans – was that they could not so easily disguise their difference. (272)

When Jews figured in travel texts, it was a mixed picture. In Eva Johanna Holmberg's major study of English travel writings and their depictions of contemporary Jews, she notes a broad range of 'early modern English understandings and engagements with the Jews' (2011: 4). For instance, noted English travel writer George Sandys (1578–1644) presents a complex, multifaceted picture of the Jews within a comparative, ethnographic frame under Ottoman rule. He is cognizant of their marginality and the anti-Semitic prejudice they have suffered:

a people scattered throughout the World, and hated by those amongst whom they live; yet suffered as a necessary mischief: subject to all wrongs and contumelies, which they support with an invincible patience. Many ... have I seen abused; some of them beaten; yet never saw I a Jew with an angry countenance ... In general, they are worldly wise, and thrive wheresoever they set footing. (qtd in Holmberg 2011: 143)

Another picture of Jews also emerges in Sandys within a comparative context with the Turks, often discussed in English texts:

> Such and more horrible blasphemies [against Christians] invent they [the Jews]; which I feare to utter. But they be generally notorious liars. Although they agree with the *Turke* in circumcision, detestation of Images, abstinency from swine's flesh, and diverse other ceremonies, nevertheless the *Turkes* will not suffer a *Jew* turn *Mahometan*, unless he first turn a kind of Christian ... Their only studies are the Divinitie and the Physick, their occupations brocage [brokerage] and usury. (qtd in Hadfield 2001: 163)

Well-known throughout Europe, the Jewish ghetto in Venice also attracted the attention of the prolific English travel writer Thomas Coryat in his famous memoir, *Coryat's Crudities* (1611), which has a separate section entitled, 'The Jews' Ghetto'. Like many European responses, his picture of the Jews is marked by contradictions, mixed with prejudice and admiration: he describes their prayers in Hebrew 'as loud yaling ... beastly bellowing' but also praises them for keeping their Sabbath so strictly (qtd in Carroll 2004: 74, 75). He offers the valuable information that Jews do not convert 'because their goods are confiscated once they embrace Christianity', and yet he argues, 'they sheare ... many a poore Christian's estate by their extortion' (qtd in Carroll 2004: 75). Overall, these conflicting strands produce a varied picture of the Jewish ghetto in Venetian Christendom, evoking many echoes in *The Merchant of Venice*. Though this was a time, ironically, when the residence of Jews in England was strongly curtailed and the Jewish community in London did not have much of a visible presence, in reality, as James Shapiro (1996) notes, there is evidence of Jews living in Shakespeare's England in the late sixteenth and early seventeenth centuries (which I take up further in Chapter 2):

> Even as some [Jews] departed, others remained, and still others, no doubt quietly arrived. There were Jews in Shakespeare's England, though probably never more than a couple of hundred ... [though] in case after case, the English

show little surprise or concern at the presence of Jews living
in their midst. (76)

Overall, it can be argued that the positioning of Jews outside of
Christendom, mostly as its 'others' but also its co-inhabitants
sometimes, could be adapted to all sorts of texts, from travel
narratives to plays such as *The Merchant of Venice*.

In addition to depicting Jews inhabiting Venice, the geo-
politics of the play also remind us of European interactions
with North Africans across the Mediterranean in the seemingly
incidental role of the Prince of Morocco. He is one of the three
suitors who come to Belmont to solve the riddle of the caskets,
laid as a condition for Portia's marriage by her dead father. His
presence would certainly have raised the question as to why
Venetian daughters like Portia must receive suitors beyond
Europe and outside their own race and religion. The Prince
of Morocco would possibly have had an exotic, attractive
presence on stage, but Shakespeare's audiences would have
also accepted the 'logic' of the plot, where the alien suitor of
a different 'complexion' fails at the riddle and is rejected and
ridiculed by Portia (2.7.79).

Another daughter of Europe, in Shakespeare's *The
Tempest*, Claribel is given a different fate; Gonzalo, the
wise counsellor, reminds Alonso and the shipwrecked party
that they had been returning from 'Tunis, at the marriage of
your [Alonso's] daughter, who is now Queen' (2.1.98–99).
Her enforced marriage to an African king, to the obvious
distress of the whole party, including her father, disrupts the
boundaries of Mediterranean Europe. The stark fault lines of
the encroachments of North African influence and power over
Europe deepen in this exchange:

ALONSO
   … Would I had never
   Married my daughter there [Tunis], for coming thence
   My son is lost and (in my rate) she too,
   Who is so far from Italy removed
   I ne'er again shall see her …

SEBASTIAN
>Sir, you may thank yourself for this great loss,
>That would not bless our Europe with your daughter
>But rather loose her to an African,
>Where she at least is banished from your eye,
>You hath cause to wet the grief on't.
>... You were kneeled to and importuned otherwise
>By all of us, and the fair soul herself
>Weighed between loathness and obedience, at
>Which end o'th' beam should bow. (2.1.108–32)

Claribel, here briefly brought to life, weighs between her repugnance, 'loathness' at marrying the African king, and her 'obedience' to her father. Remaining on the margins of the play, 'she is never present but never forgotten, is a sacrifice offered to [the new powers]' (Hulme 1986: 112). This episode is a reminder that Mediterranean North Africa, the *Maghreb*, and its associations with Muslims, had a vivid presence in English life and imagination during the reigns of Elizabeth I and James I, evoking both an attraction and a threat. Scholarly evidence indicates that the actual interactions between the English and the Moors and Turks 'involved engagement and conflict in many different kinds of situations: piracy, trade, sexual relations, slavery, diplomacy, and military combat'.[14] Westerners travelling to the Mediterranean Islamic territories produced narratives about imperial glory and power, piracy and the captivity of slaves, as well as images of sexual excess related to harems, polygamy, concubinage, and circumcision.

In *Othello*, Iago's racialized terminology – 'Barbary horse', 'black ram tupping your white ewe' – would have also evoked stereotypes taken from the stories about decadence ascribed to non-European North African cultures. And within these accounts of European interactions with Islamic Moors and Turks, not surprisingly, the daughters of Europe – Portia, Claribel, and perhaps most notably, Desdemona – would have drawn attention as potential objects of desire, caught up in the larger power struggles between Christian Europe and the Islamic cultures on its boundaries. By placing these works within English (European) histories of trade, 'discovery', and colonization, a postcolonial inquiry casts a different light on them, now more visibly peopled by characters previously on the margins of the European critical consciousness – of worlds 'elsewhere': Moors, Jews, Indians, and others. It does not imply a change in the dramatis personae, but calls for more attention to characters who were 'whited out' before.

Race, Religion, Identity

OTHELLO
>Her father loved me, oft invited me,
>Still questioned me the story of my life
>From year to year – the battles, sieges, fortunes
>That I have passed.
>I ran it through, even from my boyish days,
>To th' very moment that he bade me tell it,
>Wherein I spake of most disastrous chances,
>Of moving accidents by flood and field
>Of hair-breadth scapes i'th' imminent deadly breach,
>Of being taken by the insolent foe
>And sold to slavery; of my redemption thence
>And portance in my travailous history;
>Wherein of antres vast and deserts idle,
>Rough quarries, rocks, and hills whose heads touch heaven
>It was my hint to speak – such was my process –
>And of the cannibals that each other eat,
>The Anthropophagi, and men whose heads
>Do grow beneath their shoulders. (*Othello* 1.3.129–46)[15]

Othello's iconic speech of his 'travels' marks him as a character within the European discursive landscape of 'discovery' and colonial exploration. We have already been introduced to him as an 'extravagant and wheeling stranger / Of here and everywhere' (1.1.134–35), a figure who is also variously described as 'lascivious moor' and 'erring barbarian', despite being the 'General' of the Venetian force. Quite strikingly he casts himself as a wanderer here, inhabiting scenarios, as Kim Hall (2007) observes, 'woven from several different kinds of travel writing: captivity narratives, tales of the marvelous, and ethnography/history' (231). Typically, *The Tempest* is considered the foundational text in postcolonial explorations relating to 'discovery', travel, trade, slavery and linguistic domination within Western colonization. But as postcolonial critics (and race theorists) have obsessively returned to *Othello* as a play about race, alterity, marginalization, and exclusion, they have also recuperated the play's historical associations with colonial interactions between Europeans, North Africans, and Turks around the Islamic Mediterranean. Travellers' tales of the period were typically quasi-ethnographic, yet also invested in evoking wonder and awe – in a combination of fascination and scepticism – in their readers. Othello offers moving accounts of 'battles, sieges, fortunes', of 'disastrous chances' and 'moving accidents', fanciful and exotic to Desdemona's 'greedy ear' as well as to early modern English audiences. Here, as some critics have noted, Othello it seems 'can only gain access to his own origins through the ascriptions of European colonial discourses' (Newman 1987: 150).

Embedded within these signifiers are historical markers of European colonial expansion: Othello's experiences of 'being sold in slavery' are reminiscent of European slaving in Sub-Saharan Africa. The 'Anthropophagi' derived from Herodotus's mythical races of flesh-eating people blur into tribes encountered by Columbus in his 'discovery' of the New World – few of whom may have practiced ritual eating of flesh (Hall 2007: 231). Encounters with various others – races, religions, tribes – across an expansive colonial imaginary, covering the New World and North Africa, are embedded within Othello's set-piece speech in 1.3. Geographically, the play is Janus-faced, mapped upon dual typographies: encompassing North

Africa and its 'Moors' and, on another trajectory, it also enacts Europe's fraught engagements with the Islamic Ottomans from the outpost of Cyprus. At the end of the play, Othello, the 'Moor', attempts to claim a coherent identity: 'speak of me as I am', but then the European spectres of Islamic figures – 'Turbanned Turk', 'Circumcised dog' – intrude into his efforts at psychic wholeness. Thus, we cannot speak of Othello as he is, for his 'otherness as a black man cannot be contained within the dominant, Western fantasy of a singular, unified identity' (Singh 1994: 288).

Integral to these postcolonial critical genealogies of Othello's 'race' and ethnic identity are larger considerations of race and religion, discursively entangled within the binaries of Christianity and Islam and of Europeans and 'Turks' and 'Moors' – sometimes further elided into 'blackamoors' and 'Ethiops'. Thus, I want to further suggest that the contextual archaeology of the play – especially as it includes travel and 'discovery' texts – reveals the complexities of Western racial and religious categories in the early modern period. Hall's 'Introduction' to *Othello: Texts and Contexts* (2007) traces this unstable genealogy:

> As the *Moor of Venice*, Othello can be discussed in relation to the stories about Africans, Ethiopians, 'Mahumetans' (Muslims), 'Negroes', and Indians that appear in travel accounts, biblical exegesis, classical lore, and plays ... Like many stereotypes, the image of the Moor is malleable, responsive to the different types of political, economic, and social transactions England was involved in at any given time, particularly in the seventeenth century, when England emerged into 'nascent imperialism'. (181)

Michael Neill, in *Putting History to the Question* (2000), also problematizes the fluidity of connotation in the terms 'Moors' and Turks', intermingling race and religion, in the travel literature of the period, which also plays out in *Othello*:

> In travel literature, these two expressions are sometimes interchangeable, 'Turk' being used even in descriptions of the East Indies as a loosely generic description of the people otherwise called 'Islams' or 'Mahomettans.' The Dutch voyager William Cornelison Schouten, for example describes an encounter with the men of Tidore 'some of whom had wreathes about their heads, which they say were Turks or Moors in religion'. Turkishness or Moorishness here is a matter of religious allegiance, rendered visible (like the malignancy of Othello's 'turbanned Turk') in details of costume. (273)

Such shifting taxonomies of race and religion – the 'Moor' being associated with different colour-inflected terms, as mentioned above – persistently appear in other travel narratives, suggesting varied associations with the play. Travel accounts associated with the first English slaving voyages by John Hawkins produce telling 'tribal ethnographies' which Sujata Iyengar, in *Shades of Difference* (2005), deconstructs as rapidly producing 'what ... is already a version of racialism – a hierarchical ordering of human beings that depends upon skin color and labor, especially slavery' (13). Other contemporary representations offer a more multilayered, mixed picture of Africa and Africans. Leo Africanus, for instance, closely identified with *Othello*, produced a rich and authoritative source for descriptions of North and West Africa in *A Geographical History of Africa* (1600) in which he praises 'Arabians which inhabit in Barbary or upon the coast of the Mediterranean sea, are greatly addicted unto the study of good arts and sciences: and those things which concern their law and religion are esteemed by them in the first place' (qtd in Hall 2007: 196). But then he also exposes them for dangerous jealousy: 'No nation in the world is so subject unto jealousy; for they will rather lose their lives, than put up [with] any disgrace in the behalf of their women' (196).

George Best's 1578 description of Frobisher's search for a Northwest Passage includes speculations about people's ability to live in the world's different climactic zones, when he conjectures why Africans ('Ethiopians') were black in complexion.

> Others again imagine the middle Zone to be extreme hot, because the people of *Africa*, especially the Ethiopians, are so coal black, and their hair like wool curled short, which blackness and crooked hair they suppose to come only by the parching heat of the Sun, which how it should be possible I cannot see. (qtd in Hall 2007: 191)

More telling is Best's widely cited description of an English–Ethiopian marriage, an obvious articulation of cultural anxieties about the black presence – with its threat of miscegenation and complexion – in the English imaginary.

> Therefore, to return again to the black Moors. I myself have seen an Ethiopian as black as coal brought into England, who taking a faire English woman to Wife, begat a son in all respects as black as the father was, although England were his native Country, and an English woman his Mother: whereby it seemeth this blackness proceedeth rather of some natural infection of that man, which was so strong, that neither the nature of the Clime, neither the good complexion of the Mother concurring, could anything alter, and therefore, we cannot impute it to the nature of the Clime. (qtd in Hall 2007: 191–92)

Historical contexts such as these (and others of *The Tempest* and *The Merchant of Venice*) reveal an archive of early modern writings on travel and racial difference, which critics have mined to produce criticism with postcolonial inflections. In fact, *Othello*'s contextual history has produced a significant body of critical work linking it with European 'discovery' and travel narratives, and concomitant 'race thinking' of the period (Hall 2007: 228–32). This scholarship, partially drawn on here, includes the work of Kim Hall, Michael Neill, Ania

Loomba, Imtiaz Habib, Karen Newman, Jyotsna Singh, Ian Smith, and Daniel Vitkus, among several others, who describe Othello's identity not in terms of universalizing individualism, but rather on the terrain of early modern religious landscapes, cultural geographies, and sexual/racial taxonomies, among other contexts.[16] Via these, we can grasp at the workings of European imperialist drives as well as 'native' African analogues and sources for the materials of the play.

Yet, we are also well served to keep in mind the legacy of universalizing approaches, as mentioned earlier in relation to *The Tempest*, which continue to bracket off history or view all histories as having equal import, and in the process, inadvertently perhaps, insert stereotypical assumptions about race, gender etc. into historical and cultural records. An egregious example is Alvin Kernan's 'Introduction' to *Othello*, published by Penguin Signet Classics (1998). Given that this edition is still available in inexpensive popular reprints, it exemplifies the influence of such approaches to replace history with 'universal' symbolism. The critic acknowledges that *Othello* holds relevance to topics such as 'militarism, racism ... gender, colonialism,' but he eschews these historical contexts in order to emphasize 'the symbolic arrangement of the world that Shakespeare has constructed as a background for the characters and which sets the universal scene for their fates' (lxiii). In his reading, the world of *Othello* is clearly demarcated into East–West stereotypical binaries:

> On one side, there are Turks, cannibals, monstrous deformities of nature ... the brute force of the sea, riot, mobs, darkness ... On the other side, there are Venice, The City, law, senates, amity, hierarchy, Desdemona, love ... innocent trust. (lxxi–lxxii)

This essentialist language used by Kernan hearkens to an earlier era and seems anachronistic to us, given that postcolonial, feminist, and race theories have occasioned a paradigm shift in recognizing that Othello's tragedy reflects early modern racialism as much as his hubris or character flaw. However, in the current racial and cultural fault-lines, Kernan-style binaries persist in Anglo-American professional forums and classrooms. Such readings do not have a widespread credence, but Kernan's example exemplifies a subterranean discourse that represses colonial history in seemingly innocuous, naturalized forms.

I end with a fairly recent essay by Philip D. Collington (2005) that also seems to draw on earlier cultural biases, treating Othello's stories as fabrications and casting him as an imposter: 'much of what Othello says is fabricated and exaggerated through narrative *simulation* in order to maintain an exotic persona, which guarantees his place within Venetian society ... he overstates his foreignness in order to gain European admirers. In short, he does not fear being *other*; he fears not being *other enough*' (75). While the critic places Othello's stories within the traditions of Herodotus, Pliny, and Mandeville, he egregiously criticizes the Moor for being opportunistic: 'Othello markets himself as culturally exotic and militarily indispensable, qualities which are ultimately revealed to have been overstated' (Collington 2005: 75).

Postcolonial and race-inflected readings would empathize with Othello bearing the representational burden of Venetian (and European) racially inflected stereotypes, but Collington's reading simplistically labels him a 'liar' (79). This interpretation clearly reveals racial inflections, whereby Othello's travel stories are given no credence as Western *constructions* of race and religion, discursively shaping travel and 'discovery' narratives. Collington's fairly recent (2005) reading, once again, testifies to a dependence on a naturalized, racialized 'logic' that continues to permeate Western traditions of reading *Othello* – one that does not account for postcolonial interventions of the past two decades.

In this opening chapter, I mapped Shakespearean engagements with the era of global expansion in early modern England (and Europe), showing how plays such as *The Tempest, The Merchant of Venice,* and *Othello,* via key postcolonial responses, enable an important reappraisal of the history of emergent colonialism, though not without some resistance to postcolonial theory. In the next chapter, I explore London's early modern dramatic productions – in public and private venues – in the context of England's emerging global role, concluding with reflections on postcolonial readings of *A Midsummer Night's Dream*. Theatre audiences saw a bustling, cosmopolitan world that came alive on stage through characters (not actors) representing different hues, genders, ranks, religions, and non-human, supernatural beings, among others. Renaissance English drama encompassed 'all the world' and was not the purely English phenomenon that was for long taken for granted in the Anglo-American academy until the postcolonial 'turn'.

2

Historical Contexts 2

Shakespeare's World and Productions of Difference

HENRY IV
    This is the English, not the Turkish court:
    Not Amurath an Amurath succeeds,
    But Harry, Harry.

– Henry IV, Part 2 5.2.47–49[1]

Royal pageants: the festivities at the Princess Elizabeth's wedding in 1613 included a fight between Venetian and Turkish galleys on February 11. Another pageant for Prince Henry celebrated a 'mock fight between merchantmen and Turkish pirates on 6 June, 1610'.

– E.P. Chambers (1923: 139)

Immigrants, 'Others', and Foreign Commodities in Early Modern London

Shakespeare and Postcolonial Theory opened with an inquiry into colonial encounters, from the early sixteenth century onwards. In Chapter 1, I explored the social and cultural milieu of Shakespearean works, especially when contextualized within travel narratives that represented England's global expansion. This chapter moves to early modern London – to the city, its theatres, and society – mapping diverse, dynamic populations within a global, cosmopolitan world, the ground zero of England's incipient colonial ambitions. While historians covering political and economic histories of the period recognize Shakespearean London as a city of demographic and class realignments, including an influx strangers, yet the 'foreign' non-European elements of the city are not central to their arguments. Studies of class divisions, problems of vagrancy, and of immigrants in London, for instance, do not typically recognize or acknowledge any racial and ethnic mix of the population.[2] I want to tell a different story of early modern London through a postcolonial lens that calls for a broader geographical, commercial, racial, and cultural perspective on England's growing global contacts and imperial ambitions, including an influx of foreign commodities and peoples into the city. Drawing on recent historical work on England's interactions with its non-Western 'others', I provide selected 'snapshots' of a cosmopolitan, economically bustling city and its dynamic, popular theatres. In conclusion, I discuss postcolonial critical reappraisals of Shakespeare's *A Midsummer Night's Dream* in its imaginings of 'India'. In these readings, the play's historical reach expands as it intersects with early modern discourses of trade, 'discovery', and the commodification of goods and bodies within complex economies of exchange.

What is the significance of imagining a global London? What is the benefit of considering the racial and ethnic make-up of Shakespearean London within England's emerging proto-colonial role? These globalizing imperatives, I believe, mark a departure from the traditional 'Elizabethan World Picture' that assumed a shared community of ideas about universal order and coherence, exclusively among Europeans (Tillyard [1943] 1953). In contrast to the traditional view of a European Renaissance, a global perspective helps us to more broadly reassess productions of difference – racial, ethnic, cultural – in the early modern period and in our own times. England's forays extended in different directions on the globe: these included contacts with the Ottomans and Moors based on military conflict and religious competiveness between Christians and Muslims, and English commercial and political relations farther east with the Safavids in Persia and the Mughals in India. Quite different interactions took place in the Americas, where 'powerful men like Walter Raleigh and Richard Hakluyt ... were proponents of settlement and colonization in Guiana and Virginia; and [finally], in Sub-Saharan Africa, where John Hawkins represented England in belatedly attempting to muscle in on Spanish and Portuguese slaving activities', in his three slaving voyages: 1562, 1564, and 1567–68 (Singh 2013: 7). Nationalism and commerce collaborated in validating these trajectories of expansion, materializing in the various trading companies in England – East India Company (1600); Levant Company (1581); Muscovy Company (1555) – while often encountering their rivals among other European powers, such as the Dutch East India Company (1602).

A curious and vivid scene recounted by the European traveller Thomas Platter offers a striking 'snapshot' of the convergence of worldwide goods. Platter begins with his observations of 'tobacco' being 'lit in a small pipe, the smoke sucked into the mouth', in 'ale-houses' he visits in London. The 'English first learnt of this medicine from the Indians', he informs his readers, and goes on to mention his informant, a 'Mr. Cope', a citizen of London who has 'spent much time in the Indies' (Platter [1599] 1937: 171). Mr Cope, who inhabits 'a fine house' and owns a veritable cabinet of curiosities 'stuffed with queer foreign objects in every corner', is clearly a global collector of the period. Platter records that:

> Amongst other things I saw here, the following seemed of interest:
>
> 1 An African charm made of teeth
> 2 Beautiful Indian plumes, ornaments, and clothes from China ...
> 3 A curious Javanese costume
> 4 A felt cloak from Arabia ...
> 5 An embalmed child (Mumia)
> 6 Turkish Emperor's golden seal
> 7 ... Porcelain from China Heathen Idols
> 8 Two beautifully dyed Indian sheepskins with silken sheen ...
> 9 Numerous bone instruments
> 10 ... A long narrow Indian canoe, with the oars and sliding plans
>
> He [Mr Cope] possessed besides many old heathen coins, fine pictures, all kinds of corals and sea-plants in abundance. There are also other people in London interested in curios, but this gentleman is superior to them all ... because of the Indian voyage he carried out with such zeal. In one house on the Thames bridge, I also beheld a large live camel. (Platter 1599: 173–74)

Platter's list seems eclectic. The signifier, 'Indian', seems ambiguous as to whether it denotes the East or West Indies and trivia seems to be cluttered with an 'embalmed child'. But cumulatively, the exotic list evokes a material culture from places far beyond the West, only possible within England's growing mercantile role in the world. Mr Cope's house may seem an oddity, maybe an invention, but within the vivid narrative flow of Platter's travel memoir, London emerges as a dynamic cosmopolitan place. Once we begin to recognize early modern London as a global city in commercial and demographic flux, we can also imagine among its populations of foreigners and immigrants, more often than not people of colour – from North and Sub-Saharan Africa, the Americas, and farther to the East Indies – a global England that is a hub for exchanges and interchanges. In one instance, Queen Elizabeth I made political and commercial overtures to both 'the Turks of the Ottoman empire and the Moors of the Kingdom of Morocco', through 'emissaries and correspondence' (Matar 1999: 7). A highly documented account of a portrait of a Moorish ambassador, Abd el-Ouahed ben Messaoud ben Mohammed Anoun (known as Hamet Xerife in England), provides an iconic image of an alien 'Mahometan' figure in the streets of London. He spent six months in England beginning in the autumn of 1600, staying with a company of fifteen in the Royal Exchange, and the whole Moroccan group attended Queen Elizabeth's accession day celebrations in November 1600 (Dimmock 2017: 38). It is striking that this embassy took place just before Shakespeare wrote *Othello*, and we may imagine that Shakespeare may have had the opportunity to witness English responses to this party of elite Muslims with their unfamiliar customs, attire, and modes of worship. Such encounters probably complicated the existing discourses about 'Moors' and 'Turks', which more typically blended into the negative term 'Mahometan', emerging in travel accounts to those empires.[3]

Thus, while English images of Islamic cultures were commonly exaggerated, caught between demonization and awe, increasingly they were also based on actual contacts with Muslim empires around the Mediterranean. With the establishment of the Levant Company in 1581, English commerce and military contacts rapidly developed throughout the Mediterranean, making visible the power of Islamic empires. And with the advent of print culture, information about Ottomans and Moors was also widely disseminated, provoking complex responses, both positive and stereotypically negative:

> The Mediterranean was the setting for many stories and 'true reports' [as we have seen in *Othello*], about Islamic power at sea and in commercial ports controlled by the Ottomans. Printed accounts of Turkish and Barbary galleys attacking Christian merchantmen confirmed the traditional association of Islam with acts of violence, treachery, cruelty, and wrath ... [Yet] it was difficult for more learned Europeans, or those who lived in closer proximity to lands ruled by Muslims, to demonize Islam in such a crude way ... there were Europeans who rejected both the popular and the learned demonizations of Islam. (Vitkus 2000: 12–15)

Shakespeare 'regularly engaged imaginatively with, and was inspired by this wider world. Like many of his contemporaries he was probably interested in Islam and the challenges of staging it, but his work also indicates the extent to which he lived and worked in a city that was becoming a cosmopolitan center of global trade' (Dimmock 2017: 37). Along with Moors, historical and cultural references also signal the presence of black Africans who lived, visited, and worked in England, particularly in London. In 1596, Queen Elizabeth issued a proclamation calling for the expulsion of 'Negars and blackamoors' from England – first labelled only 'blackmoors' and in the last letter called 'Negars and blackamoors' – and licensed Dutch Captain Casper van Senden to transport them in exchange for English prisoners he had delivered from Spain.

> Whereas the Queen's majesty, tendering the good and welfare of her own natural subjects, greatly distressed in these hard times of dearth, is highly discontented to understand the great number of [Negars] and blackamoors which (as she is informed) are carried into this realm since her troubles between her and the King of Spain. (Queen Elizabeth I, *Tudor Royal Proclamations*. ([1596]1964–69) vol. 3: 221–22)

The first edict did not seem to work, and Van Senden complained that citizens refused to give up Africans 'possessed' by them. And in 1601, another warrant appeared in Elizabeth's name requiring the transportation of 'Negars' and 'Blackamoors' out of her realm. The document seems to suggest that there were large numbers of black people in England, but in actual numbers Elizabeth planned to send 'eighty-nine blackamoors' to the Iberian region for 'very good exchange' with English prisoners, and as Emily Bartels (2006) points out, 'in both sets of orders, the number of blackamoors to be expelled is obviously incommensurate with the magnitude of the problem the queen displays' (313). During this period, Africans as immigrants did not pose the kind of the threat in numbers to English livelihoods that the queen seems to imply. And overall, the efforts at expulsion did not lead to any substantive change. In fact, 'Elizabeth's efforts extended only across the short period between 1569 and 1601 and did little to diminish the size of that population. Blacks remained in England throughout the Renaissance and by the middle of the eighteenth century comprised somewhere between one and three percent of the London populace' (Bartels 2006: 307).[4]

While we cast a light on London's diverse, non-English population, we should also keep in mind the earlier expulsion of the Jews from England in 1290, which according to some historians was radical and far-reaching in its exclusionary efforts.[5] But in actual fact, this was perhaps not fully implemented, as James Shapiro's study, *Shakespeare and the Jews* (1996) demonstrates (introduced in Chapter 1). He postulates that after their expulsion from England in 1290, Jews remained in sufficient numbers 'to represent the threat of both cultural and personal miscegenation' (8). Shapiro's case is strongly supported with sixteenth- and seventeenth-century allusions to Jews in Tudor and Stuart drama, travel writings, diaries and various tracts, and other sources. Despite the official expulsion earlier, he shows that small groups of Jews were allowed to stay. Whatever the actual numbers or whether anyone knew of any Jews, England had an obsession with 'secret Jews' – a xenophobic response to an expanding global world. Shapiro explains this process of othering as a desire by early modern English people to 'define what distinguished the Jews from themselves' (14), implying their fear that Jews might infiltrate England.[6]

Not only did Moors, Ottomans, and some black Africans make an appearance in early modern London, but England's more far-reaching enterprises to the East also brought to its shores intimations of an East Indian presence. 'India', for instance, was typically viewed as a fabled site of immense riches, fantastic creatures, and other rarities of nature – an imaginary world found in the cultural mythologies created by classical and medieval writers. But by the sixteenth century India became representable as a real geographical space associated with the rich Mughal Empire. Thus, the year 1600 saw the formation of the East India Company. Queen Elizabeth I granted a formal charter to the London merchants trading to the East Indies, hoping to break the Dutch monopoly of the spice trade in the Far East. In the first few decades, its focus was to acquire trading privileges from the Mughal emperors in India. As early as 1583 the first contingent of English merchants led by John Newberry had set off for India, taking a ship as far east as Syria on a journey that would be later chronicled by Shakespeare in *Macbeth*: 'Her husbands to Aleppo gone, master o' th' Tiger' (1.3.7). On that occasion Newberry carried with him a letter from Elizabeth I addressed to the 'most mightie prince, lord Zelabdim Echebar king of Cambaia', better known as the Mughal emperor Jalaluddin Akbar. And *A Midsummer Night's Dream*, with its 'spiced Indian airs', possibly also implies a reference to the English Queen in the form of the virginal 'imperial votaress' from the West, who escaped Cupid's arrow. For early modern audiences, the 'spiced Indian air' (2.1.163) that Titania so longingly remembers may also have evoked associations with Eastern merchandise, which could, and indeed did, turn up in the marketplaces of Europe.[7]

Such entwining of mercantile and political interactions with Ottoman and Moroccan kingdoms coupled with growing trading alliances in East India instigated a growing and remarkable shift in the English world view and tastes, especially for foreign commodities (Dimmock 2017: 37). This transformation of England into a trading economy is vividly evoked by Samuel Purchas in *Purchas, His Pilgrims* (1625), when he declares: 'And now we see London an Indian Mart, and Turkie itself from hence served with Pepper, and other Indian Commodities' (vol.1: 122). From this influx of commodities noted by Purchas, it is not difficult to imagine the effects of global trade, as noted below:

> We might perhaps begin to read these references to the East Indies [in Purchas and elsewhere] in a way that acknowledges the changing reality of England's domestic space with the growing influx of foreign objects and bodies. When Purchas refers to London as 'an Indian Mart', his claims, though in some ways exaggerated, reveal a divergent view of an English city, one filled with shops and homes stocked with pepper, cinnamon, nutmegs, and later with calicoes and chintz. It also allows for us to register the presence of east Indians in London.[8]

This presence was also embodied in seventeenth-century civic pageantry in London, bringing to the fore a new 'cosmopolitan civic order', one that reflected an increasing presence of commodities and very likely people, not only from the East Indies, but also from across the globe. The growing maritime power of England during the sixteenth century and the significance of the Thames river as a highway between London and the palaces up and down stream led naturally to a development of pageantry by water. For instance, the festivities at Princess Elizabeth's wedding in 1613 included a staged fight between Venetian and Turkish galleys on 11 February. Another pageant celebrated a 'mock fight between merchantmen and Turkish pirates on 6 June, 1610' (Chambers

1923: 139). Thus, not surprisingly, pageants for the Grocers Company written by Thomas Middleton as a part of the Lord Mayor's Shows, *The Triumphs of Honor and Industry* (1617) and *The Triumphs of Honor and Vertue* (1622), staged 'both spices and Indian figures, enabling us to read within a context of civic power and pageantry, how this changing domestic appetite was altering the very "complexion" of London', and its accompanying taxonomies of racial and ethnic difference (Sen 2011b: 3):

> *The Triumphs of Honor and Industry*, called 'The Pageant of several Nations', showing even the East Indian youths dancing in the heart of London, symbolically at least, underscored the potentially cosmopolitan nature of the civic space. Thus, the prospect of 'discovering' India in a corner of Cheapside seemed to invert tropes of travel narratives wherein Englishmen ventured outside to encounter an exotic landscape. London's urban space seemed to be transformed, inviting its new Lord Mayor to identify the foreign within a familiar domestic frame. Also, apparently, 'many pounds of precious nutmeg were freely distributed by the guild), and the Indians in the pageant seem to announce England's claim over spice producing regions of the East Indies'.[9]

In *Consuming Splendor: Society and Culture in Seventeenth-century England*, Linda Levy Peck (2005) also documents how this surge in the demand for exotic commodities in the sixteenth and seventeenth centuries coincided with the development of new ways of shopping, whereby luxury commodities from both Europe and Asia helped create a new type of consumer subjectivity (2). While creating new markets, contemporary responses to such conspicuous consumption were often far from laudatory, channeling classical and biblical concerns that 'associated luxury with the subversive influence of the "other": women, favorites, foreigners, and upstarts' (Peck 2005: 6). Thus, it would be fair to assume that the allure as well as threat of 'otherness' – whether of people or commodities –

would have been integral to the social and cultural milieu of Shakespearean London, signaling an actual foreign presence in the city: not only were 'the English ... wearing Moorish or Turkish fashions, buying "strange" trinkets, displaying carpets and porcelain and consuming foodstuffs ... from elsewhere, they were also encountering non-Christians, more frequently in person, especially in London and major port cities' (Dimmock 2017: 37).

As we piece together these cultural and historical sources, we should keep in mind that the story that emerges here of a cosmopolitan, multiracial London in an era of expansion is missing in many contemporary documentary materials; for instance, William Harrison's *Description of England* (1577) and John Stowe's *Survey of London* (1598) both only offer passing references to few blacks. If postcolonial studies chart England's imperial beginnings in trade, travel, and commerce, including the slave trade, its potential can only be realized athwart studies of racial formations in early modern England – formations that have recently been illuminated by Imtiaz Habib in *Black Lives in the English Archives, 1500–1677* (2008). Using a range of documentary records – though sometimes truncated or obscure – Habib argues that these records testify to the 'size, continuity, and historical seriousness of the black presence in England in the sixteenth and seventeenth centuries' (1). Habib explains his study's aim and scope as follows:

> The book's aim is not to recover a black population of any particular size, but to establish its very presence in early modern England, in considerable plurality, range of locations, and periodic continuity, that together demonstrate black people to be a known even if denied ethnic group, rather than stray individuals encountered by few or none. (14)

Furthermore, his all-encompassing deployment of the term 'black' to include 'Negro', 'Ethiopian', 'Egyptian', 'moor/blackamoor', 'barbaree' and 'Indian' (including orthographic variations), evokes both the range of non-British 'others' who were residing in and around London at the time, while showing intersecting proto-colonial trajectories of England's expansions: from Africa, to the East Indies, to North African and Ottoman territories (1–20). His archive is fairly far-reaching. As one critic acknowledges how he tracks records of black people scattered in the documents: 'their baptisms, marriages, and burials were recorded in parish registers, the purchase of their clothes, shoes, and other necessaries lie itemized in household accounts, their presence was noted in travel accounts, legal documents and diaries' (Kaufmann 2008b: 26). However, Habib's sources are also questioned as being of 'fluctuating ethnic clarity', according to Kaufmann, who suggests that 122 of the 448 records presented are of this uncertain nature (26). Some of Habib's modes of documentation and his lack of broader historical inquiries about the social structures have come under legitimate scrutiny; despite these lacunae, his focus on retrieving material records has nonetheless reconfigured our understanding of England's racial demographic. By providing an 'accessible data base of references to Africans, Indians, and Americans in early modern England, some never published before', he has opened the way for us to add to the archival resources and to further contextualize and explain the significance and reasons of their presence.[10]

Global Imaginings on the London Stage

Tamerlanes and Tamer-chams of the late Age, which had nothing in them but the scenicall strutting, and furious vociferation to warrant them to the ignorant gapers.

– Ben Jonson, *Timber, or Discoveries Made upon Men and Matter* ... (1641: 100)

Ben Jonson's scoffing remark referring to characters from the early modern 'Turk' plays often figures in scholarship used to describe the bombastic style of actors, while casting it in a clichéd mockery of oriental despots. Specifically, the reference to 'Tamerlanes' undoubtedly evokes Marlowe's popular play in two parts (1587–88), which was at the vanguard of the craze for the 'Turk play' in London's early playhouses. Though the 'Turk' was not always appreciated, as evident from Ben Jonson's description, yet, quite tellingly, the popularity of this sub-genre was sustained for an extraordinary length of time – nearly a century, from Elizabethan to Restoration England – and theatrical companies and their dramatists offered a prolific range of productions. This was a dramatic phenomenon that drew on Islam and Muslims, with a focus on the Ottoman Empire and its threatening presence on the borders of European Christendom.

References to the popular 'Turk' plays are one indicator of London's popular stages being caught up in the new globalizing influences and their domestic impact. As a background to these changes, let me establish, more generally, how London's prolific theatres were flourishing in this increasingly global and commercial city. What was the make-up of Shakespearean audiences and the presence of foreign visitors among them? Both early modern accounts and later theatre histories offer a picture of a cosmopolitan theatre environment, fuelled by commercial expansion, as described below by Andrew Gurr (1992):

> A broad picture does appear, suggesting that while the poor, particularly the London artisan poor, grew poorer, the number of the rich grew markedly and especially in London ... Trade was especially prosperous for the London merchant. The East India Company floated in 1600, with a capital of 72,000 pounds, brought its investors a minimum return of 121 per cent on each voyage ... From that date a good deal of the wealth turned up in the form of money, not land, which was the traditional form that wealth took

until the sixteenth century. Drake's bullion ships indirectly helped the players, because the more that wealth came to hand in the readily exchangeable form of money, the more idle gallants, hangers-on at Court and Inns-of- Court lawyers were created to seek the entertainment the players were selling. (13)

Fynes Moryson's *Itinerary* (1617) also conveys a vivid sense of early modern London as a populous city with 'more Playes' as compared 'to all [other] parts of the world' and with 'Players and Comedians [that excel] all others in the world'. Moryson's text, written first in Latin and then translated by the author into English, contains 'ten years' travel' through 'twelve dominions' in Europe, with the addition of 'Turkey', and evokes a cultural milieu within a global imaginary:

> The City of London alone hath four or five Companies of players with their peculiar Theaters Capable of many thousands, wherein they all play everyday in the week but Sunday ... and other frequent spectacles ... [to which] the people flock in great numbers, being naturally more newfangled than the Athenians to hear news and gaze upon every toy, as there be, in my opinion, more Plays in London than in all the parts of the world I have seen, so do these Players or Comedians excel all other in the world. (qtd in Gurr 1992: 9)

Foreign visitors to the London theatres were noted in other accounts too. Thomas Heywood (*An Apology for Actors*, 1612) observes: 'Playgoing is an ornament to the city, which strangers of all nations repairing hither report of in their countries, beholding them here with some admiration' (52). Among the visitors, notably, were some foreign ambassadors, as recounted by Alfred Harbage (1941) from various historical sources:

> [It is] to travelers like ... De Witt of Utrecht, Platter of Basle, Busino of Venice ... we owe our most revealing descriptions

of the English theatres. Some were men of consequence ... The foreign embassies also provided playhouse patrons. We hear of the French Ambassador and his wife going to the Globe to see *Pericles*, of the Spanish Ambassador with all his train going to the Fortune and then banqueting with the players, of the Venetian Ambassador going to the Curtain ... the foreigners show no particular preference for the private as opposed to the public play houses. (86–87)

The relationship between the city of London and the stage was symbiotic and interdependent. As Jean E. Howard's study, *The Theatre of a City: The Places for London Comedy, 1598–1642* (2007), defines this process: 'Rather than simply describing London, the stage participated in interpreting it and giving it social meaning ... In these stories, specific locations are transformed into venues defined by particular kinds of interactions, whether between citizen and alien, debtor and creditor, prostitute and client, or dancing master and country gentleman. Collectively, they suggest how city space could be used and by whom, and they make "place" the arena for addressing pressing urban problems: demographic change and the influx of foreigners and strangers into the city' (cover).

The stage was set for a drama of a nation and a global city that would prove a fertile ground for explorations of difference, diversity, and alterity. Peopled by characters who often resisted the constraints of given roles and identities – social, racial, and sexual – this drama complicates Western assumptions about Shakespeare's characters all being uniformly 'white people', given the many productions of 'otherness' in his works, often involving people of colour, of higher and lower ranks, of women and of non-human subjects such as fairies, ghosts, and witches. For instance, by 'the time Shakespeare came to write *Othello* in the early 1600s the English stage had seen more than twenty plays replete with bombastic "tawny Moors" and "blackamoors" or rampaging Ottoman armies led by prancing "Grand Turks" whose "scenical strutting and furious vociferation" had become somewhat of a cliché' (Dimmock 2017: 2). This trend continued until later in the seventeenth century. Some well-known examples, other than Shakespeare's *Othello* and *Titus Andronicus*, are Marlowe's *Tamburlaine I and II* (1587–88) and *The Jew of Malta* (1589); George Peele's *The Battle of Alcazar* (1594); Thomas Heywood's *The Fair Maid of the West* – Part I (1602); Robert Greene's *Selimus* (1594); and later, William Daborne's *A Christian Turned Turk* (1612) and Philip Massinger's *The Renegado* (1630), among several others.

Fears and fantasies about Islamic culture in the form of Moorish and Turkish characters were played out in a wide range of scenarios, ideologically and nationalistically setting England apart, as summed by Henry IV in describing English practices of succession: 'This is the English, not the Turkish Court: / Not Amurath an Amurath succeeds, / But Harry, Harry' (*Henry IV, Part 2* 5.2.47–49). Considerable scholarship in the past decade on what can be cast under the rubric of early or proto-colonial encounters has been devoted to these works as well as their Turkish/Ottoman/Moorish contextual materials. The import of such globalizing, historical interventions with regard to the 'Turk' plays, described by Daniel Vitkus (2000), have general implications for the sub-genre as a whole, with its 'porous cultural mélange that made up the Islamic Mediterranean', which in turn complicates early modern identity, by presenting 'a plurality of others – Turk, Moor, Jew, Christian, renegade, heretic, pagan' (44). Matar (1999) also offers insights into English contacts with the Islamic Mediterranean. On the one hand, he points out popular negative stereotypes of Turks and Moors being deceiving, tryrannical, lustful, bombastic, etc. found in English plays, pageants, and other cultural forms implying that a 'Muslim was all that an Englishman and a Christian was not' (1999: 14); and yet these unfavourable cultural impressions were belied by actual encounters with Muslims of North Africa and the Levant 'whereby there was interaction and familiarity, along with communication and cohabitation' (14).

The popularity of the 'Turk' plays, coupled with the dissemination of travel narratives involving Moors and Turks in early modern England (described in Chapter 1) leave no doubt that people identified as belonging to Ottoman and North African territories figured prominently in the Orientalizing, proto-colonial imaginary of the period. Thus, the appeal of *Othello* as a play also becomes obvious. However, given their sense of expanding geographical and cultural horizons, Shakespeare's audiences must also have been intrigued by references to Africans, 'blackamoors', 'Indians', and to the idea of 'India' itself. As mentioned earlier, 'India' was a fabled land as well as a representable place associated with new commodities, such as spices, and with written and oral accounts of travellers and merchants involved with the East India Company.

Shakespeare's audiences may have been comprised of individuals who were acquainted with travel narratives, but 'also of people for whom India may have been the stuff of a sailor's tavern tale, a map made in the human imagination' (Hendricks 1996: 45). Shakespeare refers to 'India' and 'Indians' in several places in his oeuvre, though with some referential slippage sometimes connoting New World inhabitants: Stefano and Trinculo's 'Dead Indian' in *The Tempest* (2.2) or more elegiacally, 'Her bed is India; there she lies, a pearl' in *Troilus and Cressida* (1.1). In one particular – and unlikely – play, however, *A Midsummer Night's Dream*, figurations of 'India' have opened the way for recent (from the mid-1990s onwards) and innovative critical engagements with race, sexuality, and emerging colonialism in the early modern period. If London was an 'Indian Mart', where the consumption of Indian commodities as well as imagined figurations of 'India' had a palpable presence, postcolonial perspectives – combined with analyses of 'race' in the play – have given it a new historical significance within these Indian – both mercantile and cultural – contexts (further picked up in recent Indian-themed productions of the play discussed in Chapter 6).

In her essay, '"Obscured by Dreams:" Race, Empire, and Shakespeare's *A Midsummer Night's Dream*' (1996), Margo

Hendricks provocatively lays out a set of questions regarding the role of the changeling Indian boy:

> What are we to make of the Indian boy? On the textual level, the Indian boy is simply a plot device: he figures as the origin of the conflict between Oberon and Titania (a conflict that presumably begins in India). But why does he have to be Indian? ... Why does Shakespeare initially identify the child as 'stol'n from an Indian king' and later expand on this identification with an elaborate narrative about the boy's maternal ethnic origins [with his mother, the 'Indian votaress']? ... What implications about race and early modern England's mercantilist and/or colonialist-imperialist ideology might we draw from Shakespeare's use of India? (41)

Addressing these issues, Hendricks argues that the deployment of Indian themes can be found in the very structure of the play: the 'spatial layout is not so much a bipolar (Athens and Forest) as a tri-polar configuration, with India sitting as the symbolic and ideological hub of departure and convergence for all the business of fairyland' (44). Interestingly, the critic not only focuses on the play's engagement with mercantilism, but also on how it sheds light on 'early modern representations of race and racist ideologies' (41). Ambiguity and complexity mark evocations of 'race', whether of a 'class-based concept of genealogy', an essential nature, or [of] the ambiguity of ethnic typology', akin to a 'shaping fantasy', whereby 'India' accrues multiple associations to geography, sexuality, and skin colour (42–43).

In many ways, while the changeling boy still continues to puzzle viewers (though in some productions he is reduced to a prop), critics like Margo Hendricks, and later, Shankar Raman, Ania Loomba, Gitanjali Shahani, and Abdulhamit Arvas regard his presence (with some sense of his being a problematic figure) as a metaphor for the demand for Eastern commodities within a mercantilist economy, sometimes evoking an exchange between goods and bodies. Shankar Raman (2001) argues that some psychoanalytical readings of the 'lovely' Indian boy, who is the object of desire for both Titania and Oberon, ignore the Indianness of the boy and substitute for him a universalized Oedipal subject (246). Instead, Raman views the Indian boy in relation to historically specific practices of colonialism: 'If the Indian Boy represents his absent mother and her relationship to Titania, colonial discourse concretely represents his value through the foreign merchandise destined to be consumed in the home country ... Despite their differences, Oberon and Titania's economies both rest upon commodifying the East' (244–45).

Ania Loomba (2016) also 'examines the play's ideological investments in the discourses of travel, trade, and colonialism even though it was produced five years before the setting up of the East India Company in 1600'. According to Dympna Callaghan (2016), Loomba interweaves 'gender issues' with 'questions of race and colonialism' and reads 'the dynamics of Titania and Oberon's tussle over the Indian boy in terms of a contest about colonial goods [such as Indians spices] set in the context of familial strife' (9).

The play's evocation of Indian 'merchandise' comes to life in the activities of the Indian 'votaress' in the 'spiced Indian air by night', as Titania recounts:

> Full often hath she gossiped by my side,
> And sat with me on Neptune's yellow sands
> Marking th' embarked traders on the flood,
> When we have laughed to see the sails conceive
> And grow big bellied with the wanton wind,
> ... (her womb rich then with my young
> squire)
> Would imitate and sail upon the land
> To fetch me trifles, and return again
> As from a voyage, rich with merchandise. (2.1.125–34)[11]

Critics often identify a colonial analogy here: 'the Indian woman's pregnant womb is obviously analogous to the fullness of trading ships, the boy and merchandise being the "riches" carried by each of them' (Loomba 2016: 185). In addressing the sexual inflections of the play, also in Indian contexts, both Hendricks and Loomba refer to travel accounts by Ludovico di Varthema (or Lewes Vertomannus/Barthema as he is called in English translations): at the centre of both readings of Barthema is his recounting of a practice whereby the King of Calicut's wife was 'deflowered' by 'one of the priests' who was paid 'fiftie pieces of gold' (Loomba 2016: 195). Hendricks does not offer a counterpoint to Barthema's European assumptions of 'rampant female sexuality as a recurrent feature of eastern lands', even though she views him as a biased ethnographer (51). Moreover, while pointing to Barthema's 'Eurocentric bias in dealing with gender relations' (50) she makes her own Eurocentric lapse in confusing 'Calicut' with 'Calcutta', collapsing two similar sounding (yet different) names that refer to distinct and separate cultural, linguistic, and geographical regions in India. Loomba offers a different view of this 'deflowering' as a 'part of a larger system of matrilineal descent' so that 'subsequently women could choose their own (usually temporary) mates in their own community' (195). While for Europeans, the 'specter of female choice' suggested 'absolute male dominance' (195), Loomba explains to (Western) readers how sexual autonomy in a matrilineal culture was the driving factor of this 'deflowering' practice. The lesson from these reflections on Barthema is that postcolonial readings must explain native practices on their own terms, even when they are being stereotyped and denigrated by early modern Western witnesses and travellers.

Representations of 'India' and 'the Indian boy' have also appeared in newer readings of *A Midsummer Night's Dream*, showing a postcolonial paradigm shift occurring cumulatively, though gradually. The play's 'spiced Indian air', reminiscent of the spice trade with the East Indies, evokes 'a particular set of responses to the early modern spice trade [in which] a conflicted discourse of fear and desire ... attached itself to commodities like pepper, nutmeg, mace, and cloves as they infiltrated the English marketplace via the newly formed East India Company' (Shahani 2014: 122).

Finally, Abdulhamit Arvas (2016) takes a different approach to the Indian boy in *A Midsummer Night's Dream*, via configurations of East–West struggles and homoerotic economies of desire and exchange. Drawing on the historical context of the abduction, conversion, and circulation of young boys in the early modern period, he emphasizes the racial and homoerotic inflections of the Titania–Oberon–Indian boy triangle within the master/servant matrix. Thus, the boy becomes a commodity – a signifier in the discourses about 'India' in the context of cross-cultural exchanges and emerging colonialism. Abductions of young boys must be seen within Anglo-Ottoman relationships involving mercantilism, trade, and so forth, as well as the abductions of boys taking place in the Mediterranean, as Arvas explains:

> While English sources are critical of the Ottoman practices of abduction, we [also] see a rise in the presence of abducted boys from other lands in England, shortly after the English presence is apparent in the Mediterranean in the 1580s ... [And] the Indian boy in *A Midsummer Night's Dream* from the last decade of the sixteenth century exemplifies the abduction of boys on the English stage, responding to the logic of abduction connecting the practice to mercantilism, Mediterranean trade, and piracy activities. (2016: 150)

While we may consider connections between the changeling boy and English commodities somewhat obliquely, Arvas brings them together in provocative and productive ways, showing the commodification and circulation of the boys themselves between the two kingdoms. 'India' becomes a metaphoric space of a global erotic imaginary, while also embodying the changeling boy whom Oberon desires to abduct. By tracking evocations of 'India' via references to race, sexuality, and mercantilism, specifically the 'spice trade', as an aspect of early colonialism, as outlined above, such postcolonially inflected readings interrogate the standard, English-centred interpretations of the play. Some might question whether these readings are too embedded in an ideological grid, focusing on a minor character, the 'Indian boy', often without an embodied presence on stage and never given a voice. However, many productions and 'native', multilingual adaptations of *A Midsummer Night's Dream* that have emphasized the Indian themes and settings belie the implied dismissal of the concept of 'India' in critical explorations of the production of difference (see also Chapter 6). 'India' in the sixteenth and seventeenth centuries carried multiple resonances: of distant lands, strange people and customs, a mart for spices, silks, and calicoes, and a fantasy of forbidden desire. As such, as we have seen, it evokes both desires and fears in the early modern English imagination. *A Midsummer Night's Dream* seems similarly to traverse proliferating contexts and depictions of 'India' and Indians.

When brought to life on stage, the oriental, Indian allusions and images in Shakespeare's *A Midsummer Night's Dream* clearly add another mutation to its metamorphic form. Furthermore, such readings enable us to map a complex cultural geography, which encompasses the various 'worlds' of the play – worlds which generations of Western critics simply identified within European contexts and sources: Ovid's *Metamorphoses,* Chaucer's *Canterbury Tales,* Plutarch's *Lives of the Romans*, Apuleius' *Golden Ass,* to name a few. A postcolonial lens allows us to imagine Shakespearean audiences as cosmopolitan and worldly, enjoying imaginings about 'India' in images of an 'Indian boy', an 'Indian votaress' and her 'rich' womb, of the 'farthest step of India', the 'rich merchandize', and the 'spiced Indian air'.

PART TWO

Shakespeare, Decolonization, Postcolonial Theory

PROSPERO
   This thing of darkness I
   Acknowledge mine.

   – *The Tempest* (5.1.275–76)

3

Past and Present

Shakespeare–Postcoloniality

ARIEL
 Let me remember thee what thou hast promised,
 Which is not yet performed me ...
PROSPERO
 What is't thou canst demand?
ARIEL
 My liberty.
– *The Tempest* 1.2.242–244

Legacies of Decolonization: Aimé Césaire, George Lamming, Roberto Fernandez Retamar, Kamau Brathwaite, and Ngũgĩ Wa Thiong'o

A key imperative of postcolonial theory is to question and reinvent the way in which a culture or society is represented, especially within the histories of colonialism. In the case of early modern England, my aim in Part I was to re-configure the culturally bounded narratives of the English nation. During the sixteenth and seventeenth centuries, English national identity figured prominently in its social structures as well as cultural forms and texts such as Shakespearean drama, travel narratives, and public entertainments. Typically, we think of these national impulses in terms of Western contexts. However, as I showed in the opening chapters, the picture that emerges via a postcolonial lens is of an English society – and especially in London – that is diverse, global, cosmopolitan, and heavily influenced by proto-colonial intimations of cross-cultural encounters taking place across the early modern world.[1] Such a postcolonial, *proleptic* gaze on the period via Shakespearean drama is particularly potent in questioning teleological historical time; it enables us to consider an anti-colonial future, whereby we can de-naturalize the earlier, anticipated destiny of the English nation as a colonial power. In thus refracting earlier Western history, a postcolonial perspective enables us to re-think the relationship between the past and present – the conundrums posed by historical paradigm shifts – as we move from Shakespeare's works on the early modern stage to their reappraisals from the 1950s onwards, born from the decolonization movement's interrogations that led to the applications of postcolonial theory and criticism to Shakespeare's works in the 1980s onwards.

Western responses to Shakespeare's works from the early modern period to the twenty-first century run the gamut from diverse performance histories of specific plays to source studies, rhetorical analyses, and appropriations of the plays for social and political movements. In this chapter, we make a temporal leap to the era of decolonization in the 1950s and beyond that produced strong reactions from non-Western intellectuals and former colonial subjects who challenged associations between Shakespeare's works and the colonial 'civilizing mission' that promoted English and implicitly 'white' values as justifications for empire. Overall, these decolonizing movements underpinned the emergence of postcolonial theory under Edward Said and others, but equally, they problematized Shakespeare's iconic and canonical status, particularly by appropriating key texts such as *The Tempest* and *Othello*, which were crucial in shaping the discursive milieu of anti-colonial literature and cultural critique. I draw on representative texts of five early figures, Aimé Césaire, George Lamming, Roberto Fernandez Retamar, Kamau Brathwaite, and Ngũgĩ Wa Thiong'o, to chart the trajectory of the decolonization movements shaped by the Shakespearean imaginary, *especially* as it was haunted by specters of *The Tempest*. Since names like Césaire, Ngũgĩ and others may seem familiar among indigenous populations of their own regions and countries, but less so to Western readers and historians, we need to return to their politically-motivated appropriations of Shakespeare. In fact, I would argue that these bold forays into dismantling and reassembling the Shakespearean text – in radical forms of appropriation – serve as important precursors to the inter-cultural, trans-cultural, and global Shakespeare movement that we have been witnessing in recent years (as is evident in other examples in the following chapters). Crucial to these liberationist writings was 'the centrality of language – the colonial signifying system – in both the phenomenological violence and the resistance to it, which was key in anti-colonial resistance strategies' (Singh 2016: 5). Overall, however, these authors and their movements cannot *all* be essentialized as singularly Utopian in aims and effects. Feminist readings of Miranda and Sycorax in Césaire's play, for instance, observe reified gender and sexual hierarchies, whereby the women have no substantive roles in the power struggle between Prospero and Caliban.[2] And Retamar's essay reveals the limits of anti-colonial positions within decolonization in its implicit acceptance of the flawed regime of Fidel Castro in Cuba, with its repressive record, despite the promise of an egalitarian society.

We begin with Aimé Césaire, whose 1969 play *Une Tempête* (*A Tempest*) captured the pulse of the anti-colonial movements of the 1950s and 1960s. 1969 was the momentous year when Brathwaite's book of poems, *Islands*, and Retamar's essay 'Caliban' also appeared. However, *Une Tempête* serves as the focal point of this chapter, given its iconic status around which decolonization and the American civil rights movements coalesced. Born in Martinique, a Caribbean island-colony of the French, in 1913, Césaire was a colonial subject, a French-educated intellectual and writer who, after his immersion in a Western humanistic education in Paris, experienced a cultural and psychic alienation from the colonial culture of his birthplace. And like other students of colour from France's colonies, he began to radically interrogate European civilization and its claims to superiority. He coined the term 'Negritude' as a literary and ideological response to the 'colonial situation, a psychological and cultural search for a black, pan-African identity untainted by colonial domination' (Irele 1965: 499). The concept of 'Negritude', the rallying cry for a liberated black identity, is evident in *A Tempest*, where we can see his idea of Negritude being played out through Caliban and Ariel – through the tensions between revolutionary and assimilationist drives on the part of colonial subjects. An adaptation of Shakespeare's *The Tempest*, the play was first performed at the famous Festival d'Hammamet in Tunisia, directed by Jean-Marie Serreau in 1969. My point of reference to and citations are drawn from the text of Richard Miller's translation (1985), which had its American premiere in New York, at the Ubu Repertory Theatre, in 1991, and was published in 1992.[3]

In general terms, Césaire's revision deploys all of the characters from Shakespeare's version, identifying Prospero as a white master, while Ariel is a mulatto slave and Caliban a black slave. He also introduces a Master of Ceremonies who takes on the role of Eshu, identified as a 'black devil-god' in Miller's translation. The Shakespearean text is infiltrated and re-claimed by multiple contexts emerging from contemporary Caribbean history, African, Yoruba mythology – referencing deities Eshu and Shango – and the African-American experience ('call me X', Caliban tells Prospero, evoking Malcolm X). Some important departures from Shakespeare include a disruption by Eshu, 'a black devil-god' from an African tradition, of a dance scene involving the classical goddesses Ceres, Juno, and Iris, while revealing the limits of Prospero's magic; the rejection of Miranda by Caliban; and perhaps most provocatively, while Caliban finds his freedom through his anti-colonial consciousness that repudiates Prospero's power, Césaire's Prospero also remains on the island to illustrate the lasting effects of colonization.

While it is an adaptation of a Western canonical literary work, Césaire's play offers a broad, inclusive historical span, as one critic observes referencing the New York production:

> The first performance of *A Tempest* in English [(Trans. Richard Miller 1985) 1991, New York City], was set in the United States ... but the play ... exhibits elements of all three major theatres of the Africa homeland and diaspora – Africa, the Caribbean, and the United States – so that the central paradigm of the colonizer/colonized relation, as it is constructed in *A Tempest*, embraces the totality of the black experience in the new world.[4]

Though ending in an on-going power struggle between its two protagonists, *A Tempest* signals a triumph for 'decolonizing the mind', the compelling imperative of anti-colonial writers (mentioned in reference to Ngũgĩ below) who shaped or participated in liberation movements of the 1950s, 1960s, and 1970s, while imaginatively raising new political, social, and psychic possibilities *beyond* colonialism. Césaire's Caliban (echoing Shakespeare) resists the colonizing role of language: 'I won't answer to the name Caliban ... it is a name given to me by your hatred and every time it is spoken it is an insult' (14–15). To Prospero's claims that 'I educated, trained, dragged you from ... bestiality', Caliban retorts: 'You didn't teach me a thing! Except to jabber in your own language so I could understand your orders ... And as for your learning, did you ever impart any of *that* to me? No, you took care not to. All your science you keep for yourself alone, shut up in those big books' (11–12). In a sense, not unlike as in Shakespeare's play, Césaire reminds audiences of the powerful Western knowledges that naturalized native subjection. While, like Césaire himself, Caliban is given the European language, his enslavement is reinforced within the twentieth-century colonialist Caribbean context.

As Caliban describes the 'theft' of his identity, when Prospero labels him a 'cannibal':

> Like a man without a name. Or, to be more precise, a man whose name has been stolen. You talk about history ... well that's history ... Every time you summon me it reminds me of a basic fact, the fact that you've stolen everything from me, even my identity. (15)

Sycorax is invoked by Caliban not as the 'witch' and 'ghoul', as Prospero labels her, but as an embodiment of the earth, 'I respect the earth because I know that it is alive and I know that Sycorax is alive. / Serpent, rain, lightning. / And I see thee everywhere' (12). Representing time's passage, an aged Prospero calls to Caliban: 'Well, Caliban, it's just us two now, here on the island', while reminding us that he stays to protect 'civilization' (68). The play ends to the familiar call of 'Freedom HI-DAY' by Caliban in a continuing, master–slave power struggle between the two. Césaire's explanation of this ending suggests he wanted to 'de-mythify' and 'demystify' the tale and yet extend its relevance to multiple histories of Western domination. As he explains in an interview:

> Demystified, the play [is] essentially about the master–slave relation [with echoes of Hegel] a relation that is still alive, and which ... explains a good deal of contemporary history: in particular, colonial history, the history of the United States'. ('Interview' qtd in Frassenelli 2008: 176)

Like Césaire, the Barbadian author George Lamming, in his collection of essays, *The Pleasures of Exile* ([1960] 1992), also draws on the Prospero–Caliban relationship, though covering less expansive histories than the former. In an extended biographical meditation, he describes the legacy of colonialism in shaping the identity of the West Indian man: 'Lamming locates himself in autobiographical time and space as a Caribbean writer in self-imposed exile in London at the age of thirty-two ... The discursive space of the text shifts continually from multiple sites of marginality – London, Africa, the Caribbean, and North America, contesting old notions of self and story' (Paquet 1992: xii). Shakespeare's play proves key to Lamming in explaining shifts from one cultural context to another, as he states: I 'make use of *The Tempest* as a way of presenting a certain state of feeling which is the heritage of the exiled and colonial writer from the British Caribbean' (9).

In offering a rich mixture of personal biography, colonial history, and postcolonial cultural appropriation of Shakespeare's play, Lamming offers us a complex view of the power dynamic of the colonizer and colonized; it is both hierarchical and mutually constitutive, as they are locked in a continual struggle, as the writer explains:

> Caliban is his [Prospero's] convert, colonized by language, and excluded by language. It is precisely this gift of language, this attempt at transformation, which has brought about the pleasure and paradox of Caliban's exile. Exiled from his gods, exiled from his nature, exiled from his own name! Yet Prospero is [also] afraid of Caliban. He is afraid because he knows his encounter with Caliban is, largely, his encounter with himself ... Caliban plots murder against Prospero, not in hatred, and not in fear, but out of a deep sense of betrayal. Prospero threatens Caliban with pain; but he never mentions murder; for he knows that the death of Caliban is the death of an occasion which he needs in order to escape the purgatory which has been crystallized by their encounter. (15)

Lamming then elaborates on Caliban's multiple subject positions within a colonial economy and its relationship to nature:

> Caliban is a child of nature and a slave. These are not synonymous. A child of Nature is an innocence, which is enslaved by a particular way of learning ... But a slave is not a child. Nor is a slave in a state of Nature. A slave is a project, a source of energy, organized in order to exploit Nature. (15)

Overall, while Lamming offers an astute and often sardonic critique of the structures of colonial domination, especially via language, he ultimately claims the colonizer's language, while accepting his own identity as 'a direct descendant of slaves' and also of Prospero, as he explains:

> I am a direct descendant of slaves, too near to the actual enterprise to believe that its echoes are over with ... emancipation ... I am [also] a direct descendant of Prospero worshipping in the same temple of endeavor, using his legacy of language – not to curse our meeting – but to push it further, reminding the descendants of both sides that what's done is done, and can only be seen as a soil from which other gifts, or the same gift endowed with different meanings, may grow ... (15)

I consider Lamming's appropriation of *The Tempest* as offering us an apt analogue for the processes of dialogic postcolonial re-readings. His engagement with Shakespeare's play is deeply personal as a black man from the West Indies in Britain, and yet he also is keenly aware of the historical forces that shape him. Even while he is deploying the play to expose the entangled history of colonial encounters – and to usher in decolonization – he also creatively draws on Shakespeare's poetic palette to complicate colonial relationships, viewing the 'cursed' colonial language as a 'gift'.

Like George Lamming, other Caribbean and Latin American writers in the wake of decolonization in the 1960s also imaginatively identified with Caliban in their rewritings of Shakespeare's play. Noted Cuban writer and intellectual Roberto Fernandez Retamar, in his iconic essay-cum-manifesto 'Caliban', originally published in 1971, turns to the 'savage' of Shakespeare's play as a metaphor for the cultural situation of former colonial subjects – a situation distinctive in its marginality and revolutionary potential. Recalling a history of varied Latin American responses to *The Tempest* through the twentieth century – some of which valorize Ariel as a native intellectual – Retamar argues that new non-European perspectives on the play were only enabled by the gradual emergence of these newly liberated nations:

> Our symbol then is not Ariel ... but rather Caliban. This is something that we, the *mestizo* inhabitants of these same isles where Caliban lived, see with particular clarity: Prospero invaded the islands, killed our ancestors, enslaved Caliban, and taught him his language to make himself understood. What can Caliban do but use that same language – today he has no other – to curse him ... I know no other metaphor more expressive of our cultural situation, of our reality ... what is our history, what is our culture, if not the history and culture of Caliban?[5]

Such an identification with Caliban conveys a vivid sense of Shakespeare's seventeenth-century New World character being frequently reincarnated within 'third world' movements of liberation. In these engagements, Ariel's role is also complicated, as Retamar reminds us, by drawing on varied Latin American (including Césaire and Lamming) deployments of Shakespeare's text. Ariel can play the role of a native 'intellectual tied to Prospero', in a less 'burdensome and crude way than Caliban', though the intellectual himself could be a mixture of 'slave and mercenary' (11–12).[6]

In Retamar's account of appropriations of Caliban, he draws attention to yet another name, 'the Barbadian poet, E.P. Kamau Brathwaite, who in 1969 (the same year as the publication of Retamar's essay and Césaire's *Une Tempête*) published a poem, "Caliban" in his book of poems, *Islands* (1969)' (13). This comprises the third section of his New World Trilogy, later published as a collection, *The Arrivants*, in 1973. *Islands* is concerned with the survival and retention of aspects of African cultures in the Caribbean, thus reflecting the then-predominant interest in ancestral culture and the rediscovery of Africa in the Caribbean. And in the poem, 'Caliban', the influences of orality, performance, and popular traditions of the West Indies and Africa come together, given that Brathwaite interpreted Shakespeare's Caliban as a Caribbean slave from Africa who has to adapt to the New World and to invent new rituals to make sense of his changed existence. Three key dates in his region's history mark the end of the first section of the poem: 'December second, nineteen fifty-six'; 'the first of August eighteen thirty-eight'; and 'the twelfth October fourteen ninety-two' (192).[7]

According to Doumerc (2014), 'These three dates correspond respectively to the beginning of the Cuban revolution, the abolition of slavery in the English-speaking Caribbean, and the first landfall made by Christopher Columbus on his first voyage to the Caribbean. These three "revolutions" are presented in reverse chronological order in order to encourage the reader/listener to go back in time and experience the upheavals that have made today's Caribbean what it is and who have made Caliban the creature he is today'.[8]

The second section of the poem introduces the character of Caliban in a dramatic fashion and through vertical lines:

Ban
Ban
Cal-
iban
like to play
pan
at the Car-
nival. (193)

Brathwaite uses vertical typography to evoke the slave passage as a journey to hell, as well as to represent a spiritual transmutation undertaken by the slaves and their descendants when performing the famous Caribbean limbo dance. Caliban's journey involves going back into the past: Carnival music provides a link with the slave past and the limbo dance in Brathwaite's invocation:[9]

> Down
> ... and the dark-
> ness fall-
> ing; eyes
> shut tight
> and the whip light
> crawl-
> ing round the ship
> where his free-
> dom drown. (192–93)

In these varied reincarnations and 'travels' of *The Tempest*, the Shakespearean text proves to be capacious and polyphonic, articulating various anti-colonial histories. While these responses did not take shape under the auspices of postcolonial theory, per se, which only emerged after Edward Said's *Orientalism* (1978), when viewed retrospectively, they function as precursors to the formal colonial discourse analysis of the 1980s onwards (discussed further below). It is also noteworthy that underpinning these radical appropriations is the broad impulse to 'decolonize the mind', as a form of resistance. This term gained currency among the authors of the anti-colonial movements, who acknowledged the power of Western cultural products such as literature – often constituting a 'civilizing mission' – by which the non-Western subjects were colonized. Ngũgĩ Wa Thiong'o, the noted Kenyan writer and revolutionary, sums up this process in his ground-breaking book, *Decolonizing the Mind: the Politics of Language in African Literature* (1986):

> The colonial child was made to see the world and where he stands in it as seen and defined by or reflected in the culture of the language of imposition ... it does not matter that the imported literature carried the great humanist tradition of the best of Shakespeare, Goethe, Balzac, Tolstoy, Gorky, Brecht, Sholokhov, Dickens. The location of this great mirror of imagination was necessarily Europe and its history and culture and the rest of the universe was seen from that center. (17–18)

Here, Ngũgĩ makes visible the ideological impact of Western literature in the production of colonial subjects, who then consider their own language and culture as inferior or marginal, even while admiring the Western 'humanist tradition'. Ngũgĩ's *oeuvre* has been consistently marked by interrogations of colonial power and its self-justifications, though clearly via thoughtful revisions, as he does in his acclaimed novel, *A Grain of Wheat* (1967); here Ngũgĩ follows in the tradition of anti-colonialist works from the Caribbean and Latin America, demonstrating yet another compelling appropriation of Shakespeare's *The Tempest*. Published in 1967 by Heinemann, *A Grain of Wheat* is set in the wake of the indigenous Mau Mau rebellion and on the cusp of Kenya's independence from Britain, following a group of villagers whose lives have been transformed by the 1952–60 Emergency. However, rather than evoke the presence of Caliban as a representative of the Kenyans in confinement, he creates and transports a Prospero-like, cruel, but idealistic colonial functionary to Kenya under British rule. This character, John Thompson, plans to write a book about Kenya, called *Prospero in Africa*, a project that, according to Cartelli (1987), clearly embodies a 'paternalistic ideology that is basic to the material aims of western imperialism', which is apparent in his resolve toward his goal:[10]

> Thompson was excited, conscious of walking on this precipice of a great discovery ... 'My heart was filled with joy,' he wrote later. 'In a flash, I was convinced that the

growth of the British Empire was the development of a great moral idea: it means, it must surely lead to the creation of one British nation, embracing people of all colors and creeds ... Transform the British Empire into one nation ... From the first, as soon as he set his hands on a pen ... the title of the manuscript floated before him. He would call it PROSPERO IN AFRICA'. (47–81)

But Thompson's idealism belies the cruel authority he imposes on the Kenyan Mau Mau movement for independence; while heading the concentration camp where the resistance figures are interned, he is implicated in the deaths of eleven prisoners. Even then, facing the failure of his idealism, he justifies his role in Kenya via a colonial binary of civilization and barbarism:

> One must use a stick. No government can tolerate anarchy; no civilization can be built on this violence and savagery. *Mau Mau* is evil; a movement, which if not checked, will mean complete destruction of all the values on which our civilization has thriven. (49)

It is telling that in this novel Ngũgĩ chooses Shakespeare's iconic and supposedly all-knowing magus-like patriarch in order 'to bring European assumptions of cultural superiority into unflattering contact with the history those assumptions have imposed on the culturally dispossessed ... In this respect, it may be said that if Thompson and Ngũgĩ misread Shakespeare at all, they do so in consistency with the way colonial history has inscribed itself on colonizer and colonized alike' (Cartelli 1987: 105).

Following these vignettes in rewritings of *The Tempest,* tracking the wave of decolonization, we can see how these revisions complicate and disrupt the play's aesthetic associations with a pastoral romance or with a story of a benevolent Magus, among others; instead, they crucially relocate it within revisionist histories of the 'discovery' of the Americas, the ensuing Atlantic slave trade, and the struggles for decolonization in the Caribbean, Latin America, and Kenya (East Africa). Such versions of Shakespeare's play, as one critic notes, offer unique examples of 'transculturation' – whereby this body of work demands that 'we return to the Shakespeare text ... not as a fetishized aesthetic artifact, but as a cultural object caught up in complex processes of inter-cultural and transnational exchange, adaptation, and transformation'.[11] While *The Tempest* was the iconic text in these stories of resistance, all these writers and intellectuals were cognizant of the cultural power of Shakespeare's works within the context of the humanist Western canon itself. Like Caliban himself, they deployed the languages of the colonizers (English, French, Spanish) to appropriate Shakespeare, via resistance, ambivalence, and creative transmutations.

Edward Said's *Orientalism* and the Paradigm Shift in Shakespeare Studies

While these decolonizing cultural energies from the 1950s onwards imaginatively evoked new national and cultural communities, often disrupting singular Western identities and Eurocentric modes of thought, the disciplinary formation of postcolonial studies only took off in the West in the late 1970s, with the publication of *Orientalism* (1978) and later, *Culture and Imperialism* (1993).[12] Other contemporary and subsequent critics, including Gayatri Spivak and Homi Bhabha, among numerous others, developed postcolonial arguments in varied directions,[13] but Said's seminal argument in the first text provided the inaugural challenge to Western literary academia, which had 'declared the serious study of imperialism and its culture off limits' (1979: 13). Instead, he drew attention to a new discourse, 'Orientalism', which he defined as a 'distribution of geopolitical awareness into aesthetic, scholarly, economic, sociological, historical, and philological texts' (1979: 12). In terms of its methodology, postcolonial theory and practice, following Said, was intent on the 'unmasking, the making and operation of colonial discourses – an undertaking which ... shared a concern with the specific historical conditions and social purposes of ideological representation' (Parry 2004: 6). Central to colonial discourse analysis, then, the practical methodology drawn from Said's theory was an abiding recognition of the rhetorical power of language and culture and their imbrication within networks of power, knowledge, and history, as Said explains:

> Culture, of course, is to be found operating within civil society, where the influence of ideas, of institutions, and of other persons, works not through domination, but by what [Antonio] Gramsci calls consent. In any society, not totalitarian, then, certain cultural forms predominate over others. (1979: 7)

The discourse of 'Orientalism' that Said defines here and elsewhere as a Western project for representing and producing the East, particularly during the eighteenth and nineteenth centuries, may not be directly applicable to the proto-colonial stirrings in early modern England, but it nonetheless has a political relevance and conceptual applicability to early modern studies, as I addressed in Chapter 1. Here, I want to stress that at its *inception* postcolonial theory participated in and occasioned a paradigm shift, discursively and intellectually intertwined with a set of inter-disciplinary methodologies, broadly coming under the rubric of *critical theory*: new historicism, cultural materialism, critical race studies, feminism, and Lacanian psychoanalysis to name a few. And Shakespeare studies as a field was very much at the nexus of this tectonic shift in how we locate his works within history, ideology, and other cultural formations.

While I further discuss some selected theoretical intersectionalities in Chapter 4, here I want to zoom in on the historical moment following *Orientalism*. In what ways did Shakespeare studies take a postcolonial 'turn' from the late

1970s through the mid-1990s? It is apparent that following a Saidian influence the 'serious study of imperialism and its culture' came to the forefront (Said 1979: 13). Colonial and postcolonial history interacted with politically-inflected approaches to Shakespeare. Some seminal works – books and articles – began to appear, relating the appropriation and dissemination of Shakespeare's works to Western colonial legacies and their aftermath. Furthermore, and perhaps crucially, in drawing attention to representations of race, ethnicity, and various forms of 'otherness', this early body of postcolonial Shakespearean work also disrupted the standard associations between the Bard and an essential 'Englishness' and/or 'whiteness'.

We have already noted (in Chapter 1) some of the scholarship on *The Tempest* and the history of Western colonialism from the 1960s to the 1980s by Paul Brown and Peter Hulme. Another critical strain, marking the genesis of postcolonial criticism of Shakespeare as we know it today, mapped the 'travels' of Shakespeare's works in colonial and postcolonial India and South Africa. This included *Race, Gender, Renaissance Drama* by Ania Loomba (1989), which declared its colonial and postcolonial inflections on its cover: '[this book] inter-relates racial and sexual differences to explore the constructions of Renaissance authority and the politics of English studies, particularly Renaissance drama in post-colonial education, [particularly in India]'. Identifying her own location at that time as 'a teacher of English literature in Delhi university', which she 'shared with more than 700 others', Loomba suggests that this was 'an indication of the massive presence of the subject in colonial education and its tenacity in the post-colonial situation' (3). With this assumption, she emphasizes the 'encounter between the Western text and Indian readers as the site of a complex drama where imperialism, colonialism, postcolonialism, and patriarchy intersect' (3). Another essay laying the ground work for Postcolonial Shakespeare studies, 'Different Shakespeares: The Bard in Colonial/Postcolonial India' (Singh 1989), also follows an inquiry into appropriations and disseminations of Shakespeare in colonial and postcolonial India: 'What was the precise nature of the Empire's investment in Shakespeare?' In addressing this question, this article first examines English Shakespearean productions in colonial Calcutta, as a 'part of a political strategy of exporting English culture in the nineteenth century', and later it covers 'indigenous performances ... [in the vernacular] mediated by heterogeneous forces of race, language, and native culture' (Singh 1989: 446–47). Overall, it pointedly questions assumptions of Shakespeare's universality, a myth that perpetuated a universal humanism underpinning colonial literary studies, continuing through the 1980s – and lingering even today. In the colonial context in India, ironically, this myth helped to buttress the elite native power structures even while Shakespeare was promoted as a part of the civilizing mission of empire. But this essay also shows how, in in the postcolonial era, the transcendental status of the Bard's works was gradually disrupted by the varied, heterogeneous Shakespeares across classes, languages, and cultures, among other factors, though these movements have been uneven and eclectic at best.

Another essay informed by similar postcolonial imperatives – taking us back to the historical legacy of apartheid in South Africa – was Martin Orkin's 'Othello and the "Plain Face" of Racism' (1987a). Quoting a nineteenth-century advertisement relating to productions of *Othello* in the Cape at the outset, Orkin reveals the racist attitudes of the time. Even though, apparently, it was a popular play in the region, Othello was consistently demonized:

> In listening to Othello, do they not necessarily contract a horrible familiarity with passions and deeds of the most fiendish character ... and give up their minds to be polluted by language so gross? (166)

The history of race and racism, we learn in this article, has many mutations and permutations when inflected through the reception of *Othello*. In a wide-ranging analysis, Orkin examines attitudes toward colour and Africans in Shakespeare's England and in *Othello*; the formation and influence of racist mythologies on criticism; and finally, the silence and the racist tendencies prevailing in South African critical responses to the play:

> South African critics generally avoid *Othello*; when they do write about it, they hardly touch upon its concern with color, and seek refuge instead in a focus upon idealist abstractions or upon interiority ... [and as a result] such emphases ... upon the 'truths' of human nature, in the South African situation, encourages by a process of omission and avoidance continuing submission to the prevailing social order, [of apartheid in this case]. (180)

Orkin's essay was ground breaking in several ways, in exposing the varied modes of 'race thinking' that a play like *Othello* could demonstrate, and more strikingly it showed us how a seemingly innocuous cultural artifact, like a play, can be distorted and mobilized to implicitly endorse a repressive political system like apartheid. These selected examples cast a light on the gradual diversification and expansion of non-Western contexts or modes of knowledge within which Shakespeare's works were placed – what Orkin described in his later book, *Local Shakespeares*, as 'non-metropolitan knowledge'.

These three essays, like the earlier interventions of Césaire, Retamar, Lamming and others, reveal that the postcolonial paradigm shift did not occur by institutional edict from the Western Shakespeare establishment, but rather by individuals who interrogated canonical disseminations of his works within the context of their *own* 'local' or marginal histories.

Through the emergence of postcolonial theory that gave a distinctive intellectual and political 'turn' to the field, Shakespeare was no longer seen as if existing in an impermeable European sphere. Here, it is important to recall that postcolonial theory evolved and mutated in constant conversation with other theoretical shifts in feminism, new historicism, and race theories, among others, which I will explore further in Chapter 4. Finally, we must recognize that in this *paradigm shift* of the 1980s, Shakespearean studies also became more *global* and cosmopolitan, especially in its inclusions of non-Western receptions, a trend that has continued till the present – in criticism, performance, and in film – whereby the poetic language of the plays continues to represent and enrich human experience in increasingly expansive and varied domains.

4

Intersectionalities

Postcoloniality and Difference

LEAR
  Poor naked wretches, whereso'er you are,
  That bide the pelting of this pitiless storm,
  How shall your houseless heads and unfed sides,
  Your looped and windowed raggedness, defend you
  From seasons such as these?

  – *King Lear* 3.4.28–32[1]

Shakespeare–Postcoloniality – Johannesburg, 1996

In the last chapter, we saw how various decolonization movements – from the 1950s through the 1970s – exposed the colonial value system, representing colonized voices who spoke back in Shakespearean accents. This preceded the political 'turn' in Anglo-American Shakespeare studies through the 1980s onwards that marked a break with the liberal humanist consensus around a 'timeless' and 'universal' Shakespeare. In South Africa, for instance, the initial break from its colonial past – and white cultural dominance – only took place in 1994 when the first democratic elections were held. It was when South Africa was under an African National Congress (ANC) government – a time optimistically seen as a transition away from apartheid rule. An international conference appropriately titled 'Shakespeare–Postcoloniality' took place at the University of Witwatersrand, Johannesburg, on 3–7 July 1996. This conference marked a crucial, post-apartheid moment that remains vivid in my memory. I was a participant, presenting work on Shakespeare in former colonies such as India. If not explicitly, in effect the agenda of the conference seemed to be shaped by imperatives of *intersectionality*. There was a general recognition that the promotion of Shakespeare within colonial and postcolonial contexts inevitably intersected with prevailing forms of difference, hierarchy, and exclusion (Crenshaw 1991).[2] Not surprisingly, then, the 'discussions on Shakespeare ... led to impassioned debates on the nature of subaltern agency, post-structuralist theory, the possible connections between South Asian and South African historiography, or indeed ANC policies on landownership' (Loomba and Orkin 1998: 19).

While the main organizer was Professor Martin Orkin, a noted Shakespearean and pioneering postcolonial scholar, the event was not sponsored by the Department of English, University of Witwatersrand in Johannesburg, but by an intersectional array of departments across the social sciences and humanities. The English Department, it seems, was ambivalent about claiming this conference.[3] The fissures of race and class – and of differing investments in Western canonical works – were not bridged by the title of 'Shakespeare–Postcoloniality'. After all, it was only in the late 1980s that the country had witnessed the darkest period of the State of Emergency in South Africa. Remnants of these earlier divisions became even more evident at the conference's conclusion, creating a productive dissonance, as another participant, Margo Hendricks, noted:

> Varying cultural, political, and ethnic points of reference surfaced ... the theory and praxis of 'postcoloniality' itself was subject to interrogation ... Can expatriates from former colonies, now living in the metropolis or its surrogate (England or the US) speak for those who remain in the former colonized spaces that marked the boundaries of the British Empire? Is it appropriate for Black Americans to express kinship with the black South African? Should there have even been a conference on Shakespeare and postcoloniality, given the uses to which Shakespeare's writings have been put throughout the history of English/British imperialism?[4]

By the time we got to these final 'confessional' reflections, what became increasingly apparent was that when joined with postcoloniality, interpretations of Shakespeare's works emerged from varied subject positions responding to different material conditions. One of the designated speakers at the 'Shakespeare–Postcoloniality' conference in Johannesburg, for instance, came from outside of academia; Hugh Lewin, the author of the memoir *Bandiet* (1981), was a former member of the South African resistance. He was among many white South Africans who fought against apartheid, for which he was imprisoned for seven years, from 1964 to 1971. What did Lewin, a former *bandiet* (prisoner), have to say to us Shakespeareans? He told us a compelling story of participating in makeshift productions of Shakespeare (and other Western playwrights) in the apartheid prison, an ironic occasion, given that the choice of Shakespeare (and other Western works) was not unusual for men of European descent who had studied English canonical works in their white education curriculum in apartheid South Africa of the 1950s. In 1968, however, all performances were banned in the South African prison.[5] Given that climate, it was moving to hear him tell us that while they had felt the harsh grip of the apartheid state, Shakespeare's theatrical works had offered them powerful illusions of rebellion in a world of rigid boundaries and limits.[6]

I open with 'Shakespeare–Postcoloniality' in Johannesburg in 1996 to tell a story about an event in which Shakespearean postcolonial theory took shape 'on the ground' so to speak. As an important qualification to the orientation of this chapter, my aim is not to elide postcolonial theory with critical race theory, economic theory, and feminist or gender theory, etc., given the distinct conceptual and historical underpinnings of each critical project.[7] As already noted, the impassioned and often heated exchanges at 'Shakespeare–Postcoloniality' produced a dissonance that sometimes raised more questions than it provided answers, for instance, regarding the ways in which race, class, and gender were being theorized. In an essay published in 1997, written prior to the conference, the late Nicholas Visser warned against premature celebrations in post-apartheid South Africa. Before and after the Johannesburg conference, he notes with some ironic sarcasm, South Africa saw a 'proliferation of institutional venues and publications devoted to postcolonial inquiry ... we were colonial; we have become postcolonial ... and with the election of 1994, racial settlement has been largely effected ... and there is no need to be concerned with the fact that class relations remain unaltered in the "new" South Africa' (Visser 1997a: 82–93). From what I recall, the discussions at the conference were also caught up in similar political and theoretical concerns: interrogations of colonization, empire, and their aftermath in relation to Shakespeare were intersectionally linked to continuing material struggles for racial, economic, social, and gender equity in the global north and south. A first-hand encounter with these experiences included a visit by the participants to the black township of Soweto, where we could see the social and economic isolation of the inhabitants as a legacy of apartheid, though in 1997 the population was beginning to see some movement both in and out of the township.

Postcoloniality and Difference: *King Lear*, *Antony and Cleopatra*, and *Cymbeline*

Continuing in this vein, and extrapolating from and beyond the story of 'Shakespeare–Postcoloniality' in Johannesburg (1996), the rest of this chapter examines representations of intersectional struggles in postcolonially themed criticism and reviews of different works of Shakespeare. Earlier chapters in this book examined critical readings and cultural histories of works such as *Othello, The Merchant of Venice*, and *The Tempest*, centrally concerned with race, colonialism, and empire, and *A Midsummer Night's Dream* with its connections to 'India'. In this chapter, I deploy a postcolonial, hybridized perspective on varying responses to *King Lear, Antony and Cleopatra*, and *Cymbeline* – plays having no obvious postcolonial affiliations. I work within critical frameworks in which past and present representations of hierarchy and difference are brought into productive conversations, rather than mapped along a historical continuum, bringing to bear 'local, non-metropolitan knowledges' and different histories in understanding Shakespeare's works outside canonical, Western frameworks (Orkin 2005: 3–4). Thus, in diachronic approaches to these plays, I focus on readings of private property, capital, and class struggles represented in *King Lear*, specifically when inserted into South African history of colonization and racial apartheid; on shifting deployments and interrogations of racialist and sexual discourses in representations of Cleopatra, especially on the Western stage; and on critical interpretations of imperial and gendered nation formations in Shakespeare's *Cymbeline* in the early modern period, and on presentist readings of the discursive links between patriarchy in the play and postcolonial 'reconciliations' and debates about national identity in Israel and South Africa. And finally, I briefly extrapolate on the 'masculine embrace' of nation and empire in *Cymbeline*, highlighted in the above readings, exploring some interconnections between sexual exchange, rape and empire evoked by the play.

King Lear

Among the important interventions into the Shakespearean canon at the Johannesburg conference was a paper on *King Lear* that read the play through the lens of South African history of colonization, apartheid, and postcolonial land 'reform'. Nicholas Visser, as mentioned earlier, was one of the early critics of the variants of postcolonial theory deployed by liberal South African theorists in the post-apartheid era. He had argued, in 'Postcoloniality of a Special Type' (1997a), that 'the politics of identity and cultural practice for postcolonial theory is organized almost exclusively along racial lines; and [on] the belief that identity and subjectivity are [only] racially constructed' (1997a: 92–93). This approach elided links between and race and class. Drawing on these issues, Visser's postcolonial reading of Shakespeare's *King Lear* intertwined struggles for land use and ownership in early modern England and in post-apartheid South Africa. This talk was subsequently published in *Textual Practice* (1997b), as 'Shakespeare and Hanekon: *King Lear* and land'.

Of course, Lear's acknowledgement of the dire physical conditions of his companions in the hovel and of his subjects – of their 'houseless heads and unfed sides' – often draws connections to social problems of homelessness and poverty, and typically to the subject of 'progressive' interpretations of the play. Kozintsev's *Lear* (1971) comes to mind in considering the play's treatment of poverty. But in most productions and interpretations of *King Lear*, 'race' or racial difference never figures as a category of analysis. In Visser's essay, however, 'the issue of land – of its control, its ownership … its relation, crucially, to power as well as to powerlessness and poverty', reflects the *racial* fault-lines of apartheid, a system based on racial exclusion and discrimination (1997b: 26). The land labourers who are shortchanged in Minister Hanekom's land 'reform' are more than likely to be black, and he gives an eloquent voice to them in the epigraph citation from an indigenous poet, St. J. Page Yako: 'This land will be folded like a blanket / Till it is like the palm of a hand' (25). To bring *King Lear* to a different enunciation about the experience of homelessness into a location of *racial apartheid* is to expand the empathies of audiences toward South African black populations. The play's racial tenor becomes even more clear with Visser's insertion of the play into a longer history of colonization, 'discovery', and capitalism in South Africa. The early modern European 'discoveries' of non-Western lands often evolved into a claim for land and its uses as property (see Chapter 1); Walter Raleigh's 'discovery' and claim of Guiana for Queen Elizabeth I and Caliban's claim, 'This Island's mine / by Sycorax my mother', are but two instances of struggles for landownership in European expansionist drives. Thus, Visser seems to ignore the traditional critical focus on *King Lear's* sources in the ancient British tale and its fairy tale tenor – drawn from 'King Leir' in Holinshed's *Chronicles*. Instead, he links Lear's feudal kingship with its property entitlements to proto-capitalist land rights aligned with colonization in South Africa.

Going back to the 'originary' moment of the South African nation, Visser invites us to recall the moment of European 'discovery' of what became South Africa. On 21 February 1657, Jan Van Riebeeck, commander of the Dutch East India Company's recently established re-victualling station at the Cape, announced his first freehold grants of land to nine Dutch burghers: 'They were in all likelihood the earliest freeholding properties on the continent of South Africa,' whereby 'the land would be their property forever to do with as they like' (27). Three years later, Riebeeck fortified and enclosed the land forcibly occupied by the Company from the now dispossessed natives. Thus, we learn that 'within five years of the establishment of the European settlement at the Cape, and within few decades ... of the performance of *King Lear* before James I at Christmastide in 1606, South Africa experienced its first colonial division of the kingdom' (26). Subsequent European settlements of South Africa were also premised on further entitlements to the supposed 'waste' land, as Martin Orkin earlier pointed out in his study *Shakespeare Against Apartheid* (1987b), connecting the play's concern with land to a history of dispossession.[8] Visser acknowledges his debt to Orkin, but moves to presentist concerns (late 1990s) with the South African Constitution and the discursive networks in which land is represented and contested in the world of the play as well as in South Africa itself.

Visser's (1997b) essay exposes the whites' incremental claims to land within South Africa's colonial history, thus denaturalizing the notion of private property through an emphasis on the early modern transition of land into property in *King Lear*. It shows how the traditional 'set of relations of homage and care, obligation and reciprocity' (30) are replaced by Edmund's more opportunistic claim 'Let me, if not by birth, have lands by wit' (1.2.181). Finally, the critic segues into Minister Hanekom's Land Reform (Labour Tenants) Act of 1996 to expose it as not speaking 'to the problem of greater security of tenure for certain categories of land laborers ... [rather] the law simply seeks to extend access to private property rights to more people' (30). Similarly in the play, the critic reminds us, 'The language of commerce and law ... debases the everyday discourse of the play, such that Lear can express his angry rejection of Cordelia as if she were just so much no-longer valued goods: "When she was dear to us, we, did hold her so,/But now her price is fallen"' (28). While the 'language of bonds' is often seen as familial and affective, Visser argues that in Lear's apportionment of dowries, 'land is spoken of as disposable property, something properly considered in contractual dealings and settlements' (29).

Visser's prescient article on *King Lear* (1997b) continues to reverberate in the neo-liberal world of selective prosperity and land ownership in South Africa – and within the world global economy. *King Lear* returns to the status quo at the end, with not a bit of 'superflux' or redress for the poor; similarly, colonial legacies of racial inequities are still intact in new global realignments. Overall, his reading posits a postcolonial methodology in which colonizing paradigms of the past and present – with their overlapping inequities of race and class – are brought into a productive conversation with one another. While the author would perhaps identify his approach as Marxist or materialist, I would argue that casting the shadow of South African colonialism on to *King Lear*, in a kind of anamorphic effect, he demonstrates the validity of postcolonial readings drawn from specific colonial histories.

Antony and Cleopatra

In a powerful recent production of *Antony and Cleopatra* at the RSC (director, Iqbal Khan), the black British actor Josette Simon received many accolades for her role as the Egyptian queen. In this memorable version of a multi-layered behemoth of a play, the affective contrast between Rome and Egypt (evoked by the musical score of Laura Mvula, for instance) was in flux. The martial Roman self-representations were punctured by decadent resonances in the bacchanals and steam baths, suggesting 'light homoeroticism' as one reviewer observes (Marmion 2017). Since the vaunted Roman masculinity was given a sensual edge, it added a 'twist' to Antony's supposed 'decadence' in Egypt. The production seemed to ask: do the Romans conform to their own narratives of a heroic masculinity, or embody the very decadence they ascribe to Egypt? In Josette Simon's role as the Egyptian queen, the play also seemed to challenge its audiences as to whether Cleopatra could be anything but black, or a racial 'other'. The visual effect of her presence is evident in Figure 1.

I begin with Josette Simon, as her story historically connects to the intersections of race, sexuality, gender, and empire and, in terms of performance history, to the challenges and promise of multi-racial, non-traditional casting. She has been cast in Shakespearean roles at the RSC from the mid 1980s to the late 1990s, and her career has been important to 'debates about inclusive casting'.[9] It is also noteworthy that Cleopatra's race has not consistently taken centre stage in the Western critical tradition or in the choices in varied productions – in part because some critics focus on a pre-Shakespearean 'historic Cleopatra' who was most likely Macedonian and presumably white.[10] I would argue (supported by critical perspectives below) that Shakespeare's play offers significant evidence to identify Cleopatra in the play as black or as a racialized 'other'; that premise, importantly, would make her the only black female character in the Shakespearean canon. But the question of who plays Cleopatra has a problematic stage history in Britain and America, as feminist critics have pointed out: 'There are no ... iconic leading female Moor roles in Shakespeare save for the controversial issue of whether the Egyptian Queen, Cleopatra, should rightfully be played by a black actress.'[11] Josette Simon's black Cleopatra offers a portrayal that supports that 'rightful claim'. With her affective and psychic complexity, and despite the reviewers' stereotypical and orientalized depictions of her raced body, she brings to life the rich possibilities of a black Cleopatra. And in so doing, she frees the character from the snares of a static 'otherness' – sexual and racial – imposed on her by the Romans in the play as well as by dominant Western cultural appropriations.[12]

Reviewers responded to Simon generally with admiration, but with racialized and gendered inflections, whereby even positive comments seem to fall back on stereotypes, as here: 'Josette Simon's capricious Egyptian queen, whose vocal eccentricities tower over the evening like the pyramids at Giza. She briefly strips, full-frontal fashion, near her asp-inflicted end, before re-robing into something yet more imposing'.[13] She is also described as a 'Cleopatra to die for' in a review that states: 'She lives up to Enobarbus's report of her "infinite variety". Simon's feline grace – this is an extraordinarily

FIGURE 1 Antony and Cleopatra, *2017. Josette Simon as Cleopatra. Directed by Iqbal Khan. Photo by Helen Maybanks, RSC.*

physical performance – is a match for the Egyptian cat that is part of Robert Innes Hopkins's design'.[14] Another critic offered qualified praise for an 'erotic, mercurial' Cleopatra, with a racial comparison with Eartha Kitt: 'Simon seems born to play Cleopatra and she gives us a hypnotically mercurial figure whose eroticism is expressed through a permanent restlessness. For my money, she puts on too many different voices, ranging from guttural power to Eartha Kitt croon'.[15] Another reviewer seems to cross some fine lines of stereotyping – racial and sexual:

> Simon ... is sublime – born to be Cleopatra and hotter than a horde of cats on a particularly hot tin roof. She fidgets, frets, and threatens; a brilliantly neurotic queen whose self-doubt combined with her inclination to despotism leads to a fantastically schizophrenic performance: from playful kitten to lacerating lion, delivered in a variety of voices – from Eartha Kitt to a semi-Brian Blessed.[16]

Reviewers seemed to emphasize, above all, Simon's rendering of a histrionic and passionate woman, falling back on Western sexual stereotypes about 'exotic' women of colour, while not considering Cleopatra a multi-dimensional character, as described by Simon herself:

> This is not just a play about passion, it's a play about politics – and she's [Cleopatra] as much a player in the political narrative as Octavius or Antony ... We forget this woman has a mind. One of the attractions for Antony is not just the sex and the passion, but a meeting of minds, which can be very, very sexy.[17]

Clearly, Simon resists the one-dimensional, sexualized exoticism often ascribed to the role and evident in the trends of the reviews of the RSC production. In the same interview, though, she also is uneasy with the term 'black actor' as an essentialist label. The fine point one can take away here is the need to make a *distinction* between desiring a 'black Cleopatra' – a raced body – on stage and a black actor only being assigned roles in terms of their racial identity. Inclusive, yet race and gender-sensitive casting practices must address issues such as these. But let us first cast a look back to a stage history of Cleopatra and race.

To understand the import of a black Cleopatra on stage, we just need to consider appropriations of the Egyptian queen in various twentieth-century productions, given the curious tradition of English actresses playing seemingly 'white' Cleopatras. Performance histories observing English (white) Cleopatras have produced some dissonances in reviewers trying to reconcile the 'white' body of actresses such as Vivien Leigh with a 'foreign' character, as is recounted below (Macdonald 2002):

> In British productions of *Antony and Cleopatra,* Constance Benson made 'a most difficult character, and one most foreign to English ideas – comprehensible, pathetic, fascinating'; Dorothy Green in 1921 had 'a personality too English, and, if I may say so, too correct, for the exotic languors of the East'. In 1951, Vivien Leigh performed the 'archetypal English Cleopatra, cold, smooth, pale, and dazzlingly beautiful'. For much of the first half of the twentieth century, the look of English Cleopatras was formalized 'in terms of highly Anglicized notions of wantonness: pale skinned, frequently red-haired and often clingingly or scantily clad'.[18]

The cultural and racial anachronism of casting an English Cleopatra in another case, the 1999 RSC production of *Antony and Cleopatra,* was aptly summed by Katherine Duncan-Jones, who stated that the white actress Frances de la Tour, playing the part of the Egyptian queen, 'simply cannot represent the charismatic "serpent of old Nile;" she is entirely European in physique ... [whereas] Caesar's astonishment at the erotic beauty and splendor of Cleopatra and her women in death ... [should be] the amazement of an arrogant European dazzled by the mystique of a great African queen' (Duncan-Jones 1999: 18).

Such concerns have led to selective casting changes, of having black actresses play the role of Cleopatra, even before Josette Simon's *tour de force* performance in 2017; for instance, some black actresses appeared in the role in the late 1980s through the 1990s, and recently, Yanna McIntosh and Geraint Wyn Davies were cast as the title characters in *Antony and Cleopatra* in Stratford, Ontario (Canada) in 2014, with McIntosh being the first black actress to play the role there; Shirine Babb played a stunning black Cleopatra in the Folger Shakespeare production in 2017; and another instance, a 2013 co-production between the RSC, the Public Theatre, New York, and the Gable Stage, Miami, had a multi-racial cast drawn from both the US and UK, to be performed in all three venues. Set in the eighteenth century in St Domingue (as Haiti was known then), it had a black Cleopatra, Charmian, and Enobarbus, evoking a complicated racial mix in the Caribbean island of the period. However, from most reviews, it seems that Shakespeare's play was adapted into a Caribbean 'escape' rather than affording us any serious re-working of racial and sexual politics.[19]

Whether a white or black actress plays Cleopatra, her iconic role evokes racial and cultural instabilities. Literary critic Arthur Little gives us early modern examples of a 'raced' Cleopatra with varied permutations of 'colour':

> Even though Shakespeare's Cleopatra would be the only black Cleopatra ... [in] early modern drama, she nonetheless remains no racial anomaly in early modern English literature, where for example, Robert Greene's *Ciceronis Amor* (1589), Aemilia Lanyer's *Salve Deus Rex Judaeorum* (1610) ... refer to her as black; ... George Gascoigne's 'In Praise of a Gentlewoman' (1575) as 'nutbrowne' and Samuel Brandon's *The Virtuous Octavia* (1598) as 'sunne-burnt' (1341). Sometimes this racially othered Cleopatra occupies a number of cultural and

racial positions in a single text, as she does in Elizabeth Cary's *Tragedy of Mariam* (1613), where she is variously described as brown, black, Egyptian, and Ethiopian. (2000: 167)

Such racialized incarnations of Cleopatras signal the ambivalence toward embodiments of Cleopatra as 'white' in later centuries: 'Her [Cleopatra's] tendency toward cultural and racial polymorphous perversity extends too, to white Cleopatras, who are no less secure in their cultural and racial positions and often seem just a step away from the cultural/racial border or having about them at least a hint of color' (Little 2000: 167–68). White female bodies on stage carry their own cultural expectations. Thus, the 'dazzlingly beautiful' whiteness of Vivien Leigh or other white actresses playing Cleopatra would always already be distanced or estranged from the Eastern, Egyptian world. Given this history, Cleopatra's race continues to preoccupy scholars with a nagging question, aptly summed up by Francesca T. Royster (2003: 2): 'Was Cleopatra Black?' This question is particularly pressing since there has been a series of striking black Othellos since Ira Aldridge's success in the mid-nineteenth century, but no sustained history of black Cleopatras. Another view by Michael Neill acknowledges the play's treatment of various modes of 'otherness', but in the overall design 'how relatively insignificant' is 'the issue of racial difference'. According to the critic, the stereotypes involved are the product of Roman perception so that 'while the Roman view is given a strategic advantage ... it scarcely goes unchallenged' (1994: 87).

Neill's implicit repression of Cleopatra's race and colour is not uncommon in the responses of generations of critics, readers, and viewers of *Antony and Cleopatra*. However, as critical interest in the early modern emergence of colonialism and imperialism has grown in recent decades, discussions of Cleopatra's race and colour and of the Romans' 'orientalizing' strategies have provided new colourations to the play, merging concerns of race theory with those of postcolonial theory. These changing conceptualizations of race and imperialism focus on the political ramifications of Cleopatra's 'otherness', illuminating early modern contexts as well as contemporary critical discourses.[20] As Shakespearean race theorist Francesca Royster demonstrates in *Becoming Cleopatra: The Shifting Image of an Icon* (2003), the Egyptian queen is given a distinct, racial identity in Shakespeare's play:

> Shakespeare's construction of her [Cleopatra] counters history and figures her as black-skinned, the product of a monstrously strong sun. Like *The Aeneid's* Dido, the historical Cleopatra was an exile of sorts, the ruler of an adopted land. But if Shakespeare can transform the legendary daughter of exiled Greeks into not just 'Egypt's Queen', but 'Egypt' itself by setting her on Egyptian soil, having her rule over Egyptian people, and perform Egyptian rites (riding in golden barges or dressing as Isis, for example), just where does her national and racial identity begin and end? (48)

The issue of Cleopatra's racial origins is woven *into* the play via her identification with Egypt, a source of darkness, fecundity and a primal place of origins – with the Nile at its source and the crocodile, born from its slime, its organic symbol.[21] Cleopatra's colour and race find reference in the play at several points, as when she pleads with her absent lover:

> Think on me
> That am with Phoebus' amorous pinches black,
> And wrinkled deep in time? (1.5.28–30)[22]

In the opening scene of the play, as the Roman followers of Antony discuss their captain's rapture for the Egyptian queen, Philo expresses disgust as Antony's formerly martial eyes 'now turn / The office and devotion of their view / Upon a tawny front' (1.1.4–6). Later, he labels Cleopatra 'a gipsy', as Antony's 'Captain's heart' has now become nothing more than 'the bellows and the fan / To cool a gipsy's lust' (1.1.8–9). Shakespeare's Gypsies in the early modern period were often marked as racial 'others' elided with 'Egyptians'. After Cleopatra turns her ships away and flees, resulting in Antony's defeat, he also labels her a 'gipsy':

> O this false soul of Egypt! This grave charm
> … Like a right gipsy hath at fast and loose
> Beguiled me to the very heart of loss. (4.12.25–28)

English audiences at the time would have instantly associated 'gypsies' with dark, lustful Egyptians, as the belief was that gypsies came from Egypt, an exotic fertile place of the Nile teeming with poisonous asps and man-eating crocodiles.[23] On the Jacobean stage, as theatre historian Richard Madelaine (1998) notes in *Shakespeare in Production*, 'Cleopatra was most likely performed by a young man with a "tawny front" – that is in brown face' (3). While the play does not consistently code her as 'black' (as in the case of Othello), whatever the colour of her skin, it is different from the Romans: 'To Shakespeare's audience, what probably mattered is that she was darker than they were' (Adelman 1973: 188).[24] Cleopatra's colours change too, when she refers to her 'bluest veins' to kiss her hand, or emphasizes whiteness, when she hears of Antony's marriage to Octavia: 'I am pale Charmian' (2.5.59). After his marriage to Octavia, Antony quickly reveals his true colours to the audience when he says:

> I will to Egypt;
> And though I make this marriage for my peace,
> I' th' East my pleasure lies. (2.3.37–39)

The Romans designate the 'East' as a place of decadence resulting in Antony's weakened masculinity. But these associations with the 'east were reinforced by mostly male and white critics, more drawn to Antony than to Cleopatra, with whom they could identify as a fallen and seduced male self'.[25]

More recently, Edward Said's formulation of 'Orientalism' gave Shakespearean critics a new, postcolonial vocabulary whereby they recognized Cleopatra as an orientalist 'icon [who] has been coded in Western eyes in a way necessarily controlled by a discourse of power that served to strengthen the European self by distinguishing itself from the Orient' (Royster 2003: 11). Evelyn Gajowski, in an early application of Said's theory, complicates the play's treatment of gender difference, drawn from Petrarch and Ovid, pointing to the intersections of gender with 'Roman constructions of cultural difference or what Edward Said calls "Orientalism". All three are constructions of colonized or sexual others by imperialistic or patriarchal ideologies' (1992: 89).

Overall, postcolonial perspectives recognize how Cleopatra has been produced as a racialized, orientalist icon, both within the play and beyond. Similar associations appear in early modern English travel writings, as in George Sandys and Leo Africanus, as well as in the classical imaginary of Ovid. Egypt figures as the source of natural evolution, but cumulatively, it also becomes a 'frightening fantasy' of overwhelming fecundity, 'endowed with a prurience that affects all that is reproduced within it'.[26] Shakespeare's Cleopatra is represented in association with a fecund Nile, a lust-driven Egypt, and the goddess Isis as much as with the goddess Venus. In sum, her racial and orientalist associations are intertwined in a variety of discourses through the centuries. Finally, returning to the present, Cleopatra's 'encoded associations with orientalism' have become even more complex in terms of her role in popular African American culture and other racial constituencies. In popular culture, in films and other media, on the stage, and in literary scholarship, she is constantly appropriated within varying and complex racialist discourses.[27] But a singular finding I hope we can arrive at is that Josette Simon's Cleopatra should serve as an *inaugural* moment (like that of Ira Aldridge) when all *future* Cleopatras should be played by actresses of colour.

Cymbeline

Shakespeare's *Cymbeline* is not a play one considers 'postcolonial', yet increasingly, it is viewed in terms of an emergent British ethnicity or nation. Writing in 'Postcolonial Shakespeare: British Identity Formation and *Cymbeline*' (1999), Willy Maley provocatively states: 'I want to stake a claim for the space of "Britain" in the time of Shakespeare [in *Cymbeline*] as an exemplary postcolonial site' (146). Applying the concept of 'mimicry', he argues that 'the process of national liberation in an early modern English context involves a repetition of the colonial project, a common feature of postcolonial discourse. This act of repetition – greatly feared and eagerly awaited in equal measure – is implicit in Shakespeare's Roman/British plays [here notably *Cymbeline*]' (146). Maley's postcolonial reading goes as follows:

> In *Cymbeline* three versions of union [primarily Anglo-Scottish] coexist in the shape of a marriage threatened then resolved, long-lost brothers reunited with their natural father, and a *pax Britannica* that mirrors the *pax Romana* of pre-Reformation days. The play's complexity stems in part from its multilayered treatment of the problem of British origins and the troubled issues of union and empire ... With a foot in both camps, Roman Britain and Reformation England, *Cymbeline* marks the accession of James not as the advent of the Other ... but as the eternal return of the Same, coming to fruition ... ripely and rightly through ancient lineage. (Maley 1999: 148)

Maley's attention to repetitive mimicry, a central feature of postcolonial discourse, productively engages with the complexities of the British–Roman relationships via the union of England and Scotland in *Cymbeline*. Thus, the postcolonial paradigm serves him well in historicizing the explorations of a nationalist 'Britishness' in the play in the context of imperial

'Romanness'. Moreover, it enables us to proleptically view *Cymbeline* as marking the birth of Britain with a vision of its imperial destiny – an invention of the early modern colonizing imagination with which Shakespeare's culture had to come to terms (see Chapter 1). Incantations of the name of 'Britain' recur in the play, as Maley recounts, though in ways that problematize its identity, for instance, as Innogen asks:

> Hath Britain all the sun that shines? Day, night,
> Are they not but in Britain? I' th' world's volume
> Our Britain seems as of it, but not in't;
> In a great pool a swan's nest. Prithee think
> There's livers out of Britain. (3.4.135–39)[28]

Britain aspires to 'all the sun that shines', seeks a global place in the 'world's volume', a dying swan in a 'great pool', but the deliverance of Britain seems tied to fantasy, as it is of the world but not 'in it'. The final vision of Britain is one that is Janus-faced, as the Soothsayer hails 'a new Roman Britain, one that both pays tribute to Rome, and yet is paid tribute by Rome, as Rome's successor' (Maley 1999: 147).

> For the Roman eagle,
> From south to west on wing soaring aloft,
> Lessened herself, and in the beams o'th' sun
> So vanished; which foreshadowed our princely eagle,
> Th'imperial Caesar, should again unite
> His favor with the radiant Cymbeline,
> Which shines here in the west. (5.4.467–74)

Nation, state, empire: all these concepts are caught up in the characters' desired Britain in Shakespeare's *Cymbeline*. Intersecting his reading of the play with British history from the mid-seventeenth century onwards, Maley goes on to argue:

> These [late Stuart] plays are postcolonial in so far as Shakespeare is working through England's post-Reformation

history, the history of a nation wrested from an empire that it copied (in true deconstructive fashion) the thing to which it was ostensibly opposed, a history in which a new English nation grew into an empire virtually overnight, then sealed its fate through an act of union that resulted in a net loss of English sovereignty in favor of a British empire modelled on the Roman one that had only just been shaken off. (149)

In conclusion, Maley's postcolonial reading of *Cymbeline* – the British/Roman play – shows how the ideology of nationalism in seventeenth-century British history involves a repetition or mimicry of the colonial project, in this instance repeating a genealogy of the British imperial destiny through evocations of Rome.[29] Thus, this reading offers new understandings of the structures of colonial discourse even as it shapes an unlikely text such as *Cymbeline*.

Another approach to *Cymbeline* takes us on a journey through contemporary, postcolonial nation-formations. This recent postcolonial venture can be found in Martin Orkin's (2005) discussion of Shakespeare's late plays. Here, the critic does not directly engage with an early modern national imaginary; instead, somewhat circuitously, he focuses on the 'question of "accountability", or responsibility for or evasion of responsibility for prior speaking or action', found in the rhetorical performances of Posthumous and Iachimo in the first two acts, and then on the problematic male accountability in Act 5 of *Cymbeline* (106).

Orkin offers a 'contrapuntal mediation' of these moments in *Cymbeline* with concerns about male accountability in attempts at reconciliation, truth-telling, and peaceful compromise in Israel in October 1985 in Joshua Sobol's play, *The Palestinian Girl*, and in South Africa in 1995, with the formation of the Truth and Reconciliation Commission. Orkin's methodology may seem arbitrary and self-selecting, but his distinctive historical groundwork, as discussed earlier, demonstrates that using 'local' knowledges to explore presentations of masculinity in Shakespeare's late plays, such as *Cymbeline*, offers us additional opportunities of thinking about Shakespeare's play, at least implicitly, in relation to power and empire. In fact, the late plays themselves are particularly relevant, given that they dramatize 'travel to strange places, entailing encounters with different cultures and the unknown' (4). Traveling Europeans in the early modern period faced the imperative of asserting a national and cultural identity, while facing the challenges to their authority in encountering otherness in varied peoples and cultures (4–6). Thus, Orkin's reading shows how such contextual yokings of non-metropolitan knowledges to Shakespeare's plays disrupt the epistemological certainties of Western scholars. For instance, Sobol's play attempts to stir the conscience of 'his mainly Israeli audiences against both Israel's entanglement in Lebanon and the excesses of right wing Israeli nationalism'. But his representations of the Arabs lacks 'a cultural and historical specificity'(102). In a situation that is 'fraught and shocking' and ridden with 'multiple injustices', Sobol 'disregards or erases the lived-in complexity of the objects of his attention' (Orkin 2005: 104).

A different model of accountability, Orkin argues, is evident in the structure and proceedings of the Truth and Reconciliation Commission of South Africa, which worked 'deliberately to achieve a sense of inclusivity through testimony dealing with traumas and conflicts of the past given by victims [of apartheid]' (109). Such instances of inclusivity – of emotional and linguistic breakdown – he argues, offer a radical and important contrast to the more smooth 'truth' narratives in the 'climactic address of accountability that unfolds at the court of *Cymbeline* in 5.4' (109). All the main protagonists of the play are on stage in 5.4 delivering confessional reflections on their accountability for past misdemeanours, with the king being centre stage as these accounts unfold. He learns of his Queen's deceptions and suicide. He insists on the execution and culpability of the Roman prisoners, though he is reminded that the victory was his 'by accident'. Above all, the King does not offer any self-reflections on 'truth' or 'reconciliation'. Rejecting personal responsibility, he blames the Queen's seduction of himself and brushes off his chaste daughter's view of his 'folly':

Mine eyes
Were not in fault, for she was beautiful,
Mine ears that heard her flattery, nor my heart
That thought her like her seeming. It had been vicious
To have mistrusted her: yet, O my daughter,
That it was folly in me, thou may'st say,
And to prove it in thy feeling. Heaven mend all! (5.4.62–68)

He rejoices in the recovery of his daughter and sons, but in his exclamation, 'Heaven mend all', he accepts no responsibility for his own actions. In refusing culpability, while ordering executions and tortures, the King's (and the play's) final vision is *unlike* that of the South African Truth and Reconciliation Commission, which was based on *Ubuntu* (African humanism and reparation) not on revenge or victimization. Here one can see how the discourses of accountability, both in the play and the commission proceedings, while having *opposing* effects, are mutually constitutive in mapping the limits and possibilities of confession and reconciliation. Patriarchal entitlements to power and authority, including the power to punish, are at the forefront of Shakespeare's late plays – *Cymbeline, The Winter's Tale, The Tempest* – but significantly, the Commission proceedings denaturalize such choices, showing the rejection of overweening power, including revenge (that Cymbeline chooses).

Thus, viewing *Cymbeline* from within different histories that intertwine with the postcolonial aftermath of Afrikaner (and British) rule in South Africa and with resonances in Israel's imperial relations with Palestinians, a play seemingly far removed from these histories reveals the workings of dominant nationalisms within an imperialist agenda. As Jodi Mikalachki (1998) observes about the play's final vision, 'the masculine embrace of Roman Britain became the truly generative interaction, producing a civil masculine foundation for early modern English nationalism'.[30]

To sum up, both postcolonial readings, by Maley and Orkin, problematize the 'masculine embrace' at the end of *Cymbeline*, but do not explore all the ramifications of the distinctively gendered, male centered empire to which the play hearkens and which feminist critics point out; for instance, when Jodi Mikalachki (1995) maps the gendering of the nation in the play as follows:

> Gendering and sexualizing of the nation ... by early seventeenth century in England ... involved both an exclusion of originary female savagery and a masculine embrace of the civility of empire. (303)

Heather James (1997) also extrapolates on the imperial, gender ideology underpinning the 'masculine embrace' in *Cymbeline*:

> The radical element in Posthumous' experiences and Cymbeline's court is the role played by the 'woman's part'... At the end ... Innogen joyfully cedes her place in the succession to her brothers ... romance, women, doubt, subversion: all are subordinated to the ... play's political conclusions, in which Cymbeline's hypermasculine ... sons are restored to their father and the British court.[31]

Images of hypermasculinity and 'rape' that permeate the play are not far removed from the colonization and plunder of land, highlighting the investments of masculinity in the colonial project of discovery, seizure of land, and settlement. Walter Raleigh's 'discovery' of Guiana in 1595, entering the land that yet hath her 'maidenhead never sacked', comes to mind, as Raleigh writes in his ensuing narrative (1596). Thus, as *Cymbeline* mediates a double vision, between Roman Britain and Britain as the new Rome, it is buttressed by imperial imaginings of colonization of the New World, Africa, and the East Indies in the early modern period.

Moving to Part III, I explore disseminations of Shakespeare beyond Western experiences and modes of knowledge. Taking a global perspective, Chapters 5 to 7 follow Shakespearean engagements with 'native', non-Western cultures, thus reaching out to more hybrid and cosmopolitan communities of readers and audiences in and beyond the West.

PART THREE

Shakespeare, Postcoloniality, and Reception Histories: Performance and Film

DESDEMONA
I saw Othello's visage in his mind.

– *Othello* (1.3.253)

5

Global, Inter-cultural Shakespeares

Historical Overview: The Poetics and Politics of Appropriation and Inter-cultural Encounters

Chapter 5 charts a new 'turn' in the postcolonial journey to the Global Shakespeare movement. In the past decade or so, new interpretations, productions, and conversations about deployments of Shakespeare's works beyond its canonical uses in the West – and often within the global south – have developed into a burgeoning field[1] – a field in which issues of appropriation, representation, and power are central.[2] Today, we see an increasing scholarly interest in the uses of Shakespeare to tell stories of disparate lives, often in non-Western arenas or in culturally contested milieus in metropolitan centres themselves. Quite remarkably, this recent, postcolonially inflected, inter-cultural scholarship has expanded Shakespearean 'travels' into varied spaces and historical moments, often engaging with the local, the vernacular, and the liminal. My focus is primarily on the *discourses about* inter-culturalism emerging from performance reviews and critical sources, and less on live performances. Given the multimedia developments of our times, Shakespeare's works can also be refracted in varied mediascapes worldwide, a term that describes the influence of media in shaping how we imagine the world.[3] Thus, in scholarship, as well as on stage, film, and other media in wide-ranging locations, an interest has been growing in intercultural forms and interpretations of the plays, which seem multifarious: Chinese Shakespeares, Bollywood Shakespeares, Japanese Shakespeares, Arab Shakespeares, Black and Asian Shakespeares in Britain, among others.[4]

What is distinctive and historically significant about this cultural 'turn' is that it moves beyond the earlier ahistorical notions of a 'universal' Bard; instead, it emphasizes intercultural and intra-cultural interpretations and productions of Shakespeare that are both *global* in reach, yet also often *'native'* to distinctive, local cultures and affects. In this process, 'native' knowledges from non-metropolitan locations or liminal spaces within the Shakespearean metropolis become crucial in drawing diverse audiences. We are thus reminded that all knowledges and experiences are partially hybrid. This can be a result of colonialism and, more recently, of globalization and its effects/affects (Orkin 2005). Like Ariel's song of metamorphosis, of the 'pearls that were his eyes' (1.2.390), these Shakespearean intercultural encounters have produced rich mutations. Critics have been increasingly drawn to adaptations that dramatize or interpret Shakespeare's plays 'in voices and agents that exceed the canonical uses to which the works are put' (Dionne and Kapadia 2008: 1–2). Thus, distinctions between the 'global' and 'local' Shakespeares often get blurred in various boundary-crossing appropriations; the old colonial binaries are now refracted through our world of migrations, diasporas, exile, and East–West inter-culturalisms and transculturalisms. In this trend, any text or performance in inter-cultural settings will evoke multilateral responses, which, Margaret Litvin (2017) defines in terms of 'a global kaleidoscope of intertexts' in her study of the literary adaptation of Shakespeare in the Arab world:

It rarely happens that a would-be adapter sits down in a deliberate way for a first encounter with a Shakespeare play. Rather the first reading of the play is usually mediated by a 'global kaleidoscope' of intertexts; some combination of the films, performances, abridgements, translations, articles, conversations, versions of other Shakespeare plays ... Outside the Anglophone world this polyphony is even more striking. If the 'original' text enjoys global circulation, like Shakespeare's tragedies, then these competing intertexts come from a great variety of literary and theatre traditions, not just from the source [i.e. British, colonial] culture. (53–54)[5]

Such critical discussions about the processes and politics of appropriation have often moved along *Janus-faced* trajectories: scholars intertextually mine traditional sources, while also engaging with contemporary social realities; or they acknowledge colonial, neo-colonial, and postcolonial Shakespeares, while questioning these categories and attending to a polyphony of voices. Frequently, appropriations and adaptations serve dual and contradictory roles. They endorse and reify Shakespeare's cultural capital while simultaneously challenging its canonical and elite credentials. In sum, I argue, notwithstanding their varied perspectives and methodologies, these global/local inter-cultural encounters constitute a *legacy* of postcoloniality. 'Resistance', 'subversion', 'appropriation', 'decolonization', 'race thinking' and 'inter-cultural encounters' – terms from a postcolonial Shakespearean vocabulary mentioned in the Introduction – continue to inform recent engagements within global, inter-cultural contexts. We have moved beyond the twentieth-century binaries of colonizer–colonized, and postcolonial societies seem to want to join a world culture which includes the West. However, issues pertaining to hierarchy, difference, and inequities have not exhausted themselves, as I suggest in the Introduction, and these terms can now be productively re-deployed in exploring the new inter-cultural imperatives of Shakespearean dissemination. Some Anglo-American Shakespearean scholars may question whether the original Shakespearean text simply becomes subsumed within alien 'local' cultures, far removed from the Western early modern. Other Western, nativist impulses may consider this inter-cultural work as simply too alien and 'other'. And some who label themselves as 'progressive' may critique Shakespeare's new role in the global marketplace.[6]

Thus, it may be well worth considering the cultural credentials we ascribe to this global, inter-cultural 'turn'. Each appropriation or adaptation of Shakespeare's works both within and beyond metropolitan settings does *not* accrue scholarly, cultural or ethical value simply by its multicultural, or race-sensitive credentials. Any adaptation can easily 'flatten' or simplify the complexity of the works. The US-made 'high school' film version of *Othello*, entitled O (2001), is a case in point. It engages with the high-school culture of sports and sexual competition, but does little to explain contemporary US race politics, or to adequately convey the tragic ramifications of Shakespeare's rendering of a black man's tragedy in a dominant white culture. For instance, the film's sympathetic portrayal of Hugo (the Iago character) as a troubled teenager mutes his evil actions, weakening the racial politics of contemporary times in the US.[7]

How should we evaluate Shakespeare's inter-cultural encounters? Whether an icon of British hegemony, a product of its empire, or reclaimed and adapted according to different 'native' traditions, Shakespeare's works are *diverse* in structural and linguistic complexities and capacious in their experiential range: the characters find themselves on a shifting ground, whereby insights and consolations only seem to emanate from provisional places of knowing. A play like *Hamlet*, for instance, with its emphasis on acting, action and inaction in terms of revenge, as well as its meta-theatrical and supernatural elements, lends itself to varied cultural contexts, for instance, in China, India, and the Arab world. *King Lear*'s representations of property and land struggles, as well as familial issues, can have relevance in post-apartheid South Africa (see Chapter 4) and in Pan-Asian contexts.

Any Shakespearean work performed both within and opposed to the British canonical traditions is frequently the subject of this new global 'turn'. Alexa Huang's explorations in *Chinese Shakespeares* (2009), for instance, offers a framework based on this interactive, inter-cultural process: 'A long view of history will reveal the multi-directional processes that contribute to the mutually constructive grammar of the global and the local. Over a century of cross-fertilization has firmly rooted Shakespeare in Chinese cultural production and Chinese performance idioms in twentieth-century Shakespeare traditions' (2009: 5–6). Hence, her overarching questions: 'What does "Shakespeare" do in Chinese literary and performance culture?' Or conversely, 'how do imaginations about China function in Shakespearean performances ... in mainland China, Taiwan, and other locations?' (3). Two examples of different stage productions from Huang's study spanning several decades tell a complex story about Shakespeare in Chinese contexts. One was a Confucian, though jingoistic, production which promoted patriotism: Jiao Juyin's *Hamlet* (1942). As Huang narrates, 'in 1942 when China was at war with Japan, a Chinese-language production of *Hamlet*, set in Denmark was staged in a Confucian temple in Jiang'an in southwestern China' (3). The meanings of this wartime *Hamlet* were shaped by the interesting presence of the Confucian shrine on a rudimentary stage and the setting of the temple. Quite straightforwardly, it seems the performance 'created a communal experience during the war intended to stir patriotic spirit in Confucian moral terms' (3). Huang gives this example of Shakespeare's absorption into the political life during times of war through connections with a local venue.

In contrast, Huang gives an example of a more recent global production from East Asia: Ong Keng Sen's distinctively multi-lingual and multinational *LEAR* (1997) that reconfigured Shakespearean and Asian identity multinationally and within a post-modernist, allegorical frame. Marked by postcolonial preoccupations with the formations of hybrid identities within an inter-cultural and intra-cultural frame, *LEAR* broke new ground on many fronts – acted with English surtitles projected above the stage, actors from several Asian countries and their characters seemed to be searching for their cultural identities in this Pan-Asian production, playing to full houses in Singapore, Tokyo, and other parts of Asia and Europe (3). Huang describes the interactions between its different cultural, linguistic, and affective strands as follows:

> The power-thirsty, eldest daughter (performed cross-dressed), who spoke only Mandarin and employed *jingju* chanting and movements, confronted the Old Man (Lear) who spoke only Japanese ... The subtitles de-familiarized ... Shakespearean lines and de-corporealized Asian performance practices ... While this uniquely multi-lingual performance re-cast the questions of race and nation in a new light, its bold experiments of hybrid Asian styles were controversial ... Seen afar from the European perspective, the contrasts between the Asian languages and styles were flattened by their similarities. However, seen from an Asian perspective, the difference between Asian cultures was accentuated by the performance. (3–4)

Huang's discussion of *LEAR* and its intra-cultural complexities is a part of a larger discussion about this groundbreaking production. Ethnic and linguistic identities within the Pan-Asian context emerged as unstable and multifarious, as the inflections and sounds of Mandarin and Japanese highlighted these differences. Ong Keng Sen himself described his work in terms of a 'multicultural playground' to work 'through his ambivalence about tradition' (5). While both Jiao and Ong Keng Sen addressed national and cultural identity formation, *LEAR* brought to the fore complexities of Asian practices of intra-culturalism, providing a riposte to the historical 'one-way' Eurocentric Orientalism. For instance, despite charges of 'cultural tourism' and scepticism about whether it produces a 'politically engaged inter-culturalism', especially in the face of restricted democracies in Asian countries such as Singapore,

Ong Keng Sen's *LEAR* opened the way for denaturalizing xenophobic investments in East Asian identities, while influencing other inter-cultural and intra-cultural Pan-Asian Shakespearean experiments.[8] Nations it was performed in or represented were not liberal democracies, but its assertions of cross-cultural and multi-lingual identities, I would argue, were remarkable in highlighting issues of race and nation, while challenging the orthodoxies of nationalism itself. A testament to its continuing influence emerged in a re-adaptation of the original play, *Lear Dreaming*, a production by TheatreWorks (Singapore), which was staged for two days at the Singapore Arts Festival on 31 May and 1 June 2012. Earlier, in March 2011, with a workshop in New York City, director Ong Keng Sen started a project to re-imagine his groundbreaking 1997 production of *Lear*, the genesis of which he explained eloquently with some reflections on the aesthetic impact of the original work:

> Many people have asked why come back to this project from 1997 which I initiated then with 30 performers onstage, mostly actors even though it was an interdisciplinary work of music, dance, theatre. This time, the production is a work of music that has only one actor surrounded by eight musicians. I suppose you can say that I was hailed by Lear to respond once again ... The 1997 production was gorgeous, complete, and very material. How can it be so easy to say something so complex? What faces one at the end of life? How can we suggest the salvation, the humanity in a dictator, an authoritarian father, an oppressor? What has been oppressed? The blood lines that continue, the legacies that we inherit, that we resist – how do we open up a discussion without reducing it to a didactic 'good' and 'bad' judgment?[9]

Shakespeare's *King Lear* here undergoes two transmutations from the 1997 version to *Lear Dreaming*, 'a meditative allegory' in which the original is radically restructured, as one reviewer notes: 'the multiple characters in Shakespeare's *King Lear* and Ong's 1997 *LEAR* were distilled into one performer and eight musician/performers, while the complex musical score, combined with minimal text, framed the storytelling'.[10] This continued exploration of how contemporary performers encounter Shakespeare through ancient Asian performance traditions is now Ong Keng Sen's lasting legacy, even though often evoking controversy. In one sense, it is a humanist legacy distilled through the wrenching tragic vision of Shakespeare, but it is also modernist in its refusal to contain the play within a coherent and singular national imaginary, a important ideal of our xenophobic times.

Moving from China to India, similar concerns around intercultural exchange via indigenous encounters with Shakespeare are addressed in Parmita Kapadia's discussion of 'Jatra Shakespeare: Indigenous Indian Theatre and the Postcolonial Stage' in the anthology, *Native Shakespeares* (2008). According to the critic, the lingering influence of the ancient Indian (Bengali) theatrical tradition *Jatra,* as used by innovative Indian director Salim Ghouse in his production of *Hamlet* (Mumbai, 1992), represents a postcolonial paradox: *Jatra* is an important folk theatre, 'indigenous to India, (specifically in Bengal) but alien to most Indians, whereas Shakespeare is foreign, but familiar' (97). Kapadia offers an important reminder about how Ghouse's production was radically different from the work (however theatrically rich) of directors such as Peter Brook and Richard Schechner who mined Asian traditions to revitalize Western theatre, searching for 'new sources of energy, vitality, and sensuality', instead of engaging with them in an interactive dynamic.[11] Ghouse did *not* merely resituate the text within an indigenous context but combined alien native forms, such as *Jatra* and classical Sanskrit theatre, pairing the 'alien indigenous and familiar English-Language Shakespeare' (97). This evoked a 'pan-Indian nationhood' that could not be accommodated within vestiges of idealized 'Orientalism' that reared its presence in Brook and Schechner, whose work often evoked a simple 'alien/indigenous binary'.

Instead, as Kapadia explains, Ghouse 'foregrounded the complexities surrounding cultural interaction and national identity in India' (97), perhaps offering an uncanny model for contesting the 'nation' as a unifying term, while resisting the xenophobic Hindu nationalism in India today.

What happens to the canonical Shakespearean text of *Hamlet* in this process? In Kapadia's analysis, she describes the rift between the 'colonial and familiar language of the play' and the *Jatra* traditions that 'privilege the visual and the physical over the spoken and the oral' (98). A *Jatra* play begins with a shock and Ghouse's play highlighted 'the visceral mistrust between various characters and the intense violence with which they react' (98). In the opening, for instance, Ghouse strikingly inserted an extra-textual scene, the rehearsal for 'The Murder of Gonzago'. And given this staging of the Old King's murder at the outset, 'Hamlet's unwillingness to accept the ghost of his father's spirit [represented him] as being less ethically conflicted and more emotionally empty' (98–99). Overall, coupling the visceral performative *Jatra* staging customs with Shakespeare's play did not allow for any 'neutral spectator or pure bystander' (101). For the director, as Kapadia explains:

> All people were participants ... Ghouse emphasized that every community, every individual participates in the process of constructing a postcolonial Indian identity [in a nation] struggling to balance itself between a colonial past and a global future. (101)

In another extra-textual scene, suggestive of *Jatra*, all the characters regained 'life' at the end, with actors discarding their roles and eroding the divisions between theatrical performance and realities of everyday life. Thus, situating *Hamlet* on the 'cultural borders among the colonial [canonical], the postcolonial, the inter-cultural, and the intra-cultural', Ghouse explored new ways of engaging with contemporary audiences in a divided country (101). The term 'intra-cultural' describes interactions between local and regional elements.

As we delve into different adaptations of Shakespeare's plays, let us explore the specific appeal of Shakespeare for two *contemporary* stage and film directors who approach his works as a mirror – albeit with distortions – for contemporary, twenty-first-century global politics. Directors Sulayman Al-Bassam and Vishal Bhardwaj offer two examples of present-day *auteurs* with unique aesthetic visions through which they evoke distinctive and complex resonances in the original Shakespearean text. In the process, they produce 'a multi-layered contextualized "thickness", taking the larger function [of the productions] within their own cultures into account in ways that are remarkable for their innovation' (Knowles 2004: 12). In this task, as they transplant some of the poetic imagery and language into re-imagined, re-contextualized forms, they open up the original text to 'carry a distinct agenda, adding another authorial voice without marring the first and diluting the second' (Al-Bassam 2014: xix). But transplantations can also function as productive 'betrayals' and vehicles for completely new theatre or cinematic pieces. Exploring Shakespearean appropriations in the Arab world, Hennessey and Litvin highlight some aspects of this process, with reference to Sulayman Al-Bassam, the Anglo-Kuwaiti dramatist, who (among other works) brought to the stage three adaptations of Shakespeare:

> Arab theatre artists seeking to metabolize recent Arab-world events in or for the West have turned persistently to Shakespeare in particular ... in quest of a vocabulary their audiences (and sponsors) can understand. As state support for theatre has crumbled in many Arab countries, Shakespeare provides what [director] Sulayman Al-Bassam has called a 'playable surface', a slippery but usable platform on which an internationally mobile Arab artist can continue to produce work. In response, artists have adapted both their texts and themselves. (Hennessey and Litvin 2016: 2)

Vishal Bhardwaj, director of *Haider* (2014), the acclaimed Indian appropriation of *Hamlet*, also testifies to the relevance of inter-cultural Shakespeare, in this case within the recent histories of the Kashmiri militancy and occupation, a legacy of the Partition in the Indian sub-continent (discussed further in Chapter 7). When asked in an interview about his choice to translate the seventeenth-century writings of Shakespeare into the contemporary reality of Kashmiri politics, he explains how he transplants the 'soul' of the plays into a new locale:

> It's about the politics behind humanity, their emotions, and their conflicts. The politicians and/or ministers have changed ... The conflict remains the same ... I was not burdened with Shakespeare's name ... [Western films] are so conscious of Shakespeare's work, that they don't rise beyond it ... I always remain very true to the soul of the play rather than the text.[12]

Being 'true' to the soul of the play also reaps rich rewards for representations of the Kashmiri tragedy in *Haider*. 'All of Kashmir', like Denmark, is declared a 'prison' by the young Haider, though the plot offers a complex twist on the imperatives of revenge, far beyond Hamlet's ambivalences in Shakespeare's play. By seeking the 'soul', the director explains his use of the poetic imagery and the atmosphere that Shakespearean verses conjure to re-contextualize them in a new locale, and with new meanings *infused* into the familiar text. Though any tragic resolution eludes the film version, its vision remains 'true to the haunting opacity of Shakespeare's most opaque of tragedies'.[13]

What does it mean to not be 'burdened by Shakespeare's name'? Directors such Al-Bassam and Bhardwaj, staging inter-cultural and intra-cultural encounters with global audiences in mind, not only resist a purely English-language, canonical Shakespeare, but open new interpretive possibilities within Shakespearean language, meaning, and context (Orkin 2005); in so doing, in these two cases specifically, they enable radical political engagements with geopolitical struggles in the Middle East and Kashmir. In the following section, I explore a few key moments in a movement labelled 'Arab Shakespeares'

– encompassing the role of Arab Shakespeare translation, production, adaptation, and criticism through the twentieth and twenty-first centuries, which include the impact of Al-Bassam's dramatic offerings.

Arab Shakespeares

Within the current 'Global Shakespeare' appropriation movement, a history of inter-cultural Arab-Shakespeare encounters is attracting a growing body of scholarship.[14] The post-9/11 Middle Eastern world has brought its own confrontations with the West: Iraq, Syria, and the Israeli occupation of Palestinian territories continue to cast a large shadow. Some observers of the cultural shifts also suggest that since 9/11 a new kind of Arab Shakespeare has become possible, elicited by a new US and European interest in Arab cultural production, and new audiences in the West, and some in the region itself, as I discuss below. How do we reconcile these cosmopolitan impulses with the anti-Muslim biases reflecting vestiges of Orientalism that we *continue* to see in Western media and popular culture? I argue that if this negative vision mainly views the region as a world empty of cultural signs or as a fantasm of 'terror', the story of Arab Shakespeares offers an important counter-narrative of inter-cultural encounters and hybrid productions, of which I offer a brief snapshot/survey below.

The *Critical Survey* special issue on *Arab Shakespeares* co-edited by Katherine Hennessey and Margaret Litvin (2016) marked the subfield's coming-of-age, as it was the *second* special issue on Arab Shakespeares. When the earlier volume came out (Winter 2007), the editors observe,

> The topic was a curiosity. There existed no up-to-date monograph in English on Arab theatre, let alone on Arab Shakespeare. Few Arabic plays had been translated into

English. Few British or American theatregoers had seen a play in Arabic. In the then tiny but fast-growing field of international Shakespeare appropriation studies (now 'Global Shakespeare'), there was a great post-9/11 hunger to know more about the Arab world, but also a lingering prejudice that Arab interpretations of Shakespeare would necessarily be derivative or crude, purely local in value. (1)

But as the pioneering work of Litvin and others have demonstrated, the rich interpretive possibilities of Shakespeare's works are *not new* to Arab cultures and societies. Historically, in the nineteenth and twentieth centuries, the various regions and countries that make up the Arab world were not uniformly dominated by Western colonialism; thus, it would be fair to say that Shakespeare's works were not directly imposed as colonial texts within a single British colonial education system as they were in India, Kenya or the English-speaking Caribbean countries, for instance. In considering Arab Shakespeares, therefore, it is useful to complicate binary models, which form one strand within inter-cultural movements, and instead consider multilateral sources and inheritances. As Litvin further argues, 'Arab interpreters of Shakespeare are less like Caliban and more like Hamlet, torn between competing father figures (Claudius, the Ghost, and even the Player and Polonius). They have been enriched and confused by a multiple inheritance from the start' (Litvin 2017: 53). This is a productive formulation, informing the critic's examinations of the popular rhetorical deployments of *Hamlet* in the region. However, I offer a nuanced qualification here, namely that multiple indigenous or foreign sources should *not* block off larger considerations of any or all colonial influences or preclude the relevance of a postcolonial analysis, as I address later. The global impact of Western interventions in the region lingers. But for now, let us follow Litvin's 'multilateral' Arab engagements with Shakespeare:

Most 20th-century Arab writers and directors were not overly conscious of Shakespeare as a British writer; rather, he represented 'world' drama, a piece of '*al-turath al-alami*' (the world cultural heritage) …. [Thus] Arab audiences came to know Shakespeare through a kaleidoscopic array of performances, texts, and criticism from many directions: not just the 'original' British source culture, but through very un-English and at times more influential French, Italian, American, Soviet, and Eastern European literary and dramatic traditions. (Litvin 2017: 54)

And in this vein Litvin explores the varied histories of Arab appropriations of Shakespeare, drawing on examples from 'two periods of the Egyptian *Hamlet* tradition (the earliest extant Arab *Hamlet* from 1901, and the period of Nasserist and post-Nasser political theatre (1964–71)' (Litvin 2017: 51). Her emphasis on a 'global kaleidoscope' depicts varying Egyptian, Syrian, and Iraqi milieus and sources. The oldest surviving Arabic text of *Hamlet* (1901) is an adaptation by journalist and translator Tanyus 'Abduh, a Syrian immigrant to Egypt. This version typified the early Arab commercial theatre, where Shakespeare's name carried prestige but lacked the elitism of high culture. His translation radically altered the text, including a shift to mostly prose, an un-erotic relationship with his mother, a stronger Ophelia, a more decisive Hamlet, and a happy ending with Hamlet ascending the throne. 'For over 100 years', Arab critics have called 'Abduh a 'hack'; though recently seen as a producer of cultural capital, his work is considered as a response to the tastes of Cairo's 'emerging middle class' (Litvin 2017: 55). What is also noteworthy is that 'Abduh's *Hamlet* (happy ending and all) was adapted not directly from Shakespeare but from the French *Hamlet* by Alexandre Dumas *père*, a testimony to the popularity of Dumas in Egypt at the time.[15]

Another instance, in the same essay, offers a window into the popularity of Shakespeare in 1960s Cairo, specifically in the reception of Grigori Kozintsev's Soviet-era film version, *Gamlet* (1964), in Cairo and elsewhere. This was an Egyptian world that was cosmopolitan and at a global crossroads, even though in its non-aligned socialist identity during which period 'the privileged interlocutor of the day was the Soviet Union' (Litvin 2017: 57). However, the film's popularity 'owed more to the Egyptian lifeworld than to geopolitics as such. [For instance], with their own experience of political repression, Egyptian viewers could not miss the film's police state iconography: iron bars, eavesdroppers, armed guards, ubiquitous portraits and statues of Claudius' (57).

Litvin's emphasis on 'multilateral' Arab reception histories of Shakespeare shows that Arab responses to Shakespeare in the twentieth and twenty-first centuries were non-binary and polyphonic, rather than univocal. The Arab world was not a part of the British Empire in a sustained or consistent way. Hence, these and other examples testify to varied indigenous Arabic engagements with Shakespeare. For instance, David Moberly's essay (2016) on the first Arabic performance of *The Taming of the Shrew* in Egypt in 1930 highlights the vernacular, '"native" appropriation of the play'. Entitled 'The Taming of the Tigress: Fatima Rushdi and the First Performance of *Shrew* in Arabic', it presents a populist version of the play:

> the translator rendered the play in colloquial Egyptian Arabic rather than in the formal, classical Arabic accessible to the educated elite. As such, the play offered the uneducated Egyptian public – and women in particular – unprecedented access to this work of Shakespeare ... In this [the *Shrew*] and other roles, as one of Egypt's first renowned Shakespearean actresses, Rushdi not only effectively recast Shakespeare in an Egyptian mold, but also cast Egyptians in a Shakespearean mold, with effects that still echo today. (8)

Another essay in a similar populist vein (in the same volume) by Samer Al-Saber, 'Beyond Colonial Tropes: Two Productions of *A Midsummer Night's Dream* in Palestine' (2016), recounts the process of shedding the colonial legacy of a 'universal' Shakespeare. While initially accepting the rhetoric about Shakespeare's role in the Western civilizing mission, Al-Saber moves beyond that veneration. Exploring two Palestinian productions of *Dream* in Ramallah, Ashtar Theatre's production of 1995 and one that the author himself directed in the Al-Kasaba Drama Academy in 2011, he demonstrates the agency of the Palestinian artists:

> The two productions used their present realities as the basis for their final product: minimal sets, lighting and costumes, student actors, Palestinian vernacular and local elements to mediate the text. In both productions, the student actors appeared as themselves on stage ... [For instance] in speech, characterization, situational humor and cultural spirit, the actors played the Mechanicals and artisans as local laborers who closely resembled a commonly recognized working-class Palestinian identity. (43)

In these small 'snapshots' a vernacular and 'native' tradition of Arab Shakespeare, as opposed to a faithful rendition of the plays, comes alive. The inter-cultural and intra-cultural contexts of 'native' productions such the 1901 *Hamlet*, Palestinian *Dream,* or 1930s Egyptian *Shrew* (among numerous others), speak in many voices. Shakespeare was an iconic world figure, though the uses of his work in the Arab world could only come circuitously: in response to British colonial influences in the 1930s; through other European influences, such as French and Russian sources; or mediated through the politics of Palestine or of the political regimes of their own regions. Al-Shetawi (2013) sums up these diverse Arab Shakespearean responses in three aspects: as mimicry and admiration of Shakespeare as being part of a world culture, as anti-colonial ripostes, or as representations of the political dilemmas of their own times.[16]

How are these inter-cultural stories of Arab Shakespeares relevant to a postcolonial agenda? What is of import is that they offer us (Anglo-American readers) *counter-narratives* about Middle Eastern cultures and societies far removed from the Western popular media imaginary of the region still struggling under American imperial domination. While terms like 'terrorism' and 'Arab pathologies' have a continuing presence within American policies, with echoes of British colonialism, one figure from the Arab world, Sulayman Al-Bassam, mentioned earlier, offers an important, self-conscious counter-narrative at the intersections of Western–Arab politics and American domination through his Shakespearean adaptations. I consider him an 'auteur' like Bhardwaj, who tells stories that capture geographical and cultural particularities as much as they (according to Al-Bassam) examine a 'thematically coherent body of issues, namely: power, corruption, radical ideologies, the forces that move societies towards fracture, dissolution ...' (Litvin 2014: 223). Some reflections on his work, I believe, help us map the cultural and political fissures marking the landscape of contemporary Arab Shakespeares, especially in the light of complex and fraught Arab–West relations.

Al-Bassam's theatrical adaptations of Shakespeare into Arab settings are powerfully represented in *The Arab Shakespeare Trilogy, Three Plays: The Al-Hamlet Summit, Richard III: An Arab Tragedy, and The Speaker's Progress* (2014). Holderness, in his 'Introduction' to the *Trilogy*, sums up the process of mining Shakespeare's works for new meanings and relevance to our own times:

> These adaptations will appeal both to those interested in Shakespeare, and to those concerned with political and cultural events in the Arab world. They work upon the Shakespeare texts to produce new and unforeseen meanings; and they fashion dramatic forms that reflect in innovative ways on contemporary world events. (Holderness 2014: viii–ix)[17]

Similarly, in the 'Author's Introduction' (2014), Al-Bassam himself explains the historical relevance of his *Trilogy* to the contemporary geo-politics of the Arab–Western relationships:

> The plays are informed and inflected by concerns, issues, and events pertaining to my perception of the Arab world

during that first decade of the twenty-first century. They also address the charged, airless, and perverse relationship between the Middle East and the West. (xviii)

Al-Bassam is a controversial figure who enjoys considerable international mobility and is sometimes regarded with suspicion by other local artists who have not ventured into similar work in the West and do not share his acclaim. His productions exemplify a new type of Arabic Shakespeare, explicitly targeting the new international audience for Arabic theatre, an audience beyond the countries of the Arab world. That audience did not exist before 2001; it was galvanized by 9/11, as was Al-Bassam's work itself, and his plays are quintessential twentieth-century products. In a framing introduction to an interview with the director, we learn of the multi-faceted impact of his work: of the 'ironies' of his 'double-edged career as a bilingual, inter-cultural Anglo-Arab adaptor of Shakespeare over the past decade ... [raising issues] about the ethical dimensions of appropriation. For even while Al-Bassam has appropriated Shakespeare, the critical establishment has appropriated Al-Bassam' (Litvin 2014: 222).

Let us now consider *Richard III: An Arab Tragedy* (Summer 2006). The writer/adaptor was commissioned by the RSC in Stratford-upon-Avon, UK, to make a free adaptation of *Richard III* in Arabic (with subtitles for Anglophone audiences) under the initial working title of *The Baghdad Richard* (Al-Bassam 2014: 59–72), later titled *Richard III: An Arab Tragedy*.[18] Contemporary politics linked to both Arab despotic practices and Western imperialist interventions are key to Al-Bassam's own interpretation of this *Trilogy*, as he elaborates further in Litvin's interview with him:

> There is a unity of moral tenor, a double-edged political critique running through the *Trilogy*. All of the pieces are highly critical of dominant political practices inside the Arab world whilst also exposing the face of Western political

opportunism that has informed so much of the history of this region. The result of this double-edged moral thrust is that neither Arab audiences nor their Western counterparts can watch these pieces without feeling a sense of discomfort. (qtd in Litvin 2014: 223–24)

The director-cum-adaptor's framing essay to his Arab *Richard III* sums up the complexities of inter-cultural adaptation as well as the underlying politics. Aptly titled 'An Essay on *Richard III*, an Arab Tragedy: On the burden of Text, Nation, and Histories', in it Al-Bassam reveals the dangerous political quicksand of drawing analogies between Richard and Saddam Hussein:

However tempting it might have been to throw the book of Western literary evil – Richard III – at Saddam Hussein, this strategy could – at best – produce a freak show' ... [this analogy would] promote a reductive – and reactionary – equivalence between supreme moral evil and Arab-ness. Richard's characteristic vitality, sexual potency, wit, charm are the same tropes that suffuse the Western Orientalist fantasy of the Arab tyrant ... the combination ... would feed Western audiences' worst prejudices about Arabs. (Al-Bassam 2014: 65–66)

Richard III, as Al-Bassam saw it, was also 'a play about the nature of Kingship' and with some echoes with the 'day-to-day life of the Gulf monarchies', but of course, there could be no 'frontal criticism' of those kingdoms. Instead, ironically, only through a pronounced fidelity to the outer structure of the ancient, revered – and ostensibly harmless – Shakespearean text would it be possible to deflect the probing eye of both critic and censor' (Al-Bassam 2014: 67).

So how did Al-Bassam's *Richard III* address both its Shakespearean source as well as the multifarious contemporary allusions and linguistic variants?

Given that the play was to be performed in Arabic and hence, *a priori*, unleashed from the letter of the original text, the space for contemporary allusion created by the multiple registers of Arabic – direct, colloquial, *Qur'anic*, classical – was infinite ... Richard's opening monologue was developed with a poet skilled in Bedouin poetry, which immediately made Richard stand out from the linguistic register used by his brothers, who employed a more courtly, vanilla Arabic. Margaret's language was littered with ancient, tribal metaphors, elements of her curses were taken from Mesopotamian laments ... Suddenly, the play was not about history, or paying lip service to a world classic; it became an action painting ... with all the dizzying plethora of detail and possibilities that came with that ... From here one could legitimately populate the imaginary landscape with American ambassadors, feuding princes, immigrant workers, etc. [Thus, the play became] a crucible of internal domestic political tensions in the Gulf region whilst, simultaneously, acting as a mirror for the political expediency of the Western states. (Al-Bassam 2014: 69)

This account demonstrates how Sulayman Al-Bassam used Shakespeare's *Richard III* to stage a complex inter-cultural encounter with the Arab world, its language registers, its cultures, and above all, its recent history. Thus, he makes explicit the immense possibilities of appropriation and adaptation to rise beyond mere equivalences and flat allegories between the sources and the revised version.[19] Instead, as evident in the work of creative theatre and film practitioners such as Ong Keng Sen, Salim Ghouse, Vishal Bhardwaj, and others, Sulayman Al-Bassam explores 'thick' contextualized analogies in his productions such as *Richard III*, whereby Middle East conflicts, Western interventions, and Arab identity formations interact to complicate audience responses and expectations. One aim for him, for instance, was to encourage a response combining identification and alienation of both Western and Arab audiences – an overall experience of dual estrangement:

> Arab audiences coming to see Shakespeare in Arabic expect to see a romantic tale ... but the audiences are left looking at highly realistic political drama with no allegorical intermediary ... Western or non-Arab audiences come expecting the reverse – to see a familiar tale made distant and novel through its ethnographic re-coloring into Arabic.
> (qtd in Litvin 2014: 227)

To sum up, whether in Chinese, Indian, Arab or South African Shakespeares (discussed earlier), among others, the postcolonial journey with 'travelling' Shakespeares continues. In the remaining two chapters of this volume, I continue this exploration into inclusive, non-traditional, multi-racial Shakespeares in Britain and conclude with an extended meditation on Vishal Bhardwaj's *Haider* (*Hamlet*) and how its cultural and political contexts re-constitute the fragments of Kashmir, from the mid-1990s to the recent present.

6

Boundary Crossings on the British Shakespearean Stage

> My feelings about Shakespeare generally are that I will do everything I can to make it feel as urgent and contemporary as possible. So the more I thought about it, the more I felt modern India, particularly Northern India and Delhi, which is a place of transition, would provide a tremendously compelling way into the play *Much Ado About Nothing*.
>
> – Iqbal Khan, director, RSC, Globe, etc.[1]

Multi-racial Shakespeares in Britain

Conditions of postcoloniality pervade contemporary global Britain, perhaps most visibly in urban areas like London. Descendants of British colonial subjects from Africa, South Asia, the Caribbean, and the Middle East are integral to its cultural, racial, and ethnic diversity, even though exclusionary fault-lines still persist. How do these populations – blacks and Asians, among others – engage with Shakespeare, traditionally considered both the 'universal' Bard, and a signifier for authentic 'Britishness'? Many may believe that 'Shakespeare still belongs to an undifferentiated English society ... suffering an amnesiac response to its imperial past'.[2] Such questions call for new considerations of 'race', postcoloniality, and performance in relation to Shakespeare. From early theatre practitioners, such as those of Tara Arts (1977) and the Talawa Theatre Company (1986) in the 1980s and 1990s, who tackled discrimination and equity issues, to the twenty-first-century global diaspora generation, the range of their interventions has been – and continues to be – as diverse as their experiences. From a postcolonial perspective, it is important to recognize a body of work termed 'Black and Asian Shakespeare in Britain', as it emerged and evolved from the late 1970s through the 1980s and 1990s to the present (Jarrett-Macauley 2017).

The early artistic explorations were historic, lest we forget: whether it was Jamaican-born director Yvonne Brewster, co-founder of Talawa Theatre Company or director Jatinder Varma of Tara Arts, these practitioners reclaimed a classical Shakespeare, devising productions related to their own cultural backgrounds. For Varma, inter-cultural practice had to focus on Shakespearean language, a process for which he deployed the term 'Binglish':

> For me, theatre exists in the interplay between tradition and modernity. The new Others in British society – Blacks and Asians and other immigrant minorities – have to engage in this interplay if there is to be lasting *imaginative* change ... Specifically, this means Binglishing Shakespeare.[3]

Thus, inter-cultural Shakespeare as approached by Varma and others reflected its postcolonial legacy in being attentive to 'otherness' in British society, and confronting the 'Other [as] a vital component of the Binglish approach to the classics' (Varma 2017: 30). Yvonne Brewster's work in Talawa also meant overcoming exclusions of black actors, from classical English roles. In choosing to direct *Antony and Cleopatra*, successfully casting a black actor Dona Croll as the Egyptian queen, Brewster explained her goal: 'I really wanted to see what a Cleopatra I envisioned would look like' (qtd in Jarrett-Macauley 2017: 6). At the moment of these Black and Asian forays into previously closed cultural territory, Britain's colonial immigrants were struggling to belong to British society. As an endorsement on the Tara Arts website observes: 'Tara Arts has stretched British cultural life and helped to make those of us with different origins visible to both ourselves and others.'[4] While multiculturalism has acquired some problematic associations with ethnic and racial seclusion, it gave a crucial agenda to these early practitioners. Once the singular 'Englishness' of Shakespearean drama was disrupted, it led to further explorations in identity, race, and theatrical practice in inter-cultural settings.

My aim here is not to recount the history of Black and Asian Shakespeare, as already recorded by Jarrett-Macauley and others, like Jatinder Varma himself. Instead, I explore the less identifiably postcolonial, though strongly inter-cultural Shakespearean productions in Britain in the past decade. In my methodology, I focus on the *discourse* emanating from the critical and theatrical reviews of these productions (including some interviews with the practitioners), rather than on the live productions themselves. Born from exclusion and marginalization, more recently we can see how the multi-racial effects/affects spawned by black and Asian practitioners have mutated and proliferated, while entering previously 'white' settings such as the Globe, the National, and the RSC, among others. Some names of actors and theatre practitioners, including dramaturges (though of different generations), of the Shakespearean stage who may be familiar to theatre goers and professionals in Britain include Adrian Lester, Hugh Quarshie, Lucian Msamati, Josette Simon, Ray Fearon, Jenny Jules, David Harewood, Iqbal Khan, Samir Bhamra, Meera Syal, David Oyelowo, and Tanika Gupta, as well as other, more recent arrivals such as Ankur Bahl, Anjana Vasan, and Ncuti Gatwa. Increasingly, Shakespearean work emerging from this milieu is shaped by an ethos, a practice that rejects binaries such as 'colonial/postcolonial', invoking instead contemporary experiences of migration, diaspora, and multiracial and intercultural exchanges, in both popular and high culture.

Directors, it seems, are coming up with bold, inclusive casting, extending roles far in 'excess' of traditional affiliations between specific roles, genders, races, cultures, among other categories of difference. Changes taking place on the Shakespearean stage include the widespread practice of non-traditional casting, in a variety of versions. Ayanna Thompson identifies this practice (rather than use the throw-back term, 'colour blind') as occurring when 'actors of color are cast in roles not traditionally associated with race, ethnicity, or color to make a socio-political statement' (Thompson 2006: 6–7). Of course, any 'blind' approach would be problematic for roles in which the race of a character is central to the plot, as clearly in the case of *Othello*. Thus, for a long time now it has become impossible for white actors to play the role in black face. Overall, however, it would be fair to say that non-traditional casting evokes 'deep anxieties that pervade contemporary American and English cultures about the (in)significance of race, color, and ethnicity [as] made manifest in the slipperiness of the definitions for and practices of colorblind casting' (Thompson 2006: 7–8). Despite these unpredictable effects, I believe that the use of black, Asian, Latinx, and other actors of colour (intersecting with similar cross-overs in terms of gender and disability) complicate boundaries of familiar and alien worlds – at the intersections of the early modern period and in our own complex societies. And it is these practices that have occasioned a *paradigm shift* in our thinking about 'race' and its links to sexuality, identity formation, and power relations. The Shakespearean landscape is now peopled by diverse actors who, in turn, disrupt any essentialist identifications between bodies and roles, and between Shakespeare and 'whiteness'.

A production that, I believe, serves as a landmark in this new 'turn' in non-traditional casting on the British Shakespearean stage is the 2015 RSC version of *Othello*, directed by Iqbal

Khan. In a radical break with racial boundaries, the British actor Lucian Msamati (raised in Tanzania and Zimbabwe) made theatrical history by being the first black actor ever to play Iago at the RSC. This cross-racial casting changes the tenor of Shakespeare's play, especially given that the production, to some extent, evokes the 'modern-age' with props of technology, designer clothes, military hardware and even a scene of torture in Cyprus reminiscent of Guantanamo. This radical casting choice could certainly lead us to consider various possibilities and ramifications of its effects: how can this version *not* reinforce current racial stereotypes and hierarchies and add another racist aspect to the play? Or, does its break from a 'white' Iago enable us to challenge the 'race thinking' of our own times? Such questions offer a useful lens through which to examine this production's depiction of race relations, which unfold quite distinctly, as one reviewer notes:

> The singularity of Iqbal Khan's compelling new version is that the tragic protagonist and his nemesis are the same race in a contemporary, culturally diverse world where the army that Othello commands is multiracial but where racism still simmers below the surface ... [In one moment, for instance], a strikingly staged scene of celebratory drinking and beat-boxing in Cyprus turns ugly when a rap contest leads ... to the exposure of some very unfortunate prejudices in Jacob Fortune-Lloyd's Cassio. The fact that Othello has promoted this spuriously liberal white man over him adds a new strand of bitterness to the villain's vengeful hatred.[5]

While this explains the logic of the racial dynamics, the production, nonetheless, risked being considered 'racist', both in depicting Shakespeare's villain as a black man and in a situation in which he is attempting to destroy the life of another black man. In an interview Lucian Msamati explains Iago's vengeful nature in terms of a 'sense of betrayal ... the sense that you and I [Iago] ... we have fought in Rhodes, in Cyprus, on others' ground, Christian and heathen ... we are brothers ... but you went and chose that guy over me' (Kpade 2015). While Msamati's psychological profile of Iago's motivations as a black man is helpful, more questions arise: what role can a black Iago play in the larger story of the embattled black man in Western societies in our times? Black male bodies under threat of violence, incarceration, and exclusion figure prominently in social and cultural narratives in Anglo-American contexts today.

Msamati addresses these possible objections, in emphasizing nuances of racial specificity and difference:

> The society in which we live, it is almost as if, because of the colour of your skin, or because of the cultural currency or space you occupy, within the collective imagination, it means that you do not exist outside of those parameters, that you are not psychologically complex or interesting. In fact, you are either super-human or sub-human; you're not human. Here is Sapo and Lucian [the actors' names], two Black men from completely different parts of the African continent with completely different cultural references. Yes, of course there are similarities, but they're very different. And within those differences, there are sub-differences, and sub-differences – that's humanity. (Kpade 2015)

Here Msamati makes a call for recognizing differences among black male identities in terms of their society, nation, 'cultural references' and other factors. I concur that such specificities are useful in *preventing* the dominant culture from subsuming the identities of black men into a stereotyped collective. But they may not work uniformly. For most, though not all, reviewers of the RSC production, the cross-racial casting was convincing and seemed to offer a fascinating psychological dynamic. Though we should, perhaps, ask how many reviewers of major national publishing venues in Britain are people of colour. Did some audience members of colour feel a deep discomfort? Did they feel the dreaded ethnographic gaze directed at themselves, when the evil Iago came on?[6] Questions and issues such as these will give this production widespread currency in debates about 'race' as well as about 'whiteness' – with 'whiteness studies' a growing field in cultural and literary studies. In calling for us to 'move beyond black-and-white ideas of racism as a motivator for Iago', reviewers cannot assume that the production jettisons 'race' (Cavendish 2015). In fact, 'race' is always a factor in any discussion of this particular production. Hugh Quarshie, the British-Ghanaian actor playing Othello, who earlier resisted the role for its potential for re-inscribing 'the racist stereotype of a black man crazed with jealousy', now came to embrace its positive possibilities: 'Only by black actors playing the role ... can we address some of the racist traditions and assumptions that the play is based on' (Dickson 2015). For director Iqbal Khan, mining dissonances in this production (as in his other works) produced rewards, as he explains in an interview:

> Contradiction is, for me, peculiar to what Shakespeare does ... There's a richer music that can be made with a polyphony of voices ... Perhaps ironically, in making my Iago black, I made the play less about the black-and-white race issue ... and perhaps more about betrayal and other things. I liberated, I hope, the more complex powers within that play. (Wicker 2016)

I believe that Khan's approach, *aligning* with Msamati's own sense of a complex Othello/Iago dynamic, highlights the strength of this production: the visceral, emotionally charged scenes between the two black men resonate deeply in terms of our understanding of black male identities in Shakespeare's world and in our own times (see Figure 2). Both men seem to share deep ties embedded in the violence of their feelings, as well as in the racist hierarchies of Venice and the mercenary, multi-racial world they inhabit in Cyprus (including a South Asian Emilia). Within contingent scenarios of war, desire, jealousy and power struggles, binary racial categorizations remain elusive and the black–black dynamic between Iago and

FIGURE 2 Othello, *2015. An enraged Othello (Hugh Quarshie) with Iago (Lucian Msamati), right. Directed by Iqbal Khan. Photo by Keith Pattison, RSC.*

Othello moves along unpredictable trajectories. In this process, therefore, the effect of a black Iago on stage will always remain elusive, challenging any easy decision about whether this casting choice 'worked'.

I consider Iqbal Khan's varied Shakespearean *oeuvre* (including his latest, the RSC *Antony and Cleopatra*, introduced in Chapter 4) as embodying a range of experiences and sources, always from places of 'instability'. In his impulse to embrace the 'provisional' and 'liminal', to see every Shakespeare play as a new play, he is also an '*auteur*, or individual craftsperson possessed of a distinctive vision' (see Burnett 2013: 5). Like Sulayman Al-Bassam and Vishal Bhardwaj, Khan appropriates classical works through the prism of contingent histories and nuanced cultural formations, while rejecting any ideological agenda. Khan did not come to the theatre from an ethnically-led training to mainstream settings, but had worked with disparate materials in various locations from the outset. These included Harold Pinter at the National; Arthur Miller in the West End; and Shakespeare at the Globe, the RSC, and in the West End.[7]

In addition to Iqbal Khan's breakthrough production of *Othello*, other striking productions, evoking a 'global kaleidoscope' of intertexts, are also a part of these innovative, often intercultural trends. In the next section, we see multiple languages of the Indian sub-continent come alive through the voices of brown actors in Tim Supple's rendering of *A Midsummer Night's Dream* (2007), while Emma Rice's gender-bending, culturally mismatched *A Midsummer Night's Dream* evokes 'India' in the sitar-playing musician and Asian actors, for instance, as one aspect of the affective texture of the production (Globe 2016). Finally, we come to Shakespeare's Messina that holds a mirror up to contemporary urban Delhi, in a complex interplay of resemblances and differences, in Iqbal Khan's *Much Ado about Nothing* (RSC 2012).

Imagining 'India' on the Stage

Inter-cultural appropriations of Shakespeare with a global reach were the subject of Chapter 5. Engagements by first and second generations of immigrant practitioners in Britain, as outlined above, opened up new conversations about various kinds of boundary crossings – cultural, racial, gender and even national – as Shakespeare now took on new 'accents'. 'Multiculturalism', both in its positive and problematic aspects, fuelled early black and Asian participation in Shakespeare performance in Britain, and its growing impact was apparent in the fanfare of the London Festival of 2012, during which Shakespeare's Globe presented 37 productions of Shakespeare in different languages, and the RSC launched its own World Shakespeare Festival. Within this globalizing trend, I want to draw attention to three productions produced on different occasions: Tim Supple's early *A Midsummer Night's Dream* (2006–7) literally had a global, inter-cultural reach; Emma Rice's *A Midsummer Night's Dream* in a British venue at the Globe (2016) had a cosmopolitan flair with Indian echoes; and Iqbal Khan's *Much Ado about Nothing* (2012) (part of RSC's global endeavour), set in the postcolonial world of modern Delhi, forged connections between Shakespeare and twenty-first-century India. I chose these three plays somewhat arbitrarily, all marking passages to a 'real' and 'imagined' 'India', reflecting the burgeoning trend of using Shakespeare to bring to life 'native' voices and bodies from distinctive, often non-Western cultures. Audiences' experiences become more complex when they see Shakespearean characters and settings re-located within different, often unfamiliar, cultural idioms. Considering these three productions' wide-ranging and uneven representational range, 'India' is not a singular place or site, and neither do reviewers respond uniformly, though they are not too far apart.

How have British reviewers responded to this trend of inter-cultural, multi-racial Shakespearean productions? In our social media times, mixed critical responses in the national newspapers may not affect the popularity of a particular production at the box office or the reputation of the director in conclusive, drastic ways. Reviews in national newspapers today are supplemented by a profusion of responses, including reviews on online blogs, Twitter feeds, and Facebook pages of companies like the Globe and the RSC, and radio and TV interviews. These have all had an inclusive effect in inserting into the mix popular opinion of plays people have actually seen and, in some cases, these social media sites offer views of specific minorities and communities, such as LGBTQ. However, in the fairly compressed, overdetermined cultural space of Britain, especially that of the London stage, the theatre critics from the main *national* papers such as the *Guardian, The Times* (and *TLS*), *Telegraph, Financial Times,* and the *Independent* still wield considerable influence in affecting future careers of directors and actors.

Mainstream theatre critics, I believe, face particular challenges in their inter-cultural orientations or the lack thereof. While British Shakespeare set in locations more familiar to British audiences has been the norm for so long, productions that engage with 'local' knowledges and histories from non-Western, non-metropolitan locations and perspectives can push viewers to see difference beyond stereotypes and myths. As they try to measure the experiential immediacy of a culturally hybrid production against *their* expectations of an English Shakespearean text, their efforts to engage with the cultural alterity of those worlds may be constrained by their own cultural, linguistic, and epistemological boundaries and certainties. Figurations of 'India' as they emerge from varied reviews of three ensuing productions help me make my point, though with varying emphases.

Tim Supple, Dash Arts, *A Midsummer Night's Dream*, 2007

Let us begin with a short history of the inter-cultural genesis of this unique production:

> The director Tim Supple left England for India and Sri Lanka in 2005, not knowing what a modest British Council grant would bring. He returned with a production of 'The Dream' (Dash Arts) that must count among the most original since Peter Brook tackled the play in 1970. Apart from the spectacle and the fun, both of which are considerable, how many revivals come with actors speaking Shakespeare in no fewer than eight languages, Hindi to Tamil, Bengali to ancient Sanskrit to that great unifier of the Raj, English itself? (Nightingale 2007)

First staged in Britain in the Swan Theatre in Stratford-Upon-Avon in 2006, Supple's production later had a successful run in the newly rebuilt and restructured Roundhouse Theatre in London in 2007 (from which the reviews are taken) and again in 2008.

Tim Supple's creative vision is distinctively global and cross-cultural, with a broad range of engagements in adaptations/translations of non-Western literary works. In addition to his multilingual *A Midsummer Night's Dream*, Supple has produced several adaptations of Eastern works, ranging from *Midnight's Children* (2003), *Haroon and the Sea of Stories* (1998), and *One Thousand and One Nights* (with Hanan Shaiykh, 2011). Artistic director for the Young Vic from 1993 to 2000, in 2005, he co-founded Dash Arts with Josephine Burton, emerging 'as a unique international creative force, producing new theatre, dance, music, and art events with exceptional artists from abroad'. His *A Midsummer Night's Dream* was created for Dash Arts in 2006.[8] The discourse that emerged from the reviews of the Roundhouse production testified to the production's focus on the sensory and affective possibilities of the experience offered by the play. Cumulatively, these reviews offered an 'Orientalizing' perspective, whereby 'India-Sri Lanka' embodied ravishment, sensuality, and stereotypically 'Eastern' affects, but we learnt little about Indian theatrical traditions deployed or any other local, 'native' knowledges that the production illuminated, explained by Supple below. Their emphasis was on Shakespeare's play being 'minted anew' and on the 'freshness' of the approach in its exotic Indian-Sri-Lankan spectacle, with some recognized echoes of Peter Brook's production of *Dream*. 'Its aim was to appeal to eyes and heart rather than ears and minds – to put Shakespeare's language second to the theatrical business of suggesting in fresh ways what madness it is to fall in love' (De Jongh 2007). Others echoed a similar recognition of a 'visually ravishing' experience:

> I find Tim Supple's Indian-Sri Lankan *Dream* has lost none of its power to enchant ... it remains a visually ravishing recreation of the play, capturing all its magical strangeness.

In this setting, spectacle, music and movement inevitably take precedence. (Billington 2007)

Only one reviewer (among the main newspapers), it seems, tried to place the exoticism and sensuousness into specific Indian scenes, in a review entitled 'A delirious Dream of India':

> The lovers are rich, sumptuously silked metropolitan kids of the kind one sees in Bollywood movies. The mechanicals look exactly like the kind of traders encountered on the streets of bustling cities or squatting on their haunches in Indian village squares, while the fairies resemble faintly menacing street performers, as sure-footed shinning up ropes as they are on terra firma … I left the theatre wanting to catch the next flight to Bombay to rekindle my own dormant love affair with the subcontinent. (Spencer 2007)

FIGURE 3 *A scene from Dash Arts'* A Midsummer Night's Dream. *Directed by Tim Supple, Roundhouse Theatre London, 2007. Photo, Tristram Kenton.*

Vibrant scenes of South Asia (as in Figure 3), of brown bodies, costumes, and colour aligned with personal memories for this reviewer of his 'dormant love affair' with India. But even here, perhaps one wishes for further reflections on the ramifications of a South Asian production for British audiences in London who did not have access to the language spoken on stage. Did they have any other recourse but to exoticize their experience? Most importantly how did this production offer new access to the Shakespearean world?

It was Supple himself who answered this question in justifying the use of Indian theatrical traditions for recreating Shakespeare in a cross-pollination of the two, reminding us in an RSC interview in 2006 that there was 'no attempt to transfer or super-impose a set of cultural signs on top of a play by Shakespeare':

> I also hoped we can get closer to the full canvas of the play with Indian and Sri Lankan performers – in a theatrical culture with such a rich and vital convergence of the past and the present; the physical and the verbal; the sacred and the profane; the comedic and the tragic; the magical and the real. Mythic warrior kings and queens; daughters as goods, owned by their fathers; modern lovers cast in archetypal mold; exile in the forest; the reality of class and caste ... and of course the supernatural, the magical, the hilarious, humans transformed ...
>
> [Beyond our verbal and realistic traditions] ... there are many other possibilities in Shakespeare ... The ability to find truth in stylization, life in the ritual and beauty and form in spontaneity are all abilities ... [that] will enrich the playing of Shakespeare. In the cast, we have dancers, modern realistic actors, musicians, street artists, performers trained in forms 2000 years old and others who have ... adapted them into new forms. This is the natural make-up of a group of Indian performers for Shakespeare. India is a hybrid of a dazzling range of influences and so is Shakespeare.[9]

Supple's 2006 interview shows us *why* this production was an important landmark in intercultural, global appropriations of Shakespeare. It demonstrated that different cultures are enriched by embracing alterity and difference via the cross-pollinations of different aesthetic forms. It is also useful to note that Tim Supple's inter-cultural and intra-cultural *Dream* intersects with an earlier Indian production, even though that had *no* direct influence in Supple's conception, since he did not see it or even photos of it. This earlier production was the late Habib Tanvir's famous translation and adaptation of *A Midsummer Night's Dream* as *Kamdeo Ka Apna, Vasant Ritu Ka Sapna (The Love God's Own, A Spring Time Dream)*, in which the Indian god of love (Kamdeo) figures prominently, still considered a landmark in Indian appropriations of Shakespeare. Originally staged in 1993 as a multilingual and cross-cultural piece, it was initially planned for British actors in the royal and urban roles (speaking English) alongside the mechanicals played by rustic members of the Naya theatre from the central Indian region of Chattisgarh (speaking in dialect). The play incorporated the north Indian musical folk theatre form of *Nautanki*. In productions through the 1990s, reviewers uniformly acknowledged its success, often comparing it to Brook's production.[10]

While his *Dream* flew entirely on its own brilliantly innovative wings, with no reference to Tanvir's *Kamdeo*, Supple acknowledges Tanvir's important influence as one that is 'outside the western theatre', which he clarifies when referring to another Tanvir production, *Agra Road*, that he had seen: 'His master work, *Agra Road*, did have an influence on how I approached the Mechanicals in *Dream*. The spirit of their scenes and the quality of their performances were very much inspired by Habib and his ensemble.'[11]

In terms of its cultural and historical impact and effects, Supple's multilingual production of *A Midsummer Night's Dream* seems to mirror the impact of Ong Keng Sen's *LEAR* (see Chapter 5), in that it is both inter-cultural in its dialogic flow between the UK and the subcontinent as well as intra-cultural in its expression of multiple local languages among which specific Indian/Sri Lankan audiences would only have had access to one or two. Opening the Shakespearean *Dream* to a world of Indian polyphony, the director demonstrates (in terms underpinning this volume) the 'usefulness of local, non-metropolitan knowledges [idioms, and affects] in offering additional opportunities for thinking about Shakespeare' (Orkin 2005: 2–4). In deploying his multilingual frame, one of Supple's discoveries was that the Indian actors were closer to the world of the play than any English actor, and that his *Dream* world was not intrinsically English. Overall, in its use of cross-cultural and multilingual identities, this production's concept continues to challenge the orthodoxies of Indian nationalism itself. Since *Dream* was staged in 2007, modes of linguistic, cultural, and religious xenophobia increasingly underpin the Indian/Sri Lankan national imaginaries – as well as populist movements in the West. Another rendition of Supple's version would certainly be welcome as a riposte to all such forms of nationalistic xenophobias both in the sub-continent and in the West.

Emma Rice, The Globe, *A Midsummer Night's Dream*, 2016

Emma Rice's *A Midsummer Night's Dream*, with its complicated mutations of race, gender, and ethnicity on stage, is another striking example of a cultural boundary-crossing theatrical performance on the British Shakespearean stage. This Globe rendition of *Dream* gestured to both local (English topical references and music) and global (South Asian/Indian/Bollywood) aspects of staging, while using cross-cultural, non-traditional casting. Loudly and sensually, it drew audiences to participate in re-configuring the cultural, aesthetic, and social meanings – and meaning-making – that makes up *Dream*. Reviewers applauded the cultural 'mash-up', many highlighting the 'Indian' accents of the music and set or simply mentioning that some of the actors were Asian or black. Most reviewers also identified and approved of the gender realignments – as in the Helena/Helenus crossover – that offered a sharp 'twist' to the story of the two pairs of lovers, as one typically observed: 'The multicultural mash-up is enhanced by sexual transitioning: Helena becomes Helenus, a gay man in love with Demetrius' (Norman 2016). Mostly, however, these descriptions focused on spectacle and theatricality, offering an uncritical, stereotypical, and 'unqueered' rendering of homoerotic desires. Also, any mention of black and Asian bodies as conduits of these gender-bending desires is curiously missing in the reviews.

Typical press reviews of this successful production were celebratory, recognizing its topical and visual diversity:

> A sitar player sends music pulsing through the action. Titania swans down from the sky in chiffon. One pair of lovers is gay ... There are matted-hair fairies and a roller-skating eunuch. When Oberon casts his spell on the Fairy Queen, he seems to rape her ... There is nothing wispy about Rice's magic. It is disruptive, unnerving, highly comic. It cracks the surface of normality and lets hallucination and truth escape hand in hand. Dirty fairies dance around their Queen's flowery bed as if they had pushed their way up through the soil. Performance artist Meow Meow makes Titania a vision of sylvan sexiness. (Clapp 2016)[12]

This production did, indeed, crack 'the surface of normality', combining 'hallucination and truth', whereby the play's actions are staged on metamorphic cultural landscapes, as fleshed out vividly by another reviewer:

> Presiding over everything is an Indian matriarch, seated in cross-legged solemnity, playing an electric sitar whose headstock (the bit with the tuning pegs) resembles a Fender bass. What are we supposed to make of this weird, druggy,

space-age Bollywood mash-up? ... Nothing much. Except that Shakespeare belongs now, and then, and here and there, and everywhere. What a stylish departure from the usual updates, which tend to drag the text, bound and gagged, up some anthropological avenue that turns out to be a dead end. There are bursts of Bowie and Beyoncé, and snatches of George Formby and Marilyn Monroe, which add delicious feather-light suggestions and illuminations that link our culture with the Elizabethan age ... (Evans 2016)

The 'colourblind' casting of diverse actors aligned with the artistic versatility of the production; but the raced bodies of Asian actors as Hermia and Helenus, a black actor as Demetrius, and Titania's 'sylvan sexiness' added to the complexity of the sexual politics of the production. The visual of a traditionally-garbed Indian sitar player seated atop the stage under strings of traditional marigold garlands – evoking a floral bower – I believe gave a distinctly 'Indian' texture to the production. Some reviewers highlight the 'Indian accents' but mostly in surface, exotic effects of little thematic consequence: 'In Rice's *Dream*, Titania's Indian changeling child, a Shakespearean MacGuffin if ever there was one, has somehow become the spirit of the piece. Rice is collaborating once again with Tanika Gupta ... and the whole thing has the feel and energy of an Indian wedding' (Tripney 2016). Others observe: 'There's a strong Indian flavor (sitar music and bhangra dancing) to a show that does not, to put it mildly, defer to purists' (Taylor 2016). Another reviewer offers a more persuasive diasporic take on 'India' via London's Brick Lane (see Figure 4):

The stage is festooned with giant white globes and wafting green tubes and dressed in orange marigolds as if for an Indian wedding. It's not the first time that Shakespeare has been invested with Indian spice but with nods to 'Hoxton hipsters' this is closer to Brick Lane than Bollywood'. (Norman 2016)

FIGURE 4 A Midsummer Night's Dream, *The Globe, London, 2015. The Fairies and Bottom, with the Sitar Player. Directed by Emma Rice. Photo by Steve Tanner.*

These Indian 'accents' in the Globe production are prescient in recalling Titania's Indian votaress who gave her the changeling boy in India; hence it is somewhat disappointing the 'Indian boy' staged in this production was represented by a puppet, rather than putting a young brown body on stage.

It is clear that if love's course in *A Midsummer Night's Dream* does not run smoothly, it 'meanders into territories, we would now call "queer"' (Smith 2016).[13] Most (though not all) reviewers of the Globe production view this gender switch as having 'worked'. But as mentioned earlier, most comments are descriptive and simply tend to 'feminize' Helenus in somewhat stereotypical terms: 'The gender switch, which makes Helena into Helenus, gives an added dimension to Demetrius's reluctance to admit to his love and an added sweetness to their coming together' (Clapp 2016). Or, another reviewer notes: 'Rice's most potentially contentious change, which sees Helena becoming Helenus, yearning desperately after Demetrius, who sees marriage to Hermia as the best way to secure his place in society, works beautifully. That has a lot to do with the unaffected directness of Ankur Bahl's poignant performance as Helenus' (Gardner 2016). Overall, it seems, reviewers emphasize gender realignments over race and the colour displacements. Asian actors playing the lead roles, as stated earlier, with the Sitar play atop, take us into a distinctly Indian world (Elizabethan fairies notwithstanding). If we remain singularly 'colourblind' in this instance, we cannot mine the possibilities of an imagined 'India' representing fluid sexual drives and desires – for instance, linking Titania, the Indian votaress, the Indian changeling boy, and Oberon – as adding another dimension to our understanding of desire and sexuality as compelling forces in the play. As Titania tells her story, it was also in India that she and her 'votaress would sit by night along the sea and laugh to see the sails of passing ships conceive / and grow big bellied with the wanton wind'. Some critics have seen in that scenario 'a vision of an all-female world that seems to be possible without the intrusion of men' (Smith 2016).

In Chapter 2, I discussed the role of the changeling boy in *A Midsummer Night's Dream* through the motif of 'India' in the discourses about emerging colonialism, including the abduction and exchange of boys. Recognizing 'India' as an imagined space signals a fluidity of desires and identities. Of course, it is not the task of reviewers to yoke the play to some 'anthropological theme'. However, reducing cultural markers simply to a 'mish-mash' does not account for the Indian inspirations behind the play, as Emma Rice (2016) observed during a live stream interview with Meera Syal. From a postcolonial perspective, this production makes us *re-think* any naturalized associations between the Shakespearean plot and a purely Anglo culture, some of which we can only experience in glimmers in the range of reviews available to us.

Iqbal Khan, RSC, Stratford-Upon-Avon, *Much Ado About Nothing*, 2012

In 2012, as a part of the World Shakespeare Festival, the RSC sponsored an inter-cultural version of *Much Ado About Nothing*, described in the programme as follows: 'Iqbal Khan directs this Shakespearean comedy of love and deceit, placing it in a vibrant Indian setting, which will play in Stratford then in London at the Noel Coward in September.' It was an intriguing cultural overlay being proposed, so one is led to ask, how did the director Iqbal Khan conceive of the inter-cultural dimensions of *Much Ado About Nothing*?

> The production is set in modern Delhi, which provides a very interesting lens through which to view the play because of the parallels between early modern England and modern day Delhi: the hierarchical structures are similar; the relationships between masters and their servants are still present; the importance of honor; the centrality of women within that; the idea of bloodlines, and how daughters continue that on – if a daughter is found to be iniquitous

the bloodline is tainted. All of these ideas are absolutely still current in modern India ... So, the parallels and the opportunities to explore these aspects in *Much Ado About Nothing* in an urgent and modern context make ... them refreshingly compelling ... As the production was going to be part of the World Shakespeare Festival, Michael suggested that we might look at placing the play in an Indian context. Initially, my heart sank, because the idea of doing something exotic, for me, is anathema. (Khan 2012)

This production clearly eschews Bollywood stereotypes, as well as any form of 'exoticism' – one that is often a careless throwback to the long history of Westerners Orientalizing non-Western cultures in reductive terms. Instead, it leads us to question notions of non-Western societies as static and frozen in time, while exploring inter-cultural exchanges as dynamic and complex engagements between 'tradition' and 'modernity', as Khan explains: 'My feelings about Shakespeare generally are that I will do everything I can to make it feel as urgent and contemporary as possible ... I felt modern India, particularly Northern India and Delhi which is a place of transition, would provide a tremendously compelling way into the play.'[14]

The play's journey is to modern-day Delhi, but in critics' eyes, it seems, this production does not represent 'Shakespearean travels to India', but rather to a mediated, implicitly stereotyped Bollywood world. And in a recent reflection on *Much Ado*, Khan elaborates on his resistance to the 'exotic', explaining how he wanted to overlay the complexities of modern Delhi society with the gender politics of Messina:

I wanted to try to resist any kind of *Best Exotic Marigold* Indian Shakespeare experience ... I wanted to do it in a spiky, truthful way ... conveying something of the authentic, stratified, hierarchical mix of Indians in Delhi ... I also hoped to convey something of the range of roles women have now in India, from the entrepreneurial, cosmopolitan sexually liberated women to the indolent rich and the village girl. (Khan 2017: 141)

Yet it is quite ironic, though not surprising, that British critics of the production of *Much Ado* repeatedly fall back on 'Bollywood' as a lens, usually with minimal evidence, through which they view the play's representations of marriage, chastity, and rituals of wooing and wedding, etc. What is missing in these references is any historical engagement with Bollywood's hybrid cultural formations (Dionne and Kapadia 2014); instead the term 'Bollywood' is used as a convenient signifier for all things Indian and exotic in a seemingly timeless world. Another critic observes 'the parallels between Shakespeare's comedy and Bollywood romance, with its arranged marriages and stress on female chastity' (Billington 2012). Some touches are more nuanced: 'In Iqbal Khan's production, Shakespeare's Sicilian setting is abandoned in favor of modern Delhi. It's a bold decision to try to highlight what Khan calls the "Indianness" of Britain's most famous dramatist. Yet this reimagining, with its Bollywood textures, manages to reflect interestingly on rituals and gender roles' (Anonymous 2012). The play certainly had an eye on Delhi as a city of modernity, with self-sufficient women like Beatrice, without any distinctively exotic touches in scenes between the couple (in comparison to the wedding scene; see Figure 5). For the critics, however, a simple reductive equation of Indian life rituals to Bollywood is a convenient ploy: 'At times – as when Hero's tomb is shown translated into a smoking funeral pyre, the cast breaking into stylized movement with rain falling from the heavens – the production achieves a marriage of Bard and Bollywood that's breathtaking to behold.'[15]

To respond to these Bollywood connections made by reviewers, we have only to consider that the Delhi wedding in *Much Ado* is *not* modelled on Bollywood; Bollywood refracts rather than reflects Indian life rituals. In fact, the *Much Ado* ceremony represents a composite of hundreds of *actual* Delhi weddings that take place every day across the sprawling city. The scene of Hero and Leonato, a formally dressed, garlanded father and daughter would represent a commonplace scene at a Delhi wedding (see Figure 6). The director also recognized the

FIGURE 5 Much Ado About Nothing, 2012. *Beatrice (Meera Syal) and Benedick (Paul Bhattacharjee). Directed by Iqbal Khan. Photo by Ellie Kurttz, RSC.*

FIGURE 6 Much Ado About Nothing, 2012. Leonato *(Madhav Sharma)* and Hero *(Amara Karan)* at the Wedding. Directed by Iqbal Khan. Photo by Ellie Kurttz, RSC.

resemblances in lived experience, 'the formality of engagements and the courtship rituals around them are still very present in India' (Khan 2012). The programme notes also point to a world rooted in Indian-specific social arrangements and practices: 'The romantic, sexual, and emotional configurations underpinning the centrality of marriage in Shakespeare's comedies ... richly resonate with the Indian social milieu. *Shaadi* or marriage, together with its varied prenuptial dalliances and arrangements, emerges as a theme of endless Indian rituals, festivals, and popular culture.'[16] Finally, Khan's picture of modern Indian marriage further belies orthodoxy: 'by presenting marriage alliances in which love or at least attraction co-exists with parental arrangement, he points to hybrid forms of arranged marriages'; whether 'arranged' or not, they are always based on some form of consent.[17]

In generally positive, complimentary reviews to the theatrical experience overall, two other issues raised by critics are also telling. First is the issue that what the director describes as touches of 'grotesquery' in representing the Watch was seen as an affront to taste: Michael Billington does not approve of 'an endless procession of sight gags: the comic constable Dogberry and his Watch are particular victims of this, and [then] we got our old friend, on-stage urination ... phallic jokes ... etc' (2012). According to Cavendish, 'Khan and Co get carried away with incidental attempts to innovate. The live music is terrific but there are vulgar interpolations during the watchmen's eavesdropping scene and gimmicky antics' (2012). Khan counters this critique of his 'presentation of the Watch' directly in his recent article, insisting that the grotesque was intrinsic to Shakespeare's plays; he asserts, 'The hostile liberals took exception to our presentation of the grotesquery. It made them uncomfortable' (Khan 2017: 144).

A more amorphous sense of unease about authenticity that emerged from the main reviews focused on the 'Asian' character of the production, and on liberals searching for authenticity in identity. (I use the term 'liberal' loosely here for critics who would consider themselves attuned to and even trained to appreciate cultural difference, especially across the non-Western spectrum.) The production had a cast of twenty-two Asian actors and five musicians (Khan 2017: 140). These were diasporic Asian identities, including very famous figures like Meera Syal, and thus, in a sense, mediated by English expectations and judgments. The RSC promoted this as a sign of cosmopolitanism, but some reviewers' attacks on that very aspect are telling:

> With this production of *Much Ado*, we have a parody or pastiche of 'internationalism', with apparently second generation British actors pretending to return to their cultural roots in a decidedly colonial way. Not ever intended as offensive or racially subversive, this *Much Ado* is nevertheless unable to offer anything other than the veneer of Indian culture, served on a bed of Bradford or Birmingham Anglicized rice. (Quarmby 2012)

I end this section on Khan's work with this quote not for the shock value regarding the reviewers' use of racist clichés and stereotypes about British Asian communities. For me Quarmby's view offers a classic example of a residual English colonial thinking based on the premise of superior 'knowledge' about the 'natives'. What he is clearly revealing here is the arrogance that comes with ignorance. Overall, whether it was the reviewers' objection to the grotesquerie of Rabelaisian body humour – coupled with remarks about the accents and diction of the actors – or their mockery of British Asian actors seeking their 'cultural roots', the critical discourse about *Much Ado About Nothing* in British newspapers was largely about the reviewers' *own* expectations: about the kinds of Indians, the kinds of 'Bollywood' weddings, as well as the kinds of tasteful behaviour they wanted to see on the Shakespearean stage. It was if they wanted to re-cast the Shakespearean characters, the 'Delhi-ites', as appropriate Indian subjects under the watchful eye of their British interlocutors or patrons.

7

Shakespeare in Postcolonial Cinema

A Meditation on *Haider/Hamlet*

HAMLET
   How weary, stale, flat and unprofitable
   Seem to me all the uses of this world!
   ... 'tis an unweeded garden
   That grows to seed, things rank and gross in nature
   Possess it merely.

   – *Hamlet* (1.2.133–36)[1]

Reconstituting the Cultural Ruins of Kashmir

In this chapter I conclude the inter-cultural journey of this book by moving from the stage to the screen; specifically, to the 'travels' of Shakespeare's *Hamlet* into the landscape, histories, and cultural memories of Kashmir. In keeping with my postcolonial explorations into Global Shakespeares in scholarship and on the stage, my interest here lies in the tradition of non-Anglophone Shakespeares, found in what is defined today as 'world cinema'.[2] The term 'world cinema', drawn from Burnett (2013), approximates my usage of 'global' Shakespeares, whereby I focus on issues constellating around Shakespearean cinema from the global south, complicating our understandings of national and regional cultures, of colonial and postcolonial influences, as well as of individual figures or *auteurs*, who break away from established conventions or cultural formations. (Burnett 2013: 5). A figure in Global Shakespeares cinema who represents such an 'auteur' for an increasingly large community of inter-cultural, postcolonial Shakespeare scholars is director Vishal Bhardwaj. Introduced earlier, in Chapter 5, Bhardwaj has produced ground-breaking appropriations of Shakespeare – *Macbeth/Maqbool* (2004), *Othello/Omkara* (2006), and most recently *Hamlet/Haider* (2014) – that mediate between the elite, Western intellectual affiliations associated with the plays and the local, non-metropolitan cultures and knowledges of the Indian sub-continent.[3] The success of Bhardwaj's adaptations via 'Bollywood' shows the global reach of Shakespeare's works, as they 'circulate within the intercultural context of twenty-first-century global Shakespeare'. Thus, their success 'raises the question as to how two forces of cinema development – Shakespearean adaptation on the one hand and the global emergence of Hindi cinema – intersected and what form does that intersection take?' (11).[4] What is now called 'Bollywood' emerged from North Indian Hindi cinema, originally more locally based, both in its themes and settings. Thus, the term 'Bollywood' today is both pliant and problematic as it covers wide and disparate offerings, with an appeal that is global especially across South Asian diasporas and other non-Western populations. *Haider* represents 'Bollywood' in its international success, but it also reflects and problematizes the lyrical and affective legacy of Hindi cinema, while setting its drama of trauma in the cinematic romantic world of Kashmir (as I discuss later). Such issues have informed recent discussions of Bhardwaj's own films, showing how they reflect the 'consumption of Shakespeare and the hybrid [global] cultural product', while reminding us 'this is not Shakespeare in India, but Shakespeare in ... specific Indias'.[5]

In *Haider/Hamlet*, Bhardwaj takes Shakespeare's play (and his audience) into Kashmir – a disputed region, disjunct to the Indian State, also claimed by Pakistan. His approach expands the parameters of what constitutes inter-cultural 'appropriation' into rich, inter-textual networks of cultural and historical memories. In this process, he re-configures a mutually constitutive relationship between 'Kashmir' and '*Hamlet*' in complex ways beyond the familiar terms of the 'appropriation' and 'adaptation' debates, which imply either a resistance to or veneration of the original work. Rather, he ventures farther afield, by mapping Shakespeare's play through South Asian contextual archaeologies that affectively and imaginatively re-constitute the fragments of Kashmir – from the cataclysmic moments of the mid-1990s continuing into the present (of Bhardwaj's film). We must, of course, also recall the violent postcolonial history – the aftermath of the Indian partition between Pakistan and India in divided Kashmir – which lurks like an anamorphic shadow over the 1990s militancy and brutal occupation of Kashmir by the Indian armed forces in which the film is set – and whose effects linger today. Locating the film in the period during a time of a collective trauma, the director presents it in terms of a suggestive analogy, 'In my film, in a way, Kashmir becomes Hamlet' (Bhardwaj 2014).[6] This analogy with Kashmir has led to some questions about how the 'efforts at equating Kashmir with Hamlet, both radicalizes the film's understanding of the play, and ultimately relegates the Kashmir valley to well-known stereotypes of violence' (Sen 2017: 88). This response, perhaps, typifies some of the judgmental criticism about the film's politics, the director's intentions, and its larger implications for political interventions. In my meditation, however, I wish to consider afresh the film's politics via its *affective* and *poetic* registers.

I do so by tracing Kashmiri cultural and historical memories woven through the film's immersion of the *Hamlet* story into the 1990s occupation of Kashmir.

Regarding the relationship between *Haider* and *Hamlet*, Bhardwaj's film has demonstrated the global reach of the Shakespearean text, while at the same time, lyrically opening up the play to local knowledges, voices, and experiences of Kashmir under occupation. What is imaginatively invoked in Shakespeare's *Hamlet* – the 'unweeded garden / That grows to seed / [with] things rank and gross [possessing] it' (1.2.133–36) – is visualized quite literally in the scenes of destruction and sterility in *Haider*. After the initial bombing of Haider's home by Indian security forces and the subsequent disappearance of his father, the film moves across fast-changing vistas, taking us from dark interiors of traditional houses to blasted ruins of homes, torture chambers in prisons, scenic, though often desolate landscapes of trees and lakes, and a striking snowy graveyard, reminiscent of the gravedigger's scene in *Hamlet*. In *Haider*, though, the cemetery also becomes the site of a final bloody catastrophe with the militants battling security forces.[7] When Haider returns from college to his shattered shell of a home in Srinagar and starts rummaging for mementoes of his father's memories in the rubble, he does not express his trauma in a direct address to the audience. Unlike the closeted interiority available to Hamlet in his soliloquies, it is as if Haider's inner psychic bearings are completely disorientated. In contrast, Shakespeare's *Hamlet* is staged within firmly demarcated interiors or the battlements of the King's castle, except for the gravedigger's scene.[8]

If 'Denmark is a prison', the world of the court certainly implies the walls closing in on it, as, for instance, is famously evoked by another foreign film adaptation, Kozintsev's Russian *Hamlet* (1964). In Shakespeare's play, the protagonist seeks an affirmation of his personal identity in an elusive, contingent world that is Denmark: 'where the boundaries between naturally discrete things dissolve and opposites fuse, where uncles become fathers, mothers/aunts, funerals/marriages, where night and day are indistinguishable – merging in the graveyard scene – where the grave lacks respect for persons' (Calderwood 1983: 97–98). If Shakespeare's *Hamlet* is the ultimate metonymy for the tragic early modern – and for the formation of the individual subject as we see in Hamlet's psychic struggles – Bhardwaj's *Haider* creates a tragic subjectivity in which the personal is repeatedly imbricated in the historical, cultural, and political currents that both underlie and shape the Kashmir militancy and occupation.

Thus, in this meditation, I hope to show how these differing investments in the *personal* are crucial in understanding the *Hamlet/Haider* interrelationship. My endeavour is to capture the affective and poetic, rather than the political logic by which the film represents the traumas of occupied Kashmir. To do so, I focus on Bhardwaj's project via poetic and historical remnants of ruin, loss, and remembrance – literal, metaphoric, imaginary – constituting our experiences of the film, and resonating beyond it in Kashmiri cultural and literary works and images. I share a general recognition of *Haider* as an elegy to Kashmir but, more *specifically*, I map a network of discourses that imaginatively re-constitute the cultural and psychic fragments of Kashmir from the mid-1990s to the present. Works which interweave into the film or with which it implicitly engages in varying ways include Basharat Peer's 2010 memoir, *Curfewed Night*, his story of the Kashmir conflict, the basis of the film script; two poems by Faiz Ahmed Faiz (1950s–1980s); Agha Shahid Ali's 1997 anthology of poems, *The Country without a Post Office*; Abir Bazaz and Meenu Gaur's 2003 documentary, *Paradise on a River of Hell*; Ananya Kabir's critical work, *Territory of Desire: Representing the Valley of Kashmir* (2009); and, tangentially, images by Nilima Sheikh in her exhibit 'Each Night Put Kashmir your Dreams' (2003–10). Thus, on one level, *Haider's* tragic subjectivity is shaped by his personal angst – his quest to find his disappeared father, Dr Hilal Meer, and later to seek revenge on his uncle, Khurram, who betrays his father to the military and marries his mother, Ghazala. In this chapter I show how Haider's individual psychic trauma is interwoven with the elegiac reconstitution of cultural fragments of Kashmiri identity evoked in the works listed above. It is these inter-weavings that I explore here, and through them, I believe, the loss, grief, and remembrance experienced by Haider accrue meanings beyond his *personal* suffering and breakdown. Western viewers watching *Haider* in search of *Hamlet* may find the experience profoundly unsettling: the boundaries of Elsinore give way to the disparate, fast-moving, violent and chaotic Kashmiri locales of the film. And the plot itself emerges from the postcolonial history of the sub-continent. Cumulatively, such mutations of the original work are likely to disrupt Western viewers' epistemological certainties about the moral issues emanating from Shakespeare's play; especially since Shakespeare's tragic hero as Haider, a 'native' protagonist, does *not* confide in them through soliloquies along the way. In the process, however, I would argue, they may also recognize the *limited* frame of reference within which Hamlet, Shakespeare's iconic tragic figure, recognizes the meanings of human contingency and choice, especially when ruminating on death.

Let us begin by looking at how Shakespeare's *Hamlet* turned into Bhardwaj's *Haider* through its genesis in Basharat Peer's *Curfewed Night* (2010). As the director tells it:

> My wife, Rekha, was reading Basharat's memoir, *Curfewed Night*. One night, I saw her crying while reading it. She said, 'Hila diya mujhe iss book ne (This book shook me).' ... I didn't read the book [at this point] but *Hamlet* was very much on my mind. [Later] I contacted Basharat ... and we started work. The authentic feel in *Haider* is because of him. There are so many little things in the film which only an insider could bring in. (Singh 2014)

In choosing the Kashmiri insurgency and occupation as its theme, while including some shots of the idyllic Himalayan landscapes, Bhardwaj's film offers a riposte to the popular trend in setting romantic Hindi films in Kashmir, from the 1960s to

1980s, when they were described as Bombay Hindi films (not the more current, global term, 'Bollywood'), and their locales tended to be indigenous, Kashmir being one of them: 'the visual setting of the Kashmir valley itself became a compressed signifier for heterosexual romance' though 'it sharply diverged from the actual political situation then prevalent' in the region (Kabir 2009).[9]

As the co-script writer of *Haider*, Basharat Peer offers an explanation of their adaptation of *Hamlet* in Kashmir in terms far removed from the earlier Hindi romantic 'formula' films; instead, he explains why they adapted the Shakespearean plot to a specific practice of military surveillance during the Kashmir insurgency of the 1990s:

> Well, in the South Asian context when you think of a tragic place, of a sad place, a storied place, Kashmir is an obvious choice. When the Kashmir insurgency was going on it was at its peak in the mid-nineties ... [a policy deployed by the Indian state was to create] a militia of several thousand men, Kashmiris, who were armed and given a license to kill ... really let loose on a population and told to kill the militant groups and their sympathizers because they were part of the society, they knew who worked, and how and they knew everyone. And to me, the question of a brother betraying a brother, that the unit of a family is torn into two – the moment we thought of *Hamlet*.[10]

This central premise of 'a brother betraying a brother' offered the perfect aesthetic and moral scaffolding for holding together Shakespeare's play and Bhardwaj's film. Claudius' murder of his brother, Hamlet's father, and the seduction of and marriage to Gertrude perfectly mirrors Khurram's betrayal of his brother, Dr Meer, and his seduction of and subsequent marriage to Ghazala, his brother's wife. Thus, the film preserves the central family betrayal of Shakespeare's play. In the same interview Peer observes 'Kashmir as a place where there have been too many deaths', thus providing a context for poignant representations of cemeteries and graveyards, with the film's extended finale taking place amidst a landscape of graves and continuing violence. In Peer's *Curfewed Night* (2010), the violent history of Kashmiri is represented in several cemeteries, with one in Srinagar given the title of 'Kashmir Martyr's Graveyard', as we are led to traverse among the graves:

> We ... walked on the cobbled footpaths running between the graves and the defiant reds and violets of roses and irises. Hundreds lay buried in neat rows, each grave marked with a rectangular white marble tombstone with a green border engraved with the name of the dead ... Many of the names were familiar to me ... And there were unknown men and women from all parts of Kashmir ... Most graves named the killers: police, army, security forces, as if they, too, were to be immortalized. (121–22)

Resemblances, echoes, as well as divergences between the graveyard scene as represented in *Hamlet* and *Haider* demonstrate differing burdens of death and dying experienced by the two protagonists, as well as by the denizens of Elsinore and Kashmir. First to *Hamlet*, when the protagonist states his relationship to death while 'talking' to Yorick's skull:

> Ah poor Yorick. I knew him, Horatio. A fellow of infinite jest, of most excellent fancy. He hath bore me on his back a thousand times, and now how abhorred in my imagination it is ... Here hung those lips that I have kissed I know not how oft. Where be your jibes now – your gambols, your songs, your flashes of merriment, that were wont to set the table on a roar? (5.1.174–81)

Hamlet's mockery and abhorrence of the decaying flesh sets death far apart from his living being. When the Gravedigger tells him that the grave belongs to him, he quips: ''Tis for the dead, not for the quick. / Therefore thou liest' (5.1.118–19). Or, if 'to be [alive] or not to be' is Hamlet's dilemma, he neatly keeps the two states distinct. Panja (2017) aptly compares the renderings of the two works via references to Yorick in *Hamlet*:

> Hamlet's words on mortality are spoken because of the enormous gulf ... between his own life and that of Yorick, already rotting for many a year within the freshly dug grave ... However, in *Haider*, because of the overwhelming presence of violent death, as a result of the continuous encounters between the Indian armed forces and the Kashmiri separatists, there is no difference between ... living and ... dying ... The three old gravediggers ... welcome all to death with their song 'So Jao' (Sleep). The invitation to die, to sleep – *not* perchance to dream – is offered to all. (102–3)

Death in *Haider* is the great leveller here, not as it is in the abstract fable of Alexander's demise in *Hamlet*: 'Alexander died, Alexander was buried, Alexander returneth to dust' (5.1.198–99). Instead, in Bhardwaj's film, we literally witness a scene of freshly slaughtered bodies, with their blood splattered all over the snow. Basharat Peer's descriptions of various graveyards, honouring the dead martyrs of the region's bloody history, help to explain the film's shift from Shakespearean interiority to houses razed to the ground, desolate landscapes (including cemeteries) and reminders of violent death everywhere.

Beyond recent Kashmiri history, the film also draws upon other important cultural sources: two poems by Faiz Ahmed Faiz (1911–84), which are woven into the story at strategic moments. Faiz was both a revolutionary and romantic poet, a Pakistani though, more broadly, an iconic figure emblematic of the postcolonial world itself, with all its emotional bonds as well as fractures. The ways in which Faiz's poetry intertwines lyrical and political renderings of the division of the self are aptly summed up by Mufti (2004):

> What Faiz's love lyrics give expression to is a self in partition ... In the years following the partition of India, the

problematic of national fragmentation comes to imbue the lyric world of Faiz's verse in profound and explicit ways. But the broader problematic of a partitioned self is already present in the poems of the pre-partition years ... Faiz makes it possible to think about identity in post-partition South Asia [including Kashmir] in terms other than those normalized within the shared vocabulary of the postcolonial states. (247–48)

Within the Indian sub-continent's political and emotional ruptures, Faiz's poetry has shaped – and continues to shape – the affective memories of several generations of South Asians from the region and beyond, long after the partition of the sub-continent – itself an emblematic moment in colonial/postcolonial history. It is not incidental, then, that noted Kashmiri poet Agha Shahid Ali was one of Faiz's major translators, given that the latter's call for political and social justice would have had particular resonance for Kashmiris.[11] Let us return to the scene of Haider's bombed-out house, where he recollects in a flashback a scene with his father singing and quizzing him on an Urdu couplet (with the opening line as its title):

Gulon mein rang bhare baad-e-naubahaar chale
Chale bhi aao ke gulshan ka kaarobaar chale
[The new breeze of Spring
fills blossoms with their hue,
Come now, my love, grant the garden
leave to go about its business].[12]

This couplet is from a well-known *Ghazal* (lyric poem) by Faiz, taken from the collection *Dast-e-Saba* (Hand of the Easterly Wind), which was written and published when Faiz was in the Central Jail in Sind, Hyderabad, Pakistan. It is a call to a beloved to come to the garden of Spring, whose celebration (its 'business') is halted by their absence. The young Haider is emotionally stirred by this poem in this recollection scene of his childhood. Later, at two key moments, its lyrics evoke both a nostalgic comfort and loss: first, when Roohdar, the phantasmal militant hiding his bruises under sun glasses – the 'ghost' of the film – contacts Haider with a message from his father, he repeats the same couplet as a code of recognition; and later, in another flashback, we see Dr Meer sing this *Ghazal* for everyone's solace as a prisoner in the torture chambers of incarceration. We must remember that Roohdar also brings Haider a direct message of revenge (*Intiqam*) from his dead father, Dr Meer, whom he knew in the brutal 'camps' of the Indian military, and that clearly states:

Haider mera intiqam lena mere bhai se. Uski dono aankheno mein goliyan dagna. Jin Aankhon se usne tumhari maa pe fareb dale the
Aur Maa? –Use Allah ke insaaf ke liye chor de.
[Haider, take revenge on my brother.
 Shoot him in his eyes – those eyes with which he seduced your mother.
And your Mother? Leave her to the justice of God (Allah).]

In effect, in his emotional turbulence, Haider is moved by *two* voices of his father; the revenge message and the poetic couplet, evoking a nostalgic fullness, a call to carry on the 'business of Spring', even in the face of separation and loss. The poem offers him an affective and emotional bond not only with his father but also with the shared cultural history of his community in Faiz's poetry; thus, the revenge message of his father is countered by the solace of poetic affirmation. For Shakespeare's Hamlet, however, the revenge message is all that he hears from his father's ghost, leading to his single-minded and personal resolve to remember him:

Remember thee?
Yea, from the table of my memory
I'll wipe away all trivial fond records,
All saws of books, all forms, all pressures past ...

And thy commandment all alone shall live
Within the book and volume of my brain
Unmixed with baser matter. (1.5.97–104)

Hamlet's mind is now a book, his memory as a wax writing tablet on which items can be inscribed or erased, all familiar formulas, commonplaces, maxims. Most importantly, however, it is the edict of his father's commandment, he believes, that will lead him on a steady course to revenge. That single imperative becomes the bedrock of his drives, even as he faces the challenges of a contingent world and the psychic dilemma of 'to be or not to be', which he shares with the audience. Elsinore, with all its political and familial intrigues, remains a closed-off world. In *Haider*, by contrast, while any coherent psychic interiority for the melancholy protagonist or the people of occupied Kashmir seems out of reach, we are constantly reminded of their shared political and cultural histories – as well as of their shared duress under the surveillance of the Indian military. For instance, the soliloquies are truncated and the 'to be or not to be' speech is scattered, with Haider addressing various audiences, and not only speaking for himself as an individual: *hum hain ki nahin hain* ('do we exist or not'). Kashmiri identity as a collective is at stake throughout the film.

A second, iconic poem by Faiz Ahmed Faiz shapes the final vision of the film, which inflects the Kashmir tragedy with the postcolonial history of the subcontinent. Recited in a poetic epilogue (during the credits), entitled 'Intisaab' (Dedication), possibly written about Pakistan (though generally considered incomplete), here it is used to eulogize 'mera desh' (my country), in this instance, implying Kashmir:

Aaj ke naam
Aur, Aaj ke gham ke naam
Aaj ka gham ki hai zindagi ke bhare gulistaan se khafaa
Zard patton ka ban
Zard patton ka ban jo mera desh hai
Dard ki anjuman jo mera desh hai

[(a dedication) to this day
And to this day's sorrow ...
Today's grief that shuns the blooming garden of life,
To the forest of yellow leaves-
the forest of yellow (dying) leaves that is my country,
to the constellation of pain that is my country.]

Following this poignant opening about 'the constellation of pain', this long poem catalogues people in different professions and personal situations: addressed to 'innocent clerks', 'railway men,' 'postmen', 'peasants', 'grieving mothers', struggling 'students', 'brides' with 'unloved bodies', 'prisoners' in long incarceration; the list goes on. And the concluding couplet 'to the harbingers of days yet to come' holds little hope, as they 'like the flowers in their own fragrance / have become enthralled by their own message'.[13] The film both poignantly and defiantly keeps alive the story of social justice, even beyond the final frame. This is in contrast to Shakespeare's *Hamlet*, where, despite the many dead bodies strewn on stage and the impending conquest of Denmark, it is, in the end, largely the protagonist's tragedy, summed up by Horatio in these elegiac lines:

Now cracks a noble heart. Goodnight, sweet Prince,
And flights of angels sing thee to thy rest. (5.2.343-44)

The play does not reach to any communal vision of loss as the film does.

In addition to Faiz, another poetic voice that interweaves with his in similar lyrical renderings of pain and loss, both personal and collective, is that of Agha Shahid Ali (1949-2001), who wrote in English (and was a translator of Faiz). Ali was remembered for his poems about Kashmir through the 1990s; and their poignant images that bear witness to the Kashmiri tragedy clearly resonate in *Haider* (where Ali is mentioned in a dedication). *Curfewed Night* (2010), the title of Basharat Peer's book, is also drawn from Ali's emblematic poem about Kashmir, 'The Country without a Post Office' (1997), in the anthology of the same name. Peer eulogizes Ali's place in Kashmiri remembrances, particularly for recognizing the cataclysm of 1990s Kashmir in his poetry:

> Among the few literary responses to Kashmir, the poems of Kashmiri-American poet Agha Shahid Ali were the foremost. I often turned to his verses, which evoked the fear, the tension, the anger, and the hopelessness of our experience ... Shahid had died of cancer in 2001 in Brooklyn. Newspapers in Kashmir printed his poems every other day in the autumn of 2001, during his final days. Prayers for him rose from all the mosques of Kashmir. (95–96)

Later, in a seemingly innocuous meeting with an old Kashmiri poet, Rashid Nazki, when Peer asks him about 'poetry written in Kashmiri' after the conflict, the old poet declares, 'In English, there is Agha Shahid Ali's work ... his death was a great loss. Kashmir needs poets like him, but who can evade death?' (179). Agha Shahid Ali's poems depict curfews, villages without post offices, bombed and demolished homes, as well as the lyrical beauty of the Kashmiri landscape, infused with an affective nostalgia for a traditional composite culture in all its material and aesthetic aspects. The changing vistas of *Haider* – burning homes, torture chambers in prisons, landscapes of rivers, graveyards, bustling streets, and a population under siege and duress – find symbiotic echoes in 'The Country without a Post Office' (1997), where the tragedy of a violent occupation achieves a lyrically moving transmutation:

> Empty? Because so many fled, ran away,
> and became refugees there, in the plains,
> where they must now will a final dewfall
> to turn the mountains to glass. They'll see
> us through them – see us frantically bury
> houses to save them from fire that, like a wall
> caves in. The soldiers light it, hone the flames,

burn our world to sudden papier-mâché
inlaid with gold, then ash. (48)

The voice of a displaced population is also vividly present in another few lines of the same poem:

'Everything is finished, nothing remains' ...
Fire runs in waves. Should I cross that river?
Each post office is boarded up. Who will deliver
... My news to prisons?
Only silence can now trace my letters
to him. (49)

Houses set on fire by soldiers, the river on fire, boarded post offices and failed delivery of letters to prisons are all directly evocative of the experiences of Haider, the film's protagonist, who could very well be the speaker of several of Ali's poems. Read in relationship to the film, cross-pollinations of imagery and emotion are readily apparent. The first-person 'I', and the despairing questions offering no solutions, give an affective resonance to scenes witnessed in *Haider*.

Echoes from these contextual overlays between *Haider*, *Curfewed Night*, Faiz's poems, and Ali's 'The Country without a Post Office' also reverberate through another work, an elegiac documentary, fusing nostalgia and trauma in the aftermath of the 1990s violence in Kashmir, titled *Paradise on a River of Hell* (2002), directed by Abir Bazaz and Meenu Gaur. (It must be noted that the script and conceptualization of this documentary came from Bazaz, a Kashmiri himself, whereas Gaur lent the technical expertise.) Drawing its title from a line borrowed from Agha Shahid Ali's poem, 'Farewell' (1997): 'I am being rowed to Paradise on a River of Hell', the documentary seeks to memorialize and excavate the trauma of Kashmir in the 1990s in scenes and images similar to the ones seen in the above-mentioned works. 'The past is an absolute present trauma', the narrator declares at the outset. Travelling through collage-like vistas, *Paradise on a River of*

Hell depicts scenes of Srinagar's rubble, shells of buildings, nearly empty streets, and the Srinagar's martyrs graveyard; these are juxtaposed with images of the barren countryside, deserted houses where Kashmiris are entombed, ancient ruins, Sufi shrines and villages of contemporary massacres. The main narrative voice in English, recounting a return to the Srinagar of his childhood, tells most of the story, but native voices (subtitled) also intermittently permeate the film, as one old man asks: if so many innocents are killed, why does the sky not turn red? Another old woman simply prays aloud to God to listen to their prayers. A soundtrack that includes Kashmiri folk and Sufi music adds a tragic lyricism to the images of desolation.

While the film, it seems, offers a largely affective, emotional response to a violent history, its implicit historical resonances repeat the familiar story of Kashmir's division and occupation:

> The [documentary's] striving toward wholeness [in its lyricism] embodies a desire to excavate aspects of the 1990s in danger of being forgotten: the euphoria of the movement for *azaadi* [freedom] and the brutal retaliation by the Indian State ... [but] as the movement lost momentum through a lack of ideological cohesion ... prized aspects of their culture fell apart. (Kabir 2009: 50)[14]

In its closing moments, featuring the destruction of a Sufi shrine, Tsrar-e-Sharif, gutted in 1995 in a confrontation between militants and Indian security forces, the film is meditative in tone, eschewing any vengeance or blame. Instead the narrator repeats his call for a cultural and religious synthesis between 'Persian Sufis' (Muslims), 'Kashmiri Rishis' (Hindus), and Buddhists seeking refuge in Kashmir, calling for a morality that refused to understand 'the schizophrenia of India's Partition' which was based on the rejection of the 'other'. It is this 'morality' that Bazaz believes is at stake in Kashmir.

Finally, I end with a brief mention of the artist Nilima Sheikh's panel of paintings, which, like Bazaz and others, also focuses on the mythic, and syncretic cultural history and troubled political present of Kashmir (c. 2003–10). These panels were exhibited in a solo show in 2014, entitled *Each Night Put Kashmir in your Dreams,* a line taken from Ali's poem, 'I See Kashmir from New Delhi at Midnight'. 'Sheikh's scrolls combine Ali's poems with excerpts from myriad sources, ranging from medieval poetry to Salman Rushdie's books, along with equally widespread image references – miniatures, wall paintings, and magical Kashmiri folktales' (Sheikh 2014).

To sum up, collectively, these works draw on discursive and visual representations of Kashmir, producing a 'kaleidoscope of intertexts' – a counter-discourse to the long history of romantic Hindi 'formula' films set in idyllic Kashmiri landscapes from the 1960s through the 1980s. From an Indian perspective, these films touched a 'national chord' through 'cinematic spectacle, a version of Benedict Anderson's "Imagined Community"' (Kabir 2009: 41). But today, after the politics of the 1990s, that dream is over. When's Bazaz's narrator in *Paradise on a River of Hell* declares 'my love is burnt out', his response symbolizes the Kashmiri rejection of 'Popular [Indian] cinema's self-referential fantasy of Love in Kashmir' (Kabir 2009: 49). As Kashmiris such as Basharat Peer, Agha Shahid Ali, and Abir Bazaz strive toward a wholeness in recovering the fragments of their own history and culture, they do so with an acknowledgment that they cannot reconstitute them, but can only rehearse a history that must not be forgotten.

As I reproduce the cultural discourse of Kashmir through the voices and visions of Bhardwaj, Peer, Faiz, Ali, Bazaz, and Sheikh, I do so with the recognition that, as Kabir reminds us, 'discourse is not a seamless web through which power is uniformly diffused; rather it is striated, fragmented' (2009: 18). However, despite representational challenges, what is shared among them is a desire (excluding Faiz who died in 1984) to remember Kashmir beyond dismemberment – especially in excavating aspects of the 1990s in danger of being forgotten. Destruction, as they evoke it, also serves as a metaphor for both a nostalgic wholeness that Kashmiris are seeking and their refusal to preserve it in any idyllic, romantic Hindi film memory.

Finally, I end with a query to be addressed. In what ways does the inter-relationship between *Haider/Hamlet* illuminate the politics and poetics of appropriation and adaptation? The film moves beyond the familiar issue of a veneration or resistance toward the original. Instead, in *Haider*, Shakespeare's play is refracted through the postcolonial history of the sub-continent, with a close-up of the ravaged beauty of Kashmir. Shakespeare's *Hamlet*, in fact, offers a distinct emotional language to understand the disintegration of the characters caught in sundered relationships in the midst of betrayal and violence in *Haider*. Furthermore, it also contributes to the primal story of 'brother against brother' in Shakespeare's play to formulate and envision the workings of a surveillance state. Thus, considering *Hamlet* through the prism of the contextual histories of *Haider* complicates the personal tragedy and angst of Hamlet via cultural memories and affective histories that mediate Haider's tragic experiences. Hamlet's 'unweeded garden' expands to include a blasted paradise, a 'constellation of pain', a 'Paradise on a River of Hell', and a 'Country without a Post Office'. Political solutions regarding the Kashmir dispute continue to remain elusive and out of reach, and sharp violence continues to simmer sporadically. Bhardwaj's radical inter-cultural perspective on the postcolonial history of the sub-continent in *Haider* resonates with the works of other film and stage directors we have encountered in the journey of this book, who have challenged boundaries of national, racial, cultural and gender identities: whether it is Ong Keng Sen's *LEAR*, Al-Bassam's *Richard III*, Iqbal Khan's *Othello* and *Much Ado about Nothing*, or Bhardwaj's *Haider*, these revisions have opened up Shakespeare's plays to surprising and unexpected 'worlds elsewhere'.

APPENDIX

Podcast interviews with the authors of many of the titles in the *Arden Shakespeare and Theory* series are available. Details of both published and forthcoming titles are listed below.

Shakespeare and Cultural Materialist Theory, Christopher Marlow
http://blogs.surrey.ac.uk/shakespeare/2016/11/04/shakespeare-and-contemporary-theory-31-shakespeare-and-cultural-materialist-theory-with-christopher-marlow/

Shakespeare and Ecocritical Theory, Gabriel Egan
http://blogs.surrey.ac.uk/shakespeare/2016/05/20/shakespeare-and-contemporary-theory-24-shakespeare-and-ecocritical-theory-with-gabriel-egan/

Shakespeare and Ecofeminist Theory, Rebecca Laroche and Jennifer Munroe
http://blogs.surrey.ac.uk/shakespeare/2016/06/07/shakespeare-and-contemporary-theory-25-shakespeare-and-ecofeminist-theory-with-rebecca-laroche-and-jennifer-munroe/

Shakespeare and Economic Theory, David Hawkes
http://blogs.surrey.ac.uk/shakespeare/2016/05/05/shakespeare-and-contemporary-theory-22-shakespeare-and-economic-theory-with-david-hawkes/

Shakespeare and Feminist Theory, Marianne Novy
http://blogs.surrey.ac.uk/shakespeare/2016/05/13/shakespeare-and-contemporary-theory-23-shakespeare-and-feminist-theory-with-marianne-novy/

Shakespeare and New Historicist Theory, Neema Parvini
http://blogs.surrey.ac.uk/shakespeare/2016/08/29/
shakespeare-and-contemporary-theory-27-shakespeare-and-
new-historicist-theory-with-evelyn-gajowski-and-neema-
parvini/

Shakespeare and Postcolonial Theory, Jyotsna G. Singh
http://blogs.surrey.ac.uk/shakespeare/2016/07/19/
shakespeare-and-contemporary-theory-26-shakespeare-and-
postcolonial-theory-with-jyotsna-singh/

Shakespeare and Posthumanist Theory, Karen Raber
http://blogs.surrey.ac.uk/shakespeare/2016/09/30/
shakespeare-and-contemporary-theory-28-shakespeare-and-
posthumanist-theory-with-karen-raber/

Shakespeare and Presentist Theory, Evelyn Gajowski
http://blogs.surrey.ac.uk/shakespeare/2016/04/29/
shakespeare-and-contemporary-theory-21-the-arden-
shakespeare-and-theory-series-with-evelyn-gajowski/

Shakespeare and Queer Theory, Melissa E. Sanchez
http://blogs.surrey.ac.uk/shakespeare/2016/10/18/
shakespeare-and-contemporary-theory-29-shakespeare-and-
queer-theory-with-melissa-e-sanchez/

NOTES

Introduction

1 Whether we can consider the sixteenth and seventeenth centuries as a period of English colonialism has been debated by critics and historians. For instance, Kamps and Singh (2001) describe how the early modern 'colonizing imagination' ushered in colonialism. Richmond Barbour's *Before Orientalism* (2003) represents one critical strain which uses Said's argument as a 'straw man' to refute the viability of a 'proto-colonial' early modern. For Barbour, also see Chapter 1, note 3. For a further description of the term, 'proto-colonial'/ 'proto-colonialism', see Chapter 3, note 1.

2 For a discussion of postcolonial terms and categories, see Singh (2016: 1–9). An additional caveat: I often use the terms 'West' and 'Western' with caps throughout this volume to highlight a postcolonial perspective which perceives the 'West' in terms of asymmetrical power relations.

3 Please see Chapter 5, note 4 for a list of key Shakespearean intercultural works.

4 For an explanation of the terms, 'non-metropolitan' and 'metropolitan' knowledges, as used throughout this book, see Orkin's description (2005: 1–5).

5 My use of the term, 'intersectionality,' is based on the formulation coined by Kimberlé Crenshaw. One relevant article from her large body of work is 'Mapping the Margins: Intersectionality, Identity Politics, and Violence against Women of Color' (1991).

6 While they have overlapping concerns, my aim is not to elide postcolonial theory with critical race theory, economic theory, and feminist or gender theory, among others, given the distinct conceptual and historical underpinnings of each critical project.

7   For a full discussion of this term and related issues, see Margaret Litvin (2017). These arguments are addressed in more detail in Chapter 5.

8   I am indebted to Craig Dionne and Parmita Kapadia for this formulation in their 'Introduction' to *Native Shakespeares* (2008: 1–2).

9   For an account of the formation and dissemination of English literature within colonial and postcolonial education systems – an inventory of 'traces' (described on page 1) – including Shakespeare studies as a colonial cultural formation, see, for example: Gauri Vishwanathan (1994), Ania Loomba (1989), Jyotsna Singh (1989), Jyotsna G. Singh and Gitanjali Shahani (2010), David Johnson (1996), Martin Orkin (1987a), Ngũgĩ Wa Thiong'o (1986), and Thomas Cartelli (1987).

10 See sample syllabi: 1. Presidency University, Kolkata, India, English Honors syllabus, current 2017. Available at: www.presiuniv.ac.in/web/syllabus/ug_english.pdf (accessed 28 August 2018) and 2. University of Calcutta, India. Syllabi for General and Honours courses in English, 2010. Available at: www.caluniv.ac.in/syllabus/English.pdf (accessed 28 August 2018).

11 Among the seminal studies that occasioned the paradigm shift in the 1980s were the following: Jonathan Dollimore and Alan Sinfield (1985), Jean Howard and Marion O'Connor (1987), Jonathan Dollimore (1984), Catherine Belsey (1985), and Stephen Greenblatt (1980).

12 Some selected studies that include discussions of race and postcoloniality within the early modern period, with some references to Shakespeare (and often to his afterlives), include the following: Abdulhamit Arvas (2016), Jane Hwang Degenhardt (2010), Catherine M.S. Alexander and Stanley Wells (2000), Peter Hulme and William H. Sherman (2000), Arthur L. Little (2000), Kim Hall (1995), Sujata Iyengar (2005), Dennis Austin Britton (2014), Jyotsna G. Singh and Abdulhamit Arvas (2015), Craig Dionne and Parmita Kapadia (2008), Ian Smith (2009) and Margo Hendricks and Patricia Parker (1994).

13 Lola Olufemi, women's officer in the Cambridge students' union, sent an open letter, widely circulated, signed by

hundreds, and forwarded to the teaching forum. See the URL below and in note 15 for sources. An extract from the letter (quoted in Kennedy 2017) sums up the call for changes:

> For too long, teaching English at Cambridge has encouraged a 'traditional' and 'canonical' approach that elevates white male authors at the expense of all others. Whilst some have argued that this approach has its merits and there have been welcome attempts to address the absence of women writers, there is more that can be done. What we can no longer ignore, however, is the fact that the curriculum, taken as a whole, risks perpetuating institutional racism.

14 For a further discussion of this issue, see Michael Curtis (2017).

15 Indira Karamcheti (1995). I am indebted to Arthur Little's deployment of Karamcheti's argument in his paper, 'What's Shakespeare to Him and He to Shakespeare?' Little's nuanced analysis of the 'personal' helped me to understand my own journey as a scholar of colour (Shakespeare Association of America Annual Meeting, 2017, Plenary Session, 'The Color of Membership'. Available at: www.youtube.com/watch?v=4f8_sOAucWw, accessed 28 August 2018).

16 See Singh (1989).

17 This hybridity is also taken up by Martin Orkin in *Local Shakespeares: Proximations and Power* as he explains how local 'knowledges' and responses of North Americans and Europeans are 'partly irreversibly hybridized as a result of colonialism, and more recently globalization and its effects' (2015: 15).

Chapter 1

1 For colonial implications of the play in the 1950s and 1960s, see Chapter 3. Selected works from the 1980s and 1990s are as follows: Paul Brown (1985), Francis Barker and Peter Hulme (1985), Stephen Greenblatt (1990), Peter Hulme and William

Sherman (2000), Peter Hulme (1986), Rob Nixon (1987), Jyotsna G. Singh (1996), and Alden T. Vaughan and Virginia Vaughan (1991).
2. For a full discussion of the 'colonizing imagination' and its impact, see Ivo Kamps and Jyotsna G. Singh (2001).
3. Richmond Barbour (2003: 3–7).
4. Jonathan Burton (2005).
5. See Kamps and Singh (2001), 'Introduction' to *Travel Knowledge*, among the seminal anthologies to establish the early modern period as an era of geographical exploration, mercantile trade, nation-formation, and intercultural exchange.
6. All quotations from *The Tempest* in this volume will be taken from the Arden Shakespeare edition (2011) of the text.
7. Greenblatt's volume of essays *Learning to Curse* (1990), and his volume *New World Encounters* (1993), were also landmark works in highlighting discourses of colonialism in the early modern period, including in regards to *The Tempest*.
8. I am summarizing Frey (1979: 29–31).
9. Bruster's inclusion of Jerry Brotton's article in this list seems a bit forced. For instance, Brotton does not repress colonial contexts in the same way as is evident in Skura's piece.
10. The source texts of the play upon which most critics agree are William Strachey (1609) (also printed in Samuel Purchas (1625), *Purchas his Pilgrims*, vol. 4: 1734–58), and Silvester Jourdain (1610).
11. Richard Hakluyt (1599: Second Vol. Unpaginated Preface).
12. For a discussion of English sources for Irish stereotypes, see Vaughan and Vaughan (2011: 51–53). Dympna Callaghan (2000: 97–138) also points to affinities between the play and English accounts of Ireland.
13. A rich body of critical and historical work in the past two decades offers important reappraisals of the history of Jews in Europe, their role in early modern Europe, and the Jewish contexts of Shakespeare's *The Merchant of Venice*. Some key works include the following: Clare Carroll (2004), James Shapiro (1996), and Eva Johanna Holmberg (2011).

14 English (and European) relations with Moors and Turks in the early modern period – and their representations on the English stage – constitute a burgeoning scholarship with postcolonial inflections in the past two decades. Some key texts are as follows: Nabil Matar (1998), Daniel Vitkus (2000), Jyotsna G. Singh (2004), Gerald MacLean (2005), Matthew Dimmock (2005), Jonathan Burton (2005), and Michael Neill (2000). For a larger discussion on black presence, see also Ruth Cowhig (1985).

15 All the quotations from *Othello* in this volume will be taken from the Arden Shakespeare edition (2016) of the text.

16 Critics that explicitly describe or represent the early modern contexts of *Othello*, showing how they coalesce into a colonial imaginary, include Jonathan Burton, Imtiaz Habib, Kim Hall, Jyotsna Singh, Daniel Vitkus, Nabil Matar, Karen Newman, Ian Smith, Ania Loomba, and Michael Neill. I purport this to be more of a selective, rather than a comprehensive list.

Chapter 2

1 *Henry IV Part II*, ed. James C. Bulman (2016).

2 See David Underdown (1985), A.L. Beier and Roger Finlay (1986). Both books offer a history of the city, but do not account for its growing global role. A later edited collection on varied imaginings of the city, inspired by John Stow's *Survey of London*, covers much the same ground (Merritt 2001). It offers views of the city largely from within and does not take into account that 'the city was also the center of imperial or mercantile networks, the object of admiration, fear, praise, and scorn from outsiders in the provinces and abroad', as noted by reviewer Patrick Wallis (2002).

3 Matthew Dimmock (2017: 38–9).

4 See Emily Bartels (2006). In her nuanced analysis of these documents, Bartels observes that overall as Elizabeth's letters 'map out these transactions, they do show us a color based

discourse in the making. But significantly it is also a discourse shaped, complicated, and compromised by political and economic circumstances [including the rivalries with Spain]' (307). Bartels draws on Gretchen Gerzina (1995: 3–4). See also Peter Fryer's important work, *Staying Power: The History of Black People in Britain* (1984) cited by Bartels, who argues that 'the queen's discriminatory project failed completely insofar as [it] was a serious attempt to deport all black people from Britain' (12).

5 For another discussion of the expulsion documents above (as compared to the expulsion of the Jews), see Miranda Kaufmann (2008a). Kaufmann also points to how it differs from the earlier expulsion of the Jews: 'The Van Senden episode has been interpreted as a piece of racist immigration policy … however, it was of an entirely different nature. While in 1290 Edward's government made a tidy profit by collecting the Jews' debts on their behalf and selling their houses, no one managed to make much money in 1596–1601' (371).

6 See James Shapiro (1996: 1–15), for an account of the presence of Jews in early modern England; also, see *Kirkus Review*, 15, October, 1995 for a summation of Shapiro's argument. Available at: www.kirkusreviews.com/book-reviews/james-shapiro/shakespeare-and-the-jews/ (accessed 29 August 2018).

7 For a general background, see Amrita Sen (2011a). Associations between England's East Indian trade and evocations of 'India' in *A Midsummer Night's Dream* have produced important critical interventions, starting with Margo Hendricks's seminal essay (1996), Shankar Raman (2001), Ania Loomba (2016), Abdulhamit Arvas (2016), and Gitanjali Shahani (2014).

8 Sen (2011b: 5), quote from: Samuel Purchas (1625, Vol. 1: 20–122).

9 Sen (2011b: 97). Other sources on the Grocer's Guild and Middleton's Pageant include: David M. Bergeron (2007: 963–980), Frederick William Fairholt (1844), and John Benjamin Heath (1854).

10 See Kaufmann (2008b). Kaufmann points to lacunae in Habib's argument in not fully addressing some contextual questions: How did blacks arrive prior to English slaving voyages?

What was the treatment of black people at the time? (26). His approach, as she sees it, forgoes some historical rigour.

11 All quotations are taken from the Arden Shakespeare edition (2017).

Chapter 3

1 Here and elsewhere in the book, I occasionally use the term 'proto-colonial' as a reminder that full-blown colonialism only came into being gradually by the eighteenth century, but proto-colonial attitudes about Western domination appeared earlier in the sixteenth and seventeenth centuries, constituting Europeans as 'naturally' superior to non-European indigenous populations and cultures. I sometimes refer to an 'emerging' or 'emergent colonialism', which has similar proto-colonial implications.

2 For a critical analysis of the how Césaire leaves intact the intractable system of gender categories upheld by Prospero, see Singh (1996). Drawing on feminist and race criticism, I point out that as an allegory of colonization, *Une Tempête* fails to adequately interrogate the relationship between liberation movements, gender hierarchies, and sexual ideologies underpinning colonialism (196).

3 All quotes are from *Une Tempête* (1969) by Aimé Césaire, trans. Richard Miller (1985). This translation was used for the American premiere of the play in 1991, at the Ubu Repertory Theatre in New York City, and published in 1992. Quotes are followed by page numbers.

4 Gregson Davis (1997: 156–57).

5 Roberto Fernandez Retamar (1989).

6 Retamar's essay offers a useful survey of Latin American and Caribbean re-readings of *The Tempest*, ranging from the Uruguayan Jose Enrique Rodo's *Ariel* (1900), to the Argentine author Anibal Ponce's 'Ariel; or, The Agony of an Obstinate Illusion', the third chapter of his work *Bourgeois Humanism, Proletarian Humanism* (1932).

7   Poem cited from Edward Kamau Brathwaite ([1969] 1973). Page numbers in the text.
8   For a full analysis of Brathwaite's poem 'Caliban' and its historical contexts, see Eric Doumerc (2014).
9   According to Doumerc (2014), 'Caliban is a Trinidadian or Caribbean pan man and his very name bears testimony to the traumas of Caribbean history as the many "bangs" that punctuate Caribbean history recall the second syllable of his name, as well as the loud music produced by the steel bands'.
10 For a postcolonial reading of Ngũgĩ's *A Grain of Wheat* in relationship with Shakespeare's *The Tempest*, see Thomas Cartelli (1987: 101).
11 Pier Paolo Frasanelli (2008: 174).
12 Cited from Jyotsna G. Singh (2016).
13 Key works by Gayatri Spivak and Homi Bhabha include *In Other Worlds: Essays in Cultural Politics* (1987) and *The Location of Culture* (1994) respectively.

Chapter 4

1   All quotes from the play will be taken from the Arden Third Series edition (1997).
2   As already discussed in the 'Introduction' to this volume, the term 'intersectionality' is reminiscent of the formulation coined by American feminist legal scholar, critical race theorist, and civil rights activist Kimberlé Crenshaw, to describe overlapping or intersecting social identities and related systems of oppression, domination, or discrimination. See an article (mentioned earlier) that exemplifies her theory (1991: 1241–99). Politically inflected critical perspectives on Shakespeare from the early 1980s onwards began to recognize intersectional connections, for instance, between colonialism, race, and gender. Thus, essays in a volume such as *Political Shakespeare* cover a spectrum of politically inflected

perspectives. I am indebted to Dennis Britton for this formulation.

3   Loomba and Orkin (1998) in their 'Introduction' to the conference proceedings describe the make-up of the 'self-generating group' that called itself the 'Africa/Shakespeare Committee'. The group consisted of one member each from 'Sociology, African Literature, Theatre and Drama, Comparative Literature, and English' (19).

4   For a full discussion of the session, which functioned as a useful 'confessional', see Margo Hendricks in Loomba and Orkin (1998: 84–95).

5   Hugh Lewin, *Bandiet* (1981). I have paraphrased his talk, which was drawn from the experiences of his book.

6   For a full account of Hugh Lewin's talk in real time and its effect on the conference audience, see Jyotsna G. Singh (2008).

7   Critical race perspectives in Renaissance studies derive from and engage with a range of histories, not all of them intersecting with imperialism and colonialism. However, the work of race theorists such as Kim Hall, Ian Smith, Ayanna Thompson, Arthur Little, and Dennis Britton, to name a few, provides a crucial theoretical scaffolding for charting the constructions of difference in postcolonial studies.

8   Martin Orkin (1987b). See especially his chapter entitled, 'Cruelty, *King Lear*, and the South African Land Act of 1913'. For another important monograph on the subject, see David Johnson (1996).

9   Lynette Goddard (2017: 82). This chapter offers a complex account of how Simon navigated her race and gender in a mostly white Shakespearean theatre world from the mid 1980s to the late 1990s.

10 Sylvia Morris (2013) seeks to emphasize that the real Cleopatra was not black and that her race does not matter. The stage history of the play affirms a highly acceptable convention of white Cleopatras, as discussed in this chapter.

11 See Lynette Goddard (2017: 85). She also refers to Celia R. Daileader, *Colorblind Shakespeares* (2006), for discussions about how this role is 'whitewashed'.

12 Cleopatra in the Western imagination reveals as much about sexist stereotypes as racial typecasting. See the ground-breaking essay by L.T. Fitz (1977).
13 Dominic Cavendish, *The Telegraph*, 25 March 2017.
14 Kate Kellaway, *The Guardian*, 2 April 2017.
15 Michael Billington, *The Guardian*, 24 March 2017.
16 Gill Sutherland, 'Review: *Antony and Cleopatra*, RSC'. *Stratford-Upon-Avon Herald*, 7 April 2017.
17 David Jays, 'Interview: Josette Simon, "Powerful Women are reduced to being dishonorable"', *The Guardian*, 21 March 2017.
18 See Joyce MacDonald (2002) for a fuller discussion of changing trends that led to the racially diverse casting of Cleopatra in the 1980s and 1990s.
19 As one reviewer notes: 'The collision of cultures that comes with colonialism is built into *Antony and Cleopatra*', but here, it seems to be staged with voodoo rituals and West Indian music that simply reinforce orientalist clichés about a Caribbean island – 'such exotic touches dangle from the script like skull earrings on a woman at a formal ball, clipped on in a desperate bid to stand out.' Ben Brantley, *The New York Times*, 5 March 2014.
20 For some of the representative, early discussions of orientalism in *Antony and Cleopatra*, see John Gillies (1994: esp. 112–23); Mary Nyquist (1994) analyses the structures of 'orientalization and domestication' in representations of Cleopatra. Another key essay on the ways in which the play engages with orientalist discourses is Evelyn Gajowski (1992: 86–119). See also Ania Loomba (1996: especially pages 175–79 and 183–88), where she discusses the intersection of ideologies of gender with those of colonial conquest in *Antony and Cleopatra*. Subsequently Joyce MacDonald (2002: 45–67) offers a complex examination of Cleopatra's race and why it is sidestepped in critical history; Arthur Little (2000: 167–68) highlights Cleopatra's 'cultural and racial polymorphous perversity' both in Shakespeare's time and our own. And finally, a landmark work in this critical vein is Francesca Royster's *Becoming Cleopatra: The Shifting Image of an Icon* (2003),

which offers an extended analysis of Cleopatra and race from the early modern period to contemporary American popular culture, getting much critical mileage from the question: 'Was Cleopatra Black?'

21 See Daniel Vitkus, *Antony and Cleopatra: Texts and Contexts* (forthcoming).

22 John Wilders (2006). All quotes are from this edition of the text.

23 Vitkus (forthcoming).

24 See Joyce MacDonald's discussion of Adelman and Neill (2002: 50, note 12), where she explains the lacunae on issues of race in Adelman with a reference to Neill: 'In an apparent contradiction on the significance of Cleopatra's race, similar to Neill's, Adelman believes that it does not particularly matter what exactly Shakespeare meant to suggest by having Cleopatra call herself "blacke", but that her nonwhite skin is meant to contribute to the creation of a sense of her "ancient and mysterious sexuality"' (*The Common Liar*, 188). But according to MacDonald, 'while her sexuality would presumably be represented differently if she were white, Adelman also seems too hasty to refuse to ask what it might mean if Cleopatra and her sexuality were constructed as black'.

25 For a discussion of white male critics, ranging from Harold Bloom to T.S. Eliot, and their emphasis on Antony's racialized sexual encounter, see Francesca Royster (2003: 14–15).

26 Royster (2003: 38–50) gives a wide-ranging account of 'Cleopatra, Egypt and Origins', as well as the myths of blackness associated with Africa in the early modern period.

27 Royster (2003: 11) compares Cleopatra's relevance to African-American culture in various guises. My scope here is a bit narrower: to explore Cleopatra's race in its early modern contexts, and in terms of postcolonial and race theory – and how the various racialist discourses are played out in some instances from the recent performance history of the play.

28 Martin Butler (2005). All quotations from this play are taken from this edition.

29 I have supplemented Willy Maley's (1999) essay with ideas from a later book – see Maley (2003: 31).

30 See Martin Orkin's citation (2005) of Jodi Mikalachki (1998: 82).
31 Heather James (1997: 186–87).

Chapter 5

1 To recap the earlier chapters, let us re-invoke the originary moment in the colonial era when intellectuals and artists – Aimé Césaire, Ngũgĩ Wa Thiong'o, Roberto Fernandez Retamer, among others – pried away and re-claimed Shakespeare from his colonial contexts. 'This island's mine', they voiced Caliban's claims. Their vision opened the way for postcolonial responses to Shakespeare's works in Anglo-American scholarship from the mid 1980s onwards, as outlined in earlier chapters. These critical journeys into new territories, mostly former colonies, such as India, South Africa, Sub-Saharan Africa, and the Caribbean, were the outliers in the 1980s and 1990s, but nonetheless generated new conversations about deployments of Shakespeare beyond its canonical uses in the west.

2 The use of the term 'appropriation' in an early volume, *Shakespeare and Appropriation* (Desmet and Sawyer 1999), described 'appropriation as a [recognized] cultural practice', while making some important distinctions between a 'Big-time Shakespeare, serving "corporate goals and entrenched power structures"' and 'Small-time Shakespeare' emerging from more local, individual engagements with the plays (14–15). Colonial and postcolonial perspectives only figured marginally in this volume, though the idea of 'global' and 'local' Shakespeares first took shape here.

3 I use the term 'mediascape' as coined by Arjun Appadurai in 'Disjuncture and Difference in the Global Cultural Economy' (1990). For him the 'new global cultural economy has to be seen as a complex, overlapping, disjunctive order', composed of different inter-related, yet disjunctive global cultural flows, with 'mediascapes' being of one of them: 'the use of media… shapes the way we understand our imagined world'. Shakespeare in global cinema, for instance, has permeated the 'global cultural flows' showing Shakespeare as a site for inter-cultural encounters.

4   Some key studies in this vein (though not an all-inclusive list by any means) include: Martin Orkin, *Local Shakespeares: Proximations and Power* (2005); Craig Dionne and Parmita Kapadia, eds, *Native Shakespeares: Indigenous Appropriations on a Global Stage* (2008); Alexa Huang, *Chinese Shakespeares: Two Centuries of Cultural Exchange* (2009); Mark Thornton Burnett, *Shakespeare and World Cinema* (2013); Craig Dionne and Parmita Kapadia, eds, *Bollywood Shakespeares* (2014); Alexa Huang and Elizabeth Rivlin, eds, *Shakespeare and the Ethics of Appropriation* (2014); Katherine Hennessey and Margaret Litvin, eds, 'Arab Shakespeares', Special Issue, *Critical Survey* (2016), Jyotsna G. Singh and Abdulhamit Arvas, 'Global Shakespeares, Affective Histories, Cultural Memories' (2015); Margaret Litvin, 'Multilateral Reception: Three Lessons from the Arab *Hamlet* Tradition' (2017); and Delia Jarrett-Macauley, ed., *Shakespeare, Race and Performance: The Diverse Bard* (2017).

Also, see the MIT's pioneering digital site under the directorship of Peter S. Donaldson and Alexa Huang, a collaborative project titled: 'The Global Shakespeares Video & Performance Archive', offering online access to performances of Shakespeare, while also demonstrating the diversity of the world-wide reception and production of his plays. To see these productions, browse specific links on the MIT website, as follows: http://globalshakespeares.mit.edu/about/; http://globalshakespeares.mit.edu/hamlet-al-bassam-sulayman-2004/ (accessed 31 March 2018).

5   See Margaret Litvin (2017). For a further discussion, also see Litvin (2011).

6   See Alexa Alice Joubin (2018).

7   For a discussion of responses to the film O (2001), see Brittany Rowland (2016). Overlapping eerily with the Columbine shootings, due to which its release was postponed, O received some positive reviews. But by reifying contemporary race thinking, with its attendant stereotypes, the film offers a problematic, sympathetic portrayal of Hugo (Iago) as a troubled teenager. One critic observes: 'His jealousy and deep desire to have the attention turned on him drives him to do evil acts, but that does not make him evil himself in the audience's eyes' (Semenza 2005: 102).

8 For a detailed analysis and critique of the inter-cultural politics in Ong Keng Sen's *LEAR*, see Rustom Bharucha (2001). Bharucha's attempts 'to tease out some troubling questions that cut across the domains of inter-cultural practice and multi-racial/multicultural politics', produce a useful discussion of inter-cultural exchanges in a Pan-Asian and global context, but his criteria for evaluating inter-culturalism are somewhat doctrinaire and 'politically correct', while lacking in sensitivity to the sensual and affective impact of *LEAR*.

9 Ong Keng Sen (2015).

10 For a full discussion of the import and implications of *Lear Dreaming* and the continuing influence of Ong Keng Sen's work, see Lisa Porter (2013). The video of 'Lear Dreaming', is available at: http://globalshakespeares.mit.edu/lear-dreaming-ong-keng-sen-2012/ (accessed 1 April 2018).

11 Parmita Kapadia (2008) in '*Jatra Shakespeare*', cites Rustom Bharucha (1983: 207). Here she discusses Salim Ghouse's radical departure from Western deployments of Asian theatrical traditions, such as by Richard Schechner, Peter Brook, and others. According to Kapadia, noted Shakespearean director, Peter Brook's adaptation of the Indian epic the *Mahabharata* offered a flashpoint in highlighting the politics and ethics of appropriation in terms of East–West relations. Criticism of his work by theorists such as Rustom Bharucha and others opened up to the way to a greater self-consciousness about the politics and poetics of inter-cultural dramatic work (2008: 96).

12 Vishal Bhardwaj and TRM editors (2015).

13 Sanjukta Sharma (2014) praises the film for 'transmuting Shakespeare's poetic imagery and the atmosphere that his verses conjure into re-contextualized visuals' and considers it a success. Also, see Rachel Saltz (2014). Saltz does not consider *Haider* equal to Mr Bhardwaj's other Shakespeare films.

14 A body of writing that has demonstrated the interpretive possibilities in terms of inter-cultural adaptation and translation of Shakespeare in the Arab world includes the following samples of key works: Margaret Litvin (2011, 2014, 2017), Margaret Litvin and Katherine Hennessey (2016),

Mahmoud F. Al-Shetawi (2013), Katherine Hennessey (2018) and David C. Moberly (2016).

15 I am paraphrasing Litvin (2017: 53).

16 For a detailed discussion of a wide range of appropriations of Shakespeare in the Arab world, including many literary examples in Arabic not known in the West, see Mahmoud F. Al-Shetawi (2013), 8–9. This article compares 'known postcolonial "Shakespeares" and Arabic appropriations of his plays. It … [importantly considers] whether Arabic dramatists have been "writing back," so to speak in response to the colonial experience' (4).

17 Graham Holderness (2014). According to Holderness, '*The Arab Shakespeare Trilogy* is a uniquely innovative dramatic experiment accomplished by Anglo-Kuwaiti dramatist Sulayman Al Bassam … The plays adapted – *Hamlet, Richard III, and Twelfth Night*. There is a savage comedy in the satire of *The Al-Hamlet Summit; Richard III: An Arab Tragedy* plays out history partly as tragic farce; and [the third play], *The Speaker's Progress* strikes a delicate balance between tragic containment and comic resistance' (viii–ix). Video links to actual productions of the *Trilogy* are available at: http://globalshakespeares.mit.edu/hamlet-al-bassam-sulayman-2004/; http://globalshakespeares.mit.edu/richard-3-al-bassam-sulayman-2007/; http://globalshakespeares.mit.edu/the-speakers-progress-al-bassam-sulayman-2011/ (accessed 31 March 2018).

18 For links to videos of Al-Bassam's live productions, see note 17.

19 Margaret Litvin (2014) explains the adaptation process more fully: 'Besides Shakespeare, the other main element appropriated in the Al-Bassam *Trilogy* is the Arab world: its language registers, its cultures, and above all, its recent history' (223). His Shakespeare appropriations seek to comment on a specific, decade-long slice of historical time, (2001–2011) more than an Arab world as a fixed geographic or cultural space' (223). Litvin's introductory comments to her interview with Al-Bassam uses a 'dialogic, explicitly contextualized format' while exploring the ethical dimensions of appropriation in her dialogue with the director (222).

Chapter 6

1. Permission to use this quotation as an Epigraph from the Director's Q&A with Iqbal Khan has been given by the RSC. See the official RSC site for *Much Ado about Nothing* (2012). Available at: www.rsc.org.uk/much-ado-about-nothing/past-productions/iqbal-khan-2012-production (accessed 25 May 2018). This features a full discussion by Iqbal Khan (2017: 40) about his direction of *Much Ado About Nothing*. Khan has also directed *Othello* and *Antony and Cleopatra* at the RSC and *Macbeth* at the Globe (2016) among other Shakespearean and non-Shakespearean works in various settings, including the West End, the Barbican, and the National Theatre.
2. I am indebted to Delia Jarrett-Macauley (2017) for mapping the history of black and Asian Shakespeare performance in Britain. She offers us a genealogy of theatre practitioners ranging from Ira Aldridge to Paul Robeson and to 'those who were born and grew up under colonialism', and later devised Shakespeare productions using their cultural background. Examples include Yvonne Brewster, co-founder and Artistic Director of Talawa Theatre Company, and Jatinder Varma, director of Tara Arts, among others, who were the 1980s generation, schooled in Britain, sometimes emerging from urban theatre groups, and facing and tackling issue of diversity and equity (5).
3. Jatinder Varma (2017: 33). Also see Jarrett-Macauley (2017: 5–7) for her discussion of the role of theatre companies such as Talawa and Tara Arts. For further information on the Company, see www.tara-arts.com/about-us/history (accessed 4 September 2018). Also, for a discussion of Varma's ideas and practice, see Chandrika Patel (2012).
4. See www.tara-arts.com/about-us/history (accessed 4 September 2018) for a brief history of Tara Arts. Its repertoire is broad, though consistently evoking multicultural and multi-racial themes as well as actors of colour. For a sample of its productions, see www.tara-arts.com/search/all.
5. Paul Taylor (2015). Other notable reviews covering mainstream English newspapers include the following: Andrew Dickson

(2015), Dominic Cavendish (2015), and Michael Billington (2015). For a useful discussion of the casting of a black Iago, see Sapo Kpade (2015). Also, see the comments of black actor Adrian Lester, who played Othello at the National Theatre, on race and casting, in Lawrence (2016).

6 For a full discussion of 'whiteness studies' as a complex mode of inquiry into issues of 'race' through literature, history, and popular culture, see Stowe (1996: 69).

7 To get a full sense of Iqbal Khan's personal and professional trajectory, see sample interviews: 'Iqbal Khan, 2012 Production', Director's Q&A, *Much Ado about Nothing*, RSC, 2012. Available at: www.rsc.org.uk/much-ado-about-nothing/past-productions/iqbal-khan-2012-production; Wicker (2016); Morley (2015).

8 This quote is from a blurb on the official website for Dash Arts. Available at: www.dasharts.org.uk/archive/research.html. For other sources for Tim Supple's work, including *Dream*, several websites are available (all accessed in March 2018).

See 'An Interview with Director Tim Supple', *The Agency*. Available at: http://theagency.co.uk/the-clients/tim-supple/; Monidipa Mondal (2008), Jacob Cherian (2008) and Aasheesh Sharma (2006).

9 Tim Supple, 'Director Interview', RSC 2006. This is a comprehensive account of the production in its conception, direction, and differing audience responses in India and the UK. Available at: www.rsc.org.uk/a-midsummer-nights-dream/past-productions/tim-supple-2006-production/director-interview.

10 For an account of the Habib Tanvir production, *Kamdeo Ka Sapna*, including a clip of the opening, see the MIT Global Shakespeare Site. Available at: http://globalshakespeares.mit.edu/midsummer-nights-dream-tanvir-habib-1993/, (accessed 30 March 2018). The MIT informational page includes an abridged paper by Jyotsna Singh, 'Traveling Shakespeares in India: The genesis of Habib Tanvir's *A Midsummer Night's Dream*', presented at the 'Shakespeare in Asia' conference at Stanford University, 2004. This paper briefly traces Habib Tanvir's artistic career, giving a background to the production and its appropriation of Shakespeare's *A Midsummer Night's Dream*.

11 Quote by Supple, taken from my recent e-mail conversation with him on 4 March 2018.

12 Below is a selected list of reviews: Susannah Clapp (2016), Lloyd Evans (2016), Dominic Cavendish (2016), Neil Norman (2016), Paul Taylor (2016), and Lyn Gardner (2016).

13 According to Bruce Smith (2016), Oberon's desire for the changeling boy has mythic echoes of the Jupiter–Ganymede relationship: 'In his desire, Oberon recalls Jupiter who fell in love with a Shepherd boy, Ganymede, took on the form of an eagle, wafted him to Olympus as his page-boy, just the role Oberon imagines for Titania's changeling'. By making the 'Indian boy' into a puppet, this production evades the erotic relationship triad of Titania–changeling–Oberon.

14 Iqbal Khan's Q & A on the RSC website for the production (2012) clearly describes his conception of inter-culturalism, which eschews any kind of exoticism, drawn from Bollywood or elsewhere. Available at: www.rsc.org.uk/much-ado-about-nothing/past-productions/iqbal-khan-2012-production (accessed 30 March 2018). For a further discussion of Iqbal Khan's conception of the *Much Ado* (2012) production, see his chapter, '1960s Birmingham to 2012 Stratford-upon-Avon' (2017: 137–45).

15 Dominic Cavendish (2012). Other reviews are as follows: '*Much Ado*', *Evening Standard*, 2 August (2012); Michael Billington (2012), *Much Ado About Nothing*, Review, Courtyard Theatre, *The Guardian*, 2 August; Neil Norman (2012), *Theatre Review*, 3 August; and Kevin Quarmby (2012).

16 Jyotsna Singh (2012).

17 For an astute, non-stereotypical reading of the production's representation of 'arranged marriages' which in the popular white culture is often elided into ideas of 'forced marriages', see Varsha Panjwani (2017). She views Khan's production as an interesting use of Shakespeare to reflect marriages in the South Asian diaspora in Britain via New Delhi. She explains as follows: 'In situating the play in a foreign location, Khan's decision is no more or less contentious than Shakespeare's who set the play in Messina even as the English actors performed the parts. Moreover, it is widely understood that Shakespeare

was using these far-flung locations to hold up a mirror to issues closer to home … By presenting marriage alliances in which love or at least attraction co-exists with parental arrangement, Khan points to hybrid forms of arranged marriages that exist in the South Asian diaspora … What is also clear from each of the cases presented in Khan's production … is that no matter the motivations of the individuals involved, consent is taken as a given and an important part of the arranged-marriage process. In distinguishing between arranged marriages and forced marriage … Khan's production sheds light on a vexing socio-political issue' (97–101).

Chapter 7

1   All quotations are from the Arden Third Series edition of the text (2016).

2   Mark Thornton Burnett (2013) describes World Cinema as a 'mode of filmmaking that takes place outside the Hollywood mainstream'; while eschewing English as the dominant language, Burnett focuses on Shakespearean productions from South and East Asia, Latin America, and Africa (5).

3   Wide-ranging reviews of the film, and interviews with Vishal Bhardwaj, Basharat Peer, and others, have been followed by a growing body of critical scholarship, which includes the history of Kashmir and Indian nationalism, the legacy of Bollywood, the *Hamlet/Haider* intertextuality, and the cultural contexts of *Haider*, to name a few. An overview of writings on Vishal Bhardwaj, including *Haider*, include the following: Brinda Charry and Gitanjali Shahani (2014), Amrita Sen (2017), Shormistha Panja (2017), Paromita Chakravarti (2016), and Jyotsna Singh and Abdulhamit Arvas (2015).

4   For a full discussion of this phenomenon and comparisons between Hollywood and Bollywood, see Dionne and Kapadia (2014: 7–11).

5   See Charry and Shahani (2014: 114). This quote, which refers to *Omkara/Othello* in terms of a 'specific' region, is also applicable to Kashmir – a disputed region of India.

6. Harmeet Singh (2014). For additional interviews and reviews of Bhardwaj, see notes 12 and 13 in Chapter 5.
7. This analysis is drawn from earlier reflections in Singh and Arvas (2015: 187).
8. Also, see Singh and Arvas (2015: 187).
9. Kabir (2009: 40–41) offers an astute history of representations of Kashmir in colonial and postcolonial contexts, while critiquing the 'desire' of the Indian nation for Kashmir, which does not translate into an acknowledgement of its autonomy as a territory.
10. Scott Simon (2014).
11. For a full discussion of Faiz's poetic *oeuvre* and his contributions, see Agha Shahid Ali (1991).
12. Original poem in Urdu, 'Gulon Mein Rang Bhare', in Kuldip Salil (2015: 26–27). Translation mine.
13. Original poem in Urdu, 'Intisaab', from Hashmi and Hashmi (2012: 100–3). Translation is mine. I reference the opening couplet here. It is long poem, generally considered incomplete, and can be found in varying lengths in different editions. The version sung in *Haider* (during the credits) includes additional stanzas not found in this edition.
14. See Kabir (2009: 49–53) for her further analysis of this documentary's aesthetic form, as well as its engagement with Kashmiri history, culture, and recent politics.

REFERENCES

Adelman, Janet (1973), *The Common Liar: An Essay on Antony and Cleopatra*, New Haven, CT: Yale University Press.

Africanus, Leo John (1600), *A Geographical History of Africa*, trans. John Pory, London.

Al-Bassam, Sulayman (2014), *The Arab Shakespeare Trilogy: The Al-Hamlet Summit; Richard III: An Arab Tragedy; The Speaker's Progress*, London: Bloomsbury.

Alexander, Catherine M.S. and Stanley Wells, eds (2000), *Shakespeare and Race*, Cambridge: Cambridge University Press.

Ali, Agha Shahid (1991), 'Introduction', in Faiz Ahmed Faiz, trans. Agha Shahid Ali, *The Rebel's Silhouette: Selected Poems by Faiz Ahmed Faiz*, ix–xxvi, Amherst: University of Massachusetts Press.

Ali, Agha Shahid (1997), *The Country without a Post Office: Poems, 1991–1995*, New York: W.W. Norton.

Al-Saber, Samer (2016), 'Beyond Colonial Tropes: Two Productions of *A Midsummer Night's Dream* in Palestine', *Critical Survey*, 28 (3): 27–46.

Al-Shetawi, Mahmoud F. (2013), 'Arabic Adaptations of Shakespeare and Postcolonial Theory', *Critical Survey*, 25 (3): 4–28.

Appadurai, Arjun (1990), 'Disjuncture and Difference in the Global Cultural Economy', *Theory, Culture & Society*, 7 (2): 295–310.

Arvas, Abdulhamit (2016), 'Indian Boys in England', in 'Travelling Sexualities, Circulating Bodies, and Early Modern Anglo-Ottoman Encounters', PhD diss., Michigan State University, East Lansing, MI.

Barbour, Richmond (2003), *Before Orientalism: London's Theatre of the East, 1576–1626*, Cambridge: Cambridge University Press.

Barker, Francis and Peter Hulme (1985), 'Nymphs and Reapers Heavily Vanish: The Discursive Con-texts of *The Tempest*', in John Drakakis (ed.), *Alternative Shakespeares*, 191–205, London: Methuen.

Bartels, Emily Carroll (2006), 'Too Many Blackamoors: Deportation, Discrimination, and Elizabeth I', *SEL Studies in English Literature 1500–1900*, 46 (2): 305–322.
Bazaz, Abir and Meenu Gaur, dirs. (2002), *Paradise on a River of Hell* [film]. Production: PSBT (Public Service Broadcasting Trust, India). Available online: www.youtube.com/watch?v=9slv3Urjh88 (accessed 25 May 2018).
Beier, A.L. and Roger Finlay, eds (1986), *London 1500–1700: The Making of the Metropolis*, New York: Longman.
Belsey, Catherine (1985), *The Subject of Tragedy: Identity and Difference in Shakespearean Tragedy*, London: Methuen.
Bergeron, David M. (2007), 'The Triumphs of Truth', in Gary Taylor and John Lavagnino (eds), *Thomas Middleton: The Collected Works*, 964, Oxford: Oxford University Press.
Best, George (1578), *A True Discourse of the Late Voyages of Discovery for the Finding of a Passage to Cathaya by the Northwest ...*, London: Henry Bynneman
Bhabha, Homi (1994), *The Location of Culture*, London: Routledge.
Bhardwaj, Vishal, dir. (2014), *Haider/Hamlet*, Production: VB Pictures.
Bhardwaj, Vishal and TRM Editors (2015), 'Decoding Shakespeare: Vishal Bhardwaj on *Haider* at NYIFF', *The Review Monk*, 15 May. Available online: https://thereviewmonk.com/article/decoding-shakespeare-vishal-bhardwaj-haider-nyiff/ (accessed 29 April 2018).
Bharucha, Rustom (1983), *Rehearsals of Revolution: The Political Theater of Bengal*, Honolulu: University of Hawaii Press.
Bharucha, Rustom (2001), 'Consumed in Singapore: The Intercultural Spectacle of *Lear*', *Theater*, 31 (1): 106–127.
Billington, Michael (2007), '*A Midsummer Night's Dream* – Review', Roundhouse Theatre, *The Guardian*, 14 March.
Billington, Michael (2012), '*Much Ado about Nothing* – Review', *The Guardian*, 2 August. Available online: www.theguardian.com/stage/2012/aug/02/much-ado-about-nothing-review (accessed 29 April 2018).
Billington, Michael (2015), '*Othello* Review – History Is Made with RSC's Fresh Take on the Tragedy', *The Guardian*, 12 June. Available online: www.theguardian.com/stage/2015/jun/12/othello-rsc-stratford-hugh-quarshie-lucian-msamati-joanna-vanderham (accessed 29 April 2018).
Billington, Michael (2017), '*Julius Caesar/Antony and Cleopatra* Review – Rome Truths from the RSC', *The Guardian*, 24 March.

Available online: www.theguardian.com/stage/2017/mar/24/julius-caesar-antony-and-cleopatra-rsc-review-rome-season (accessed 29 March 2018).

Brantley, Ben (2014), 'Shakespeare Hits the Beach: An "Antony and Cleopatra" Set in the Caribbean', *The New York Times*, 5 March. Available online: www.nytimes.com/2014/03/06/theater/an-antony-and-cleopatra-set-in-the-caribbean.html?rref=collection%2Fbyline%2Fben-brantley&action=click&contentCollection=undefined&region=stream&module=stream_unit&version=search&contentPlacement=1&pgtype=collection (accessed 29 April 2018).

Brathwaite, Edward Kamau ([1969] 1973), 'Caliban', in *The Arrivants: A New World Trilogy – Rights of Passage, Islands, Masks*, Oxford: Oxford University Press.

Britton, Dennis Austin (2014), *Becoming Christian: Race, Reformation, and Early Modern English Romance*, New York: Fordham University Press.

Brown, Paul (1985), '"This thing of darkness I acknowledge mine": *The Tempest* and the Discourse of Colonialism', in Jonathan Dollimore and Alan Sinfield (eds), *Political Shakespeare: New Essays in Cultural Materialism*, 48–71, Ithaca, NY: Cornell University Press.

Bruster, Douglas (2000), *Quoting Shakespeare: Form and Culture in Early Modern Drama*, Lincoln: University of Nebraska Press.

Burnett, Mark Thornton (2013), *Shakespeare and World Cinema*, Cambridge: Cambridge University Press.

Burton, Jonathan (2005), *Traffic and Turning: Islam and English Drama, 1579–1624*, Newark: University of Delaware Press.

Butler, Martin, ed. (2005), *Cymbeline by Shakespeare*, Cambridge: Cambridge University Press.

Calderwood, James (1983), *To Be or Not to Be: Negation and Metadrama in Hamlet*, New York: Columbia University Press.

Callaghan, Dympna (2000), *Shakespeare without Women: Representing Gender and Race on the Renaissance Stage*, London: Routledge.

Callaghan, Dympna, ed. (2016), *A Feminist Companion to Shakespeare*, Oxford: Wiley Blackwell.

Carey, Daniel and Claire Jowitt (2012), *Richard Hakluyt and Travel Writing in Early Modern Europe*, London: Ashgate.

Carroll, Clare (2004), 'Between Hope and Fear: Jews in Early Modern Europe', in Vincent P. Carey (ed.), *Voices for Tolerance in an Age of Persecution*, 6–84, Washington, DC: The Folger Shakespeare Library.

Cartelli, Thomas (1987), 'Prospero in Africa: *The Tempest* as Colonialist Text and Pretext', in Jean E. Howard and Marion F. O'Connor (eds), *Shakespeare Reproduced: The Text in History and Ideology*, 99–115, London: Methuen.

Cavendish, Dominic (2012), '*Much Ado About Nothing*, RSC Courtyard Theatre, Stratford-upon-Avon, Review', *The Telegraph*, 2 August. Available online: http://www.telegraph.co.uk/culture/theatre/theatre-reviews/9447812/Much-Ado-About-Nothing-RSC-Courtyard-Theatre-Stratford-upon-Avon-review.html (accessed 29 April 2018).

Cavendish, Dominic (2015), '*Othello*, RSC Stratford, Review: "Electrifying"', *The Telegraph*, 12 June. Available online: www.telegraph.co.uk/culture/theatre/theatre-reviews/11663749/Othello-RSC-Stratford-review-electrifying.html (accessed 29 April 2018).

Cavendish, Dominic (2016), 'Emma Rice's *A Midsummer Night's Dream* had me transfixed at the Globe', *The Telegraph*, 6 May 2016. Available online: www.telegraph.co.uk/theatre/what-to-see/emma-rices-revolutionary-midsummer-nights-dream-had-me-transfixe/ (accessed 29 April 2018).

Cavendish, Dominic (2017), 'All dressed up with nowhere to go: *Julius Caesar* and *Antony and Cleopatra* at Royal Shakespeare Theatre – Review', *The Telegraph*, 25 March. Available online: http://www.telegraph.co.uk/theatre/what-to-see/julius-caesar-antony-cleopatra-royal-shakespeare-theatre-review/ (accessed 29 April 2018).

Césaire, Aimé (1969), *Une Tempête*, Paris: Editions du Seuil.

Césaire, Aimé (1992), *A Tempest*, trans. Richard Miller, New York: Ubu Repertory Theatre Publications.

Chakravarti, Paromita (2016), 'Review of *Haider*, dir. Vishal Bhardwaj', *Shakespeare Bulletin*, 34 (1): 129–132.

Chambers, E.P. (1923), *The Elizabethan Stage*, vol. I, Oxford: The Clarendon Press.

Charry, Brinda and Gitanjali Shahani (2014), 'The Global as Local: *Othello* as *Omkara*', in Craig Dionne and Parmita Kapadia (eds), *Bollywood Shakespeares*, 107–123, New York: Palgrave Macmillan.

Cherian, Jacob (2008), 'I am against actors who lie: Tim Supple', *The Economic Times*, 19 January. Available online: https://economictimes.indiatimes.com/opinion/interviews/i-am-against-actors-who-lie-tim-supple/articleshow/2712360.cms (accessed 29 April 2018).

Clapp, Susannah (2016), '*A Midsummer Night's Dream* Review – The Wildest of Dreams', *The Guardian*, 8 May. Available online: www.theguardian.com/stage/2016/may/08/midsummer-nights-dream-shakespeares-globe-theatre-review-emma-rice (accessed 29 April 2018).

Collington, Philip D. (2005), 'Othello the Traveler', *Early Theatre*, 8 (2): 73–100.

Coryat, Thomas (1611), *Coryat's Crudities: Hastily Gobbled upin Five Months Travels in France, Savoy, Italy … Switzerland*, London.

Cowhig, Ruth (1985), 'Blacks in English Renaissance Drama', in David Dabydeen (ed.), *The Black Presence in English Literature*, 1–25, Manchester: Manchester University Press.

Crenshaw, Kimberlé (1991), 'Mapping the Margins: Intersectionality, Identity Politics, and Violence against Women of Color', *Stanford Law Review*, 43 (6): 1241–1299.

Curtis, Michael (2017), 'The Canon Misfires at Cambridge University', *American Thinker*, 29 October. www.americanthinker.com/articles/2017/10/the_canon_misfires_at_cambridge_university.html.

Daileader, Celia R. (2006), 'The Cleopatra Complex: White Actresses on the Interracial "Classic" Stage', in Ayanna Thompson (ed.), *Colorblind Shakespeare: New Perspectives on Race and Performance*, 205–220, London: Routledge.

Davis, Gregson (1997), *Aimé Césaire*, Cambridge: Cambridge University Press.

Degenhardt, Jane Hwang (2010), *Islamic Conversion and Christian Resistance on the Early Modern Stage*, Edinburgh: Edinburgh University Press.

De Jongh, Nicholas (2007), 'An Eastern Enchantment: First Night', *Evening Standard*, 14 March. Excerpt available online: www.questia.com/newspaper/1G1-160554802/an-eastern-enchantment-first-night (accessed 29 April 2018).

Desmet, Christy and Robert Sawyer, eds (1999), *Shakespeare and Appropriation*, London: Routledge.

Dickson, Andrew (2015), 'Othello: The Role that Entices and Enrages Actors of All Skin Colors', *The Guardian*, 10 June. Available online: www.theguardian.com/stage/2015/jun/10/othello-actors-rsc-lucian-msamati-hugh-quarshie (accessed 8 May 2018).

Dimmock, Matthew (2005), *New Turkes: Dramatizing Islam and the Ottomans in Early Modern England*, Aldershot: Ashgate.

Dimmock, Matthew (2017), 'Bringing Strange Lands to London', Program Essay, Royal Opera House, *Otello* (Verdi), 36–39.

Dionne, Craig and Parmita Kapadia, eds (2008), *Native Shakespeares: Indigenous Appropriations on a Global Stage*, Aldershot: Ashgate.

Dionne, Craig and Parmita Kapadia, eds (2014), *Bollywood Shakespeares*, New York: Palgrave Macmillan.

Dollimore, Jonathan (1984), *Radical Tragedy: Religion, Ideology, and Power in the Drama of Shakespeare and His Contemporaries*, London: Prentice Hall/Harvester Wheatsheaf.

Dollimore, Jonathan and Alan Sinfield, eds (1985), *Political Shakespeare: New Essays in Cultural Materialism*, Ithaca, NY: Cornell University Press.

Doumerc, Eric (2014), 'Caliban Playing Pan: A Note on the Metamorphoses of Caliban in Edward Kamau's "Caliban"', *Caliban: French Journal of English Studies*, 52: 239–250. Available online: https://caliban.revues.org/664#text (accessed 27 March 2018).

Duncan-Jones, Katherine (1999), 'Caught in the Coils of Old Nile', *TLS*, 6 August: 18. Available online: www.the-tls.co.uk/articles/private/caught-in-the-coils-of-old-nile/ (accessed 29 April 2018).

Evans, Lloyd (2016), 'What an Extraordinary Debut for Emma Rice: Globe's *Midsummer Night's Dream* Reviewed', *The Spectator*, 21 May. Available online: www.spectator.co.uk/2016/05/what-an-extraordinary-debut-for-emma-rice-globes-midsummer-nights-dream-reviewed/ (accessed 29 April 2018).

Fairholt, Frederick William, ed. (1844), *Lord Mayors Pageants*, London: The Percy Society.

Faiz, Faiz Ahmed (1991), *The Rebel's Silhouette: Selected Poems by Faiz Ahmed Faiz*, trans. Agha Shahid Ali, Amherst: University of Massachusetts Press.

Faiz, Faiz Ahmed (2012), 'Intisaab' ('Dedication'), in Ali Madeeh and Shoaib Hashmi (eds), *The Way It Was Once: Faiz Ahmed Faiz: His Life and Poems*, 100–103, New Delhi: Harper Collins Publishers, India.

Faiz, Faiz Ahmed (2015), 'Gulon Mein Rang Bhare' ('Flowers Flush with Color'), in Kuldip Salil (ed. and trans.), *The Best of Faiz Ahmed Faiz*, Delhi, India: Rajpal and Sons. Translation Mine.

Fitz, L.T. (1977), 'Egyptian Queens and Male Reviewers: Sexist Attitudes in *Antony and Cleopatra*', *Shakespeare Quarterly*, 28 (3): 297–316.

Frasanelli, Pier Paolo (2008), 'Shakespeare and Transculturation: Aimé Césaire's *A Tempest*', in Craig Dionne and Parmita Kapadia (eds), *Native Shakespeares: Indigenous Appropriations on a Global Stage*, 174–86, Hampshire: Ashgate.

Frey, Charles (1979), '*The Tempest* and the New World', *Shakespeare Quarterly*, 30 (1): 29–41.

Fryer, Peter (1984), *Staying Power: The History of Black People in Britain*, London: Pluto Press.

Fuller, Mary C. (1995), *Voyages in Print: English Narratives of Travel to America, 1576–1624*, vol. 7, Cambridge: Cambridge University Press.

Gajowski, Evelyn (1992), '*Antony and Cleopatra*: Female Subjectivity and Orientalism', in *The Art of Loving: Female Subjectivity and Male Discursive Traditions in Shakespeare's Tragedies*, Newark: University of Delaware Press.

Gardner, Lyn (2016), '*A Midsummer Night's Dream* Review – Emma Rice Makes a Rowdy Globe Debut', *The Guardian*, 6 May. Available online: www.theguardian.com/culture/2016/may/06/a-midsummer-nights-dream-review-a-rowdy-night-out-but-less-can-be-more (accessed 28 April 2018).

Gerzina, Gretchen (1995), *Black London: Life Before Emancipation*, New Brunswick: Rutgers University Press.

Ghouse, Salim (1992), stage production of *Hamlet*, Bombay.

Gillies, John (1994), *Shakespeare and the Geography of Difference*, vol. 4, Cambridge: Cambridge University Press.

Goddard, Lynette (2017), 'Will We Ever Have a Black Desdemona?: Casting Josette Simon at the Royal Shakespeare Company', in Delia Jarrett-Macauley (ed.), *Shakespeare, Race, and Performance: The Diverse Bard*, 80–95, London: Routledge.

Greenblatt, Stephen (1980), *Renaissance Self-Fashioning: From More to Shakespeare*, Chicago: University of Chicago Press.

Greenblatt, Stephen (1990), 'Learning to Curse: Aspects of Linguistic Colonialism in the Sixteenth Century', in Stephen Greenblatt (ed.), *Learning to Curse: Essays in Modern Culture*, 16–39, London: Routledge.

Greenblatt, Stephen, ed. (1993), *New World Encounters*, Berkeley, CA: University of California Press.
Gregory, Derek (2004), *The Colonial Present: Afghanistan,Palestine, Iraq*, 1–15, Hoboken, NY: Wiley-Blackwell.
Gurr, Andrew (1992), *The Shakespearean Stage, 1574–1642*, Cambridge: Cambridge University Press.
Habib, Imtiaz (2008), *Black Lives in the English Archives, 1500–1677*, London: Ashgate.
Hadfield, Andrew (2001), *Amazons, Savages, and Machiavels: Travel and Colonial Writing in English, 1550–1630*, Oxford: Oxford University Press.
Hakluyt, Richard (1589 and 1598, 1599–1600), *The Principal Navigations, Voyages, and Discoveries of the English Nation*, London: George Bishop and Ralph Newberie.
Hall, Kim (1995), *'Things of Darkness': Economies of Race and Gender in Early Modern England*, Ithaca, NY: Cornell University Press.
Hall, Kim, ed. (2007), *Othello: Texts and Contexts*, Bedford: Macmillan.
Harbage, Alfred (1941), *Shakespeare's Audience*, New York: Columbia University Press.
Harrison, William (1577), *Description of England*, London: N. Trubner & co.
Heath, John Benjamin (1854), *Some Account of the Worshipful Company of Grocers of the City of London*, London: C. Whittington.
Helfers, James P. (1997), 'The Explorer or the Pilgrim?: Modern Critical Opinion and Editorial Methods of Richard Hakluyt and Samuel Purchas', *Studies in Philology*, 94 (2): 160–186.
Helgerson, Richard (1992), *Forms of Nationhood: The Elizabethan Writing of England*, Chicago: University of Chicago Press.
Hendricks, Margo (1996), '"Obscured by Dreams": Race, Empire, and Shakespeare's *A Midsummer Night's Dream*', *Shakespeare Quarterly*, 47 (1): 37–60.
Hendricks, Margo and Patricia Parker, eds (1994), *Women, 'Race', and Writing in the Early Modern Period*, London: Routledge.
Hennessey, Katherine (2018), *Shakespeare on the Arab Peninsula*, New York: Palgrave.
Hennessey, Katherine and Margaret Litvin, eds (2016), 'Introduction', *Arab Shakespeares, Critical Survey*, 28 (3): 1–7.

Heywood, Thomas (1612), *An Apology for Actors*, London: Nicholas Okes.

Holderness, Graham (2014), 'Introduction', in Sulayman Al-Bassam, *The Arab Shakespeare Trilogy*, viii–xii, London: Bloomsbury.

Holmberg, Eva Johanna (2011), *Jews in the Early Modern English Imagination: A Scattered Nation*, Farnham, UK: Ashgate.

Howard, Deborah (2005), 'The Status of the Oriental Traveler in Renaissance Venice', in Gerald Maclean (ed.), *Re-Orienting the Renaissance: Cultural Exchanges with the East*, 29–49, London: Palgrave.

Howard, Jean and Marion O'Connor, eds (1987), *Shakespeare Reproduced: The Text in History and Ideology*, London: Methuen.

Howard, Jean Elizabeth (2007), *Theater of a City: The Places of London Comedy, 1598–1642*, Philadelphia: University of Pennsylvania Press.

Huang, Alexa Cheng-Yuan (2009), *Chinese Shakespeares: Two Centuries of Cultural Exchange*, New York: Columbia University Press.

Huang, Alexa and Elizabeth Rivlin, eds (2014), *Shakespeare and the Ethics of Appropriation*, New York: Palgrave Macmillan.

Hulme, Peter (1986), *Colonial Encounters: Europe and the Native Caribbean, 1492–1797*, London: Methuen.

Hulme, Peter and William Sherman, eds (2000), *'The Tempest' and Its 'Travels'*, Philadelphia: University of Pennsylvania Press.

Irele, Abiola (1965), 'Negritude-Literature and Ideology', *The Journal of African Studies*, 3 (4): 499–526.

Iyengar, Sujata (2005), *Shades of Difference: Mythologies of Skin Color in Early Modern England*, Philadelphia: University of Pennsylvania Press.

James, Heather (1997), *Shakespeare's Troy: Drama, Politics, and the Translation of Empire*, vol. 22, Cambridge: Cambridge University Press.

Jarrett-Macauley, Delia, ed. (2017), *Shakespeare, Race and Performance: The Diverse Bard*, London: Routledge.

Jays, David (2017), 'Josette Simon, "Powerful women are reduced to being dishonourable"', *The Guardian*, 21 March. Available online: www.theguardian.com/stage/2017/mar/21/josette-simon-cleopatra-rsc-shakespeare (accessed 29 April 2018).

Johnson, David (1996), *Shakespeare in South Africa*, Oxford: Clarendon Press.

Jonson, Ben (1641), *Timber, or Discoveries Made upon Men and Matter*, London.

Joubin, Alexa Alice (2018), 'Introduction: Global Shakespeares in World Markets and Archives', *Borrowers and Lenders* (special issue), 11 (1): 1–11.

Jourdain, Silvester (1610), *A Discovery of the Bermudas, Otherwise Called the Ile of Divels*, London: John Windet.

Juyin, Jiao (1942), *Hamlet* [stage production].

Kabir, Ananya J. (2009), *Territory of Desire: Representing the Valley of Kashmir*, Minneapolis: University of Minnesota Press.

Kamps, Ivo and Jyotsna Singh, eds (2001), *Travel Knowledge: European 'Discoveries' in the Early Modern Period*, New York: Palgrave.

Kapadia, Parmita (2008), 'Jatra Shakespeare: Indigenous Indian Theatre and the Postcolonial Stage', in Craig Dionne and Parmita Kapadia (eds), *Native Shakespeares: Indigenous Appropriations on a Global Stage*, 91–103, Aldershot: Ashgate.

Karamcheti, Indira (1995), 'Caliban in the Classroom', in Jane Gallop (ed.), *Pedagogy: The Question of Impersonation*, 138–146, Bloomington: Indiana University Press.

Kaufmann, Miranda (2008a), 'Caspar Van Senden, Sir Thomas Shirley and the "Blackamoor" Project', *Historical Research*, 81 (212): 366–371.

Kaufmann, Miranda (2008b), '"Traces of Shame?": Review of Imtiaz Habib, *Black Lives in the English* Archives, 1500–1677', *TLS*, 26, 8 August.

Kellaway, Kate (2017), '*Antony and Cleopatra* Review – Josette Simon is a Cleopatra to die for', *The Guardian*, 2 April. Available online: www.theguardian.com/stage/2017/apr/02/antony-and-cleopatra-stratford-review-josette-simon (accessed 29 April 2018).

Kennedy, Maev (2017), 'Cambridge academics seek to "decolonise" English syllabus', *Guardian*, 25 October. Available online: https://www.theguardian.com/education/2017/oct/25/cambridge-academics-seek-to-decolonise-english-syllabus.

Kernan, Alvin (1998), 'Introduction', in William Shakespeare, *Othello*, second revised edition, New York: Penguin Signet Classics.

Khan, Iqbal (2012), 'Iqbal Khan 2012 Production', RSC *Much Ado about Nothing*. Available online: www.rsc.org.uk/much-ado-about-nothing/past-productions/iqbal-khan-2012-production (accessed 15 May 2018).

Khan, Iqbal (2017), '1960s Birmingham 2012 - Stratford-upon-Avon', in Delia Jarrett-Macauley (ed.), *Shakespeare, Race and Performance*, London: Routledge.

Knowles, Ric (2004), *Reading the Material Theatre*, Cambridge: Cambridge University Press.

Kpade, Sapo (2015), 'Interview with Lucian Msamati', *Media Diversified*, 3 June. Available online: https://mediadiversified.org/2015/06/03/interview-with-lucian-msamati-the-first-black-iago-at-the-royal-shakespeare-company/ (accessed 5 June 2018).

Lamming, George ([1960] 1992), *The Pleasures of Exile*, Ann Arbor: University of Michigan Press.

Lawrence, Ben (2016), 'Adrian Lester: "Soon race, class and gender won't matter"', *The Telegraph*, 24 January. Available at: www.telegraph.co.uk/theatre/actors/adrian-lester-soon-race-class-and-gender-wont-matter/ (accessed 29 April 2018).

LEAR (1997), [stage production] dir. Ong Keng Sen.

Lear Dreaming (2012), [stage production] Singapore: TheatreWorks (staged for two days at the Singapore Arts Festival on 31 May and 1 June). Available online: http://globalshakespeares.mit.edu/lear-dreaming-ong-keng-sen-2012/ (accessed 1 April 2018).

Lewin, Hugh (1981), *Bandiet: Seven Years in a South African Prison*, vol. 251, London: Heinemann.

Ley, Graham and Sarah Dadswell, eds (2012), *Critical Essays on British South Asian Theatre*, Exeter: Exeter University Press.

Little, Arthur (2000), *Shakespeare Jungle Fever: National-Imperial Re-visions of Race, Rape, and Sacrifice*, Stanford, CA: Stanford University Press.

Little, Arthur (2017), 'What's Shakespeare to Him and He to Shakespeare?', Shakespeare Association of America Annual Meeting, Plenary Session, 'The Color of Membership'. Available online: www.youtube.com/watch?v=4f8_sOAucWw (accessed 2 April 2018).

Litvin, Margaret (2011), *Hamlet's Arab Journey: Shakespeare's Prince and Nasser's Ghost*, Princeton, NJ: Princeton University Press.

Litvin, Margaret (2014), 'For the Record: Conversation with Sulayman Al-Bassam', in Alexa Huang and Elizabeth Rivlin (eds), *Shakespeare and the Ethics of Appropriation*, London: Palgrave Macmillan.

Litvin, Margaret (2017), 'Multilateral Reception: Three Lessons from the Arab *Hamlet* Tradition', *Middle Eastern Literatures*, 20 (1): 51–63.

Loomba, Ania (1989), *Gender, Race, Renaissance Drama*, Manchester: Manchester University Press.

Loomba, Ania (1996), 'Shakespeare and Cultural Difference', in Terence Hawkes (ed.), *Alternative Shakespeares*, vol. 2, London: Routledge.

Loomba, Ania (2016), 'The Great Indian Vanishing Trick: Colonialism, Property, and the Family in *A Midsummer Night's Dream*', in Dympna Callaghan (ed.), *A Feminist Companion to Shakespeare*, 181–205, Oxford: Wiley Blackwell.

Loomba, Ania and Martin Orkin, eds (1998), *Post-Colonial Shakespeares*, London: Routledge.

MacDonald, Joyce Green (2002), 'Sex, Race, and Empire in Shakespeare's *Antony and Cleopatra*', in *Women and Race in Early Modern Texts*, Cambridge: Cambridge University Press.

Maclean, Gerald, ed. (2005), *Re-Orienting the Renaissance: Cultural Exchanges with the East*, London: Palgrave.

Madelaine, Richard, ed. (1998), *Antony and Cleopatra (Shakespeare in Production)*, Cambridge: Cambridge University Press.

Maley, Willy (1999), 'Postcolonial Shakespeare: British Identity Formation and *Cymbeline*', in Jennifer Richards and James Knowles (eds), *Shakespeare's Late Plays: New Readings*, 145–157, Edinburgh: Edinburgh University Press.

Maley, Willy (2003), *Nation, State and Empire in English Renaissance Literature: Shakespeare to Milton*, Hampshire: Palgrave Macmillan.

Malone, Edmond (1808), *An Account of the Incidents, from Which the Title and Part of the Story of Shakespeare's* The Tempest *Were Derived*, London: C. and R. Baldwin.

Marmion, Patrick (2017), 'It's Sex, Chicanery and Sandals at the RSC: Patrick Marmion sees a lavish double bill of *Julius Caesar* and *Antony & Cleopatra* in Stratford', *Daily Mail*, 30 March. Available online: http://www.dailymail.co.uk/tvshowbiz/article-4366650/Review-RSC-s-Julius-Caesar-Antony-Cleopatra.html (accessed 29 April 2018).

Matar, Nabil (1998), *Islam in Britain, 1558–1685*, Cambridge: Cambridge University Press.

Matar, Nabil (1999), *Turks, Moors, and Englishmen in the Age of Discovery*, New York: Columbia University Press.

Merritt, J.F., ed. (2001), *Imagining Early Modern London: Perceptions and Portrayals of the City from Stow to Strype, 1596–1720*, Cambridge: Cambridge University Press.

Mikalachki, Jodi (1995), 'The Masculine Romance of Roman Britain: *Cymbeline* and Early Modern English Nationalism', *Shakespeare Quarterly*, 46 (3): 301–322.

Mikalachki, Jodi (1998), *The Legacy of Boadicea: Gender and Nation in Early Modern England*, London: Routledge.

Moberly, David C. (2016), 'The Taming of the Tigress: Fatima Rushdi and the First Performance of the *Shrew* in Arabic', *Critical Survey*, Special Issue, 'Arab Shakespeares', 28 (3): 8–26.

Mondal, Monidipa (2008), 'Creating a Dream: An Interview with Tim Supple', *Ex Nihilo*, 1 February. Available online: https://exnihilomagazine.wordpress.com/2008/02/01/creating-a-dream-an-interview-with-tim-supple/ (accessed 28 April 2018).

Morley, Christopher (2015), 'Director Iqbal Khan: My grim view of Birmingham has changed', *Birmingham Post*, 20 April. Available online: www.birminghampost.co.uk/whats-on/arts-culture-news/director-iqbal-khan-grim-view-9080699 (accessed 27 April 2017).

Morris, Sylvia (2013), '"Far More Fair than Black": Cleopatra, Othello, and Blacks in Renaissance England', *The Shakespeare Blog*, 28 October. Available online: http://theshakespeareblog.com/2013/10/far-more-fair-than-black-cleopatra-othello-and-blacks-in-renaissance-england/ (accessed 28 April 2018).

Moryson, Fynes (1617), *Itinerary*, London: J. Beale.

'*Much Ado About Nothing*, Courtyard Theatre, Review' (2012), *Evening Standard*, 2 August. Available online: www.standard.co.uk/go/london/theatre/much-ado-about-nothing-rsc-courtyard-review-8001453.html (accessed 28 April 2018).

Mufti, Aamir (2004), 'Towards a Lyric History of India', *boundary 2*, 31 (2): 245–274.

Neill, Michael, ed. (1994), 'Introduction', in William Shakespeare, *Antony and Cleopatra*, 1–130, Oxford: Oxford University Press.

Neill, Michael (2000), *Putting History to the Question: Power, Politics, and Society in English Renaissance Drama*, New York: Columbia University Press.

Newman, Karen (1987), '"And Wash the Ethiop White": Femininity and the Monstrous in *Othello*', in Jean E. Howard and Marion

F. O'Connor (eds), *Shakespeare Reproduced: The Text in History and Ideology*, 141–162, London: Methuen.

Ngũgĩ, W.T. Wa Thiong'o (1975), *A Grain of Wheat*, London: Heinemann.

Ngũgĩ, W.T. Wa Thiong'o (1986), *Decolonising the Mind: The Politics of Language in African Culture*, London: James Currey.

Nightingale, Benedict (2007), 'Review of *A Midsummer Night's Dream*', *The Telegraph*, 15 March.

Nixon, Rob (1987), 'Caribbean and African Appropriations of *The Tempest*', *Critical Inquiry*, 13 (3): 557–578.

Norman, Neil (2012), 'Theatre Review: *Much Ado about Nothing*, RSC Courtyard Theatre and Noel Coward Theatre', *Express*, 3 August. Available online: http://www.express.co.uk/entertainment/theatre/337099/Theatre-Review-Much-Ado-About-Nothing-RSC-Courtyard-Theatre-and-Noel-Coward-Theatre (accessed 28 April 2018).

Norman, Neil (2016), 'Theatre Review: *A Midsummer Night's Dream* at the Shakespeare's Globe', *Express*, 13 May. Available online: www.express.co.uk/entertainment/theatre/669708/Theatre-review-A-Midsummer-Night-s-Dream-at-the-Shakespeare-s-Globe (accessed 28 April 2018).

Nyquist, Mary (1994), '"Profuse, Proud Cleopatra": "Barbarism" and Female Rule in Early Modern English Republicanism', *Women's Studies*, 24 (1–2): 85–30.

Orkin, Martin (1987a), '*Othello* and the Plain Face of Racism', *Shakespeare Quarterly*, 38: 166–188.

Orkin, Martin (1987b), *Shakespeare Against Apartheid*, Johannesburg: Ad Donker Publishers.

Orkin, Martin (2005), *Local Shakespeares: Proximations and Power*, London: Taylor & Francis.

Pacquet, Sandra Souchet ([1960] 1992), 'Foreword', in George Lamming, *The Pleasures of Exile*, vii–xxvii, Ann Arbor: University of Michigan Press.

Panja, Shormistha (2017), 'Curfewed Night in Elsinore: Vishal Bhardwaj's *Haider*', in Shweta Rao Garg and Deepti Gupta (eds), *The English Paradigm in India*, 101–109, London and Singapore: Palgrave Macmillan.

Panjwani, Varsha (2017), 'Much Ado about Knotting: Arranged Marriages in British–Asian Shakespeare Productions', in Delia Jarrett-Macauley (ed.), *Shakespeare, Race and Performance: The Diverse Bard*, 96–109, London: Routledge.

Parry, Benita (2004), *Postcolonial Studies: A Materialist Critique*, London: Routledge.
Patel, Chandrika (2012), 'Imagine Indiaah ... on the British Stage: Exploring Tara's "Binglish" and Tamasha's Ethnic Approaches', in Graham Ley and Sarah Dadswell (eds), *Critical Essays on British South Asian Theatre*, Exeter: Exeter University Press.
Peck, Linda Levy (2005), *Consuming Splendor: Society and Culture in Seventeenth-Century England*, Cambridge: Cambridge University Press.
Peer, Basharat (2010), *Curfewed Night*, New York: Scribner.
Platter, Thomas ([1599] 1937), *Thomas Platter's Travels in England, 1599*, ed. Claire Williams, London: Jonathan Cape.
Porter, Lisa (2013), 'Ong Keng Sen's *Lear Dreaming*: Humanity and Power in Process', *Theatre Forum*, 43: 80–90. Available online: www.questia.com/library/journal/1P3-3113656431/ong-keng-sen-s-lear-dreaming-humanity-and-power-in (accessed 1 April 2018).
Purchas, Samuel (1625), *Purchas His Pilgrims in Five Books*, London: Henry Fetherston.
Quarmby, Kevin (2012), '*Much Ado about Nothing*', British Theatre Guide. Available online: http://www.britishtheatreguide.info/reviews/much-ado-about-rsc-courtyard-t-7732 (accessed 28 April 2018).
Raleigh, Walter (1596), *The Discovery of the Large, Rich, and Beautiful Empyre of Guiana*, London: Robert Robinson.
Raman, Shankar (2001), *Framing India: The Colonial Imaginary in Early Modern Culture*, Stanford, CA: Stanford University Press.
Retamar, Roberto Fernandez (1989), 'Caliban: Notes Toward a Discussion of Culture in Our America,' in Edward Baker (trans.), *Caliban and Other Essays*, 14, Minneapolis: University of Minnesota Press.
Rowland, Brittany (2016), 'Othello and Tim Blake Nelson's "O": Shakespearean Violence in High School', *ReelRundown*, 15 June. Available online: https://reelrundown.com/movies/Othello-and-Tim-Blake-Nelsons-O-Shakespearean-Violence-in-High-School (accessed 28 April 2018).
Royster, Francesca T. (2003), *Becoming Cleopatra: The Shifting Image of an Icon*, London: Palgrave.
Said, Edward (1978), *Orientalism*, 1st ed., New York: Pantheon Books.
Said, Edward (1979), *Orientalism*, New York: Vintage Books.

Said, Edward (1993), *Culture and Imperialism*, New York: Vintage Books.
Saltz, Rachel (2014), 'Shakespearean Revenge in a Violent Kashmir', *The New York Times*, 3 October. Available online: www.nytimes.com/2014/10/03/movies/haider-puts-an-indian-twist-on-hamlet.html (accessed 29 April 2018).
Semenza, Gregory M. Colón (2005), 'Shakespeare after Columbine: Teen Violence in Tim Blake Nelson's" O"', *College Literature*, 32 (4): 99–124.
Sen, Amrita (2011a), 'Changelings, Bottom, and Domestic Transculturation: Finding the Indian in *A Midsummer Night's Dream*', PhD diss., Michigan State University, East Lansing, MI.
Sen, Amrita (2011b), 'Trading India: Commerce, Spectacle, and Otherness in Early Modern England', PhD diss., Michigan State University, East Lansing, MI.
Sen, Amrita (2017), 'Locating *Hamlet* in Kashmir: *Haider*, Terrorism, and Transmission', in Sonya Freeman Loftis, Allison Kellar, and Lisa Ulevich (eds), *Shakespeare's Hamlet in an Era of Textual Exhaustion*, 87–98, London: Routledge.
Sen, Ong Keng (2015), *Lear Dreaming, Director's Notes*, Theatreworks. Available online: www.theatreworks.org.sg/international/leardreaming/notes.htm (accessed 18 May 2018).
Shahani, Gitanjali (2014), 'The Spiced Indian Air in Early Modern England', *Shakespeare Studies*, 42: 122–137.
Shakespeare, William (1997), *King Lear*, ed. R.A. Foakes, London: Bloomsbury Arden.
Shakespeare, William (2005), *Cymbeline*, ed. Martin Butler, Cambridge: Cambridge University Press.
Shakespeare, William (2006), *The Tragedy of Antony and Cleopatra*, ed. John Wilders, London: Bloomsbury Arden.
Shakespeare, William (2010), *The Merchant of Venice*, ed. John Drakakis, London: Bloomsbury Arden.
Shakespeare, William (2011), *The Tempest*, ed. Virginia Mason Vaughan and Alden T. Vaughan, London: Bloomsbury Arden.
Shakespeare, William (2016), *Hamlet*, ed. Ann Thompson and Neil Taylor, London: Bloomsbury Arden.
Shakespeare, William (2016), *Henry IV Part II*, ed. James C. Bulman, London: Bloomsbury Arden
Shakespeare, William (2016), *Othello*, ed. E.A.J. Honigmann and Ayanna Thompson, revised edn, London: Bloomsbury Arden.

Shakespeare, William (2017), *A Midsummer Night's Dream*, ed. Sukanta Chaudhuri, London: Bloomsbury Arden.

Shapiro, James (1996), *Shakespeare and the Jews*, New York: Columbia University Press.

Sharma, Aasheesh (2006), 'Decadent writers came after Shakespeare: Tim Supple', *India Today*, 10 April. Available online: www.indiatoday.in/magazine/interview/story/20060410-decadent-writers-came-after-shakespeare-tim-supple-783428-2006-04-10 (accessed 29 April 2018).

Sharma, Sanjukta (2014), 'Film Review | Haider', *Live Mint*, 3 October. Available online: http://www.livemint.com/Leisure/NLNfyiXDL31Dq9zF0NZU8N/Film-review–Haider.html (accessed 29 April 2018).

Sheikh, Nilima (2014), 'Each Night Put Kashmir in Your Dreams', exhibition brochure, Art Institute of Chicago, 8 March.

Simon, Scott (2014), 'Interview with Basharat Peer: New Shakespeare Movie Puts *Hamlet* in Kashmir', National Public Radio, 25 October. Available online: www.npr.org/2014/10/25/358789984/new-shakespeare-movie-puts-hamlet-in-kashmir (accessed 14 April 2018).

Singh, Harmeet (2014), '"Kashmir is the *Hamlet* of my Film", says Vishal Bhardwaj on *Haider*', *The Indian Express*, 5 October. Available online: http://indianexpress.com/article/entertainment/bollywood/kashmir-is-the-hamlet-of-my-film/ (accessed 28 April 2018).

Singh, Jyotsna (1989), 'Different Shakespeares: The Bard in Colonial/Postcolonial India', *Theatre Journal*, 41 (4): 445–458.

Singh, Jyotsna (1994), 'Othello's Identity: Post-colonial Theory and Contemporary African Re-writings of *Othello*', in M. Hendricks and P. Parker (eds), *Women, 'Race', and Writing in the Early Modern Period*, 287–299, London: Routledge.

Singh, Jyotsna, G. (1996), 'Caliban versus Miranda: Race and Gender Conflicts in Post-Colonial Rewritings of *The Tempest*', in V. Traub, M.L. Kaplan, and D. Callaghan (eds), *Feminist Readings of Early Modern Culture: Emerging Subjects*, 191–209, Cambridge: Cambridge University Press.

Singh, Jyotsna, G. (2004), 'Islam in the European Imaginary in the Early Modern Period', in Vincent P. Carey (ed.), *Voices for Tolerance in an Age of Persecution*, 85–92, Washington, DC: The Folger Shakespeare Library.

Singh, Jyotsna, G. (2008), 'Afterword', in Craig Dionne and Parmita Kapadia (eds), *Native Shakespeares*, New York: Palgrave.

Singh, Jyotsna (2012), 'Wooing and Wedding in *Much Ado about Nothing*', *Much Ado about Nothing* RSC programme.

Singh, Jyotsna, G. (2013), *A Companion to the Global Renaissance: English Literature and Culture in the Era of Expansion*, Oxford: Wiley Blackwell.

Singh, Jyotsna, G. (2016), 'Introduction', in *The Postcolonial World*, 1–32, London: Routledge.

Singh, Jyotsna G. and Abdulhamit Arvas (2015), 'Global Shakespeares, Affective Histories, Cultural Memories', *Shakespeare Survey (Shakespeare, Origins and Originality)*, 68: 183–196.

Singh, Jyotsna G. and Gitanjali Shahani (2010), 'Postcolonial Shakespeare Revisited', *Shakespeare*, 6 (1): 127–138.

Skura, Meredith A. (1989), 'Discourse and the Individual: The Case of Colonialism in *The Tempest*', *Shakespeare Quarterly*, 40 (1): 42–69.

Smith, Bruce (2016), 'Queer Goings-On', *A Midsummer Night's Dream*, programme, The Globe.

Smith, Ian (2009), *Race and Rhetoric in Renaissance England: Barbarian Errors*, New York: Palgrave Macmillan.

Spencer, Charles (2007), 'A Delirious Dream of India', *The Telegraph*, 15 March.

Spivak, Gayatri (1987), *In Other Worlds: Essays in Cultural Politics*, London: Routledge.

Stow, John (1598), *A Survey of London*, London: The History Press.

Stowe, David (1996), 'Uncolored People: The Rise of Whiteness Studies', *Lingua Franca*, September/October: 69–77. Available online: www.academia.edu/346081/Uncolored_People_The_Rise_of_Whiteness_Studies (accessed 22 May 2018).

Strachey, William (1609), 'A True Repertory of the Wracke and Redemption of Sir Thomas Gates', London.

Supple, Tim (2006), 'Director Interview: *A Midsummer Night's Dream*', RSC. Available online: www.rsc.org.uk/a-midsummer-nights-dream/past-productions/tim-supple-2006-production/director-interview (accessed 29 April 2018).

Sutherland, Gill (2017), 'REVIEW: Antony & Cleopatra, RSC', *Stratford-upon-Avon Herald*, 7 April. Available online: http://

www.stratford-herald.com/68677-review-antony-cleopatra-rsc. html (accessed 29 April 2018).

Taylor, P. (2015), '*Othello*, RSC, Stratford-upon-Avon, Review: "Racism still simmers in black Iago production"', *The Independent*, 15 June. Available online: www.independent. co.uk/arts-entertainment/theater-dance/reviews/othello-rsc-stratford-upon-avon-review-racism-still-simmers-in-black-iago-production-10320449.html (accessed 29 April 2018).

Taylor, Paul (2016), '*A Midsummer Night's Dream*, Shakespeare's Globe, Review: "Risky gender bending works like a charm"', *Independent*, 6 May. Available online: www.independent.co.uk/arts-entertainment/theatre-dance/reviews/a-midsummer-nights-dream-shakespeares-globe-review-risky-gender-bending-works-like-a-charm-a7016296.html (accessed 15 May 2018).

Thompson, Ayanna, ed. (2006), *Colorblind Shakespeare: New Perspectives on Race and Performance*, London: Routledge.

Thompson, Ayanna (2013), *Passing Strange: Shakespeare, Race, and Contemporary America*, New York: Oxford.

Tillyard, E.M.W. ([1943] 1953), *The Elizabethan World Picture: A Study of the Idea of Order in the Age of Shakespeare, Donne, and Milton*, New York: Vintage.

Tripney, Natasha (2016), 'Emma Rice's *A Midsummer Night's Dream* review at Shakespeare's Globe – "joyful"', *The Stage*, 6 May. Available online: www.thestage.co.uk/reviews/2016/a-midsummer-nights-dream-review-at-shakespeares-globe/ (accessed 29 April 2018).

Underdown, David (1985), *Revel, Riot, and Rebellion: Popular Politics and Culture in England, 1603–1660*, London: Oxford University Press.

Varma, Jatinder (2017), 'Classical Binglish in the Twenty-first Century', in Delia Jarrett-Macauley (ed.), *Shakespeare, Race and Performance: The Diverse Bard*, 30–42, London: Routledge.

Vaughan, Alden T. and Virginia Mason Vaughan (1991), *Shakespeare's Caliban: A Cultural History*, Cambridge: Cambridge University Press.

Vishwanathan, Gauri (1994), *Masks of Conquest: Literary Study and British Rule in India*, New York: Columbia University Press.

Visser, Nicholas (1997a), 'Postcoloniality of a Special Type: Theory and Its Appropriations in South Africa', *The Yearbook of English Studies*, 27: 79–94.

Visser, Nicholas (1997b), 'Shakespeare and Hanekom, *King Lear* and Land', *Textual Practice*, 11 (1): 25–37.
Vitkus, Daniel (2000), 'Introduction', in *Three Turk Plays from Early Modern England*, New York: Columbia University Press.
Vitkus, Daniel, ed., *Antony and Cleopatra: Texts and Contexts* (forthcoming).
Wallis, Patrick (2002), 'Review of *Imagining Early Modern London: Perceptions and Portrayals of the City from Stow to Strype* by J.F Merritt', *Reviews in History*, no. 281. Available online: http://www.history.ac.uk/reviews/review/281 (accessed 19 May 2018).
Wicker, Tom (2016), 'Iqbal Khan: "I want Shakespeare to speak urgently in a 21st-century context"', *The Stage*, 28 June. Available online: www.thestage.co.uk/features/interviews/2016/iqbal-khan-want-shakespeare-speak-urgently-21st-century-context/ (accessed 29 April 2018).

INDEX

Please note: page numbers in *italic type* indicate images.

Abd el-Ouahed ben Messaoud 61
actors/actresses of colour 118,
    152, 154. See also black
    actors/actresses
Adelman, Janet 207 n.24
Africanus, Leo 51
Agra Road (Tanvir) 163
Aldridge, Ira 115, 118
Ali, Agha Shahid 181, 186,
    189–91, 193
An Apology for Actors
    (Heywood) 70
anti-Semitism 41, 44
Antony and Cleopatra 111
    and the role of race in the
    casting of Cleopatra
    109–18, 150–1
apartheid 97–8, 103–4, 106,
    122. See also South
    Africa
appropriation, poetics and
    politics of 127–38
Apuleius 78
Arab Shakespeares 138–47
*The Arab Shakespeare Trilogy,
    Three Plays* (Al-Bassam)
    143
The Arrivants (Brathwaite) 90
Arvas, Abdulhamit 77
auteurs 13, 136, 143, 156, 178

Babb, Shirine 114
Bahl, Ankur 151

Bandiet (Lewin) 103
Barker, Francis 29
Bartels, Emily 63
Al-Bassam, Sulayman 136–7,
    143–4
The Battle of Alcazar (Peele)
    24, 72
Bazaz, Abir 181, 191–3
*Becoming Cleopatra: The
    Shifting Image of an Icon*
    (Royster) 116
Benson, Constance 113
Best, George 51–2
'Beyond Colonial Tropes:
    Two Productions of A
    *Midsummer Night's
    Dream* in Palestine' (Al-
    Saber) 141
Bhabha, Homi 94
Bhamra, Samir 151
Bhardwaj, Vishal 136, 143,
    178, 193
Bhattacharjee, Paul (as
    Benedick) *172*
'Binglish' 150
black actors/actresses 110, 112–
    14, 150–1, 153, 155, 166.
    See also actors/actresses
    of colour
black and Asian Shakespeare
    Emma Rice's *A Midsummer
    Night's Dream* 164–9
    familiar practitioners 151

INDEX

imagining 'India' on the stage 157–9
Iqbal Khan's *Much Ado About Nothing* 169–75
multi-racial Shakespeares in Britain 149–57
Tim Supple's *A Midsummer Night's Dream* 159–64
Black Lives in the English Archives 1500–1677 (Habib) 67
black people
 Elizabeth's expulsion order 62–3
 presence in early modern England 67–8
Bollywood 164, 171, 178, 183
Bollywood Shakespeares (Dionne/Kapadia) 5
boundary crossings, on the British Shakespearean stage 149–75. *See also* cultural boundary crossing
Brandon, Samuel 114
Brathwaite, E.P. Kamau 16, 83, 89–91
Brewster, Yvonne 150–1
Britain, multi-racial Shakespeares in 149–57
Britishness 150
Brook, Peter 134, 159
Brotton, Jerry 32
Brown, Paul 27–30, 33, 40, 96
Bruster, Douglas 31–3
Burnett, Mark Thornton 178
Burton, Jonathan 26
Burton, Josephine 160

Calderwood, James L. 180–1

'Caliban' (Brathwaite) 89–91
'Caliban' (Retamar) 89
Callaghan, Dympna 33, 75
Canterbury Tales (Chaucer) 78
Carey, Daniel 35, 37–8
Carroll, Clare 42
Cartelli, Thomas 92
Cary, Elizabeth 115
Caxton, William 35
Césaire, Aimé 16, 27
Chambers, E.P. 57
Chaucer, Geoffrey 78
Chinese Shakespeares (Huang) 131
Christianity 25, 36, 45, 50
A Christian Turned Turk (Daborne) 72
Ciceronis Amor (Greene) 114
Cleopatra, role of race in casting 109–18, 150–1
Collington, Philip D. 54
colourblind casting 152, 166, 168
Columbus, Christopher 90
Consuming Splendor: Society and Culture in Seventeenth-century England (Peck) 66
Cope, Walter 59–60
Coryat, Thomas 45
Coryat's Crudities (Coryat) 45
The Country without a Post Office (Ali) 181, 190–1
critical elaboration, Gramsci on 1
Croll, Dona 151
cultural boundary crossing
 on the British Shakespearean stage 149–75
 Emma Rice's *A Midsummer Night's Dream* 164–9

examples of non-traditional
    casting 152
imagining 'India' on the
    stage 157–9
Iqbal Khan's *Much Ado
    About Nothing*
    169–75
multi-racial Shakespeares in
    Britain 149–57
Tim Supple's *A Midsummer
    Night's Dream* 159–64
Culture and Imperialism (Said)
    94
Curfewed Night (Peer) 181,
    184, 189, 191
Cymbeline
    Maley's and Orkin's
        postcolonial readings
        119–24

Daborne, William 72
Dash Arts 160
Davies, Geraint Wyn 114
decolonization, legacies of. *See*
    legacies of decolonization
*Decolonizing the Mind: the
    Politics of Language
    in African Literature*
    (Ngugi) 91–2
Description of England
    (Harrison) 67
Dido, Queen of Carthage
    (Marlowe) 24
'Different Shakespeares: The Bard
    in Colonial/Postcolonial
    India' (Singh) 96–7
Dionne, Craig 5
Discovery of the Bermudas
    (Jourdain) 33
Dolan, Frances 32

Doumerc, Eric 90
Drake, Francis 70
Dumas, Alexandre 140
Duncan-Jones, Katherine 113
Dutch East India Company 59,
    107

'Each Night Put Kashmir your
    Dreams' (Sheikh) 181, 193
East India Company 59, 69, 73
    formation 64
El Dorado 31
Elizabeth I 47, 61–2, 64
Epistle Dedicatory (Hakluyt) 37
expulsions
    of black people 62–3
    of Jews 42–3, 63–4

*The Fair Maid of the West–Part
    I* (Heywood) 72
Faiz, Faiz Ahmed 181, 185–6,
    188–9, 191
'Farewell' (Ali) 191
Fearon, Ray 151
female sexuality, imperial
    control and regulation 28
Festival d'Hammamet 84
Fortune-Lloyd, Jacob 153
Frey, Charles 30

Gajowski, Evelyn 118
Gamlet (Kozintsev) 140
Gascoigne, George 114
Gatwa, Ncuti 151
Gaur, Meenu 181
*A Geographical History of
    Africa* (Leo Africanus) 51
Ghouse, Salim 134–5
global representations on the
    London stage 68–78

Globe Theatre 71
Golden Ass (Apuleius) 78
A Grain of Wheat (Ngũgĩ) 92
Gramsci, Antonio 1
Green, Dorothy 113
Greenblatt, Stephen 29–30
Greene, Robert 72
Gupta, Tanika 151
Gurr, Andrew 69

Habib, Imtiaz 53, 67–8
Haider (Bhardwaj) 137, 178
   reconstituting the cultural ruins of Kashmir 177–94
Hakluyt, Richard (*The Principall Navigations*) 36–8, 59
Hakluytus Posthumous, or Purchas his Pilgrims (Purchas) 36, 38, 65
Hall, Kim 28, 34, 36, 41, 49, 52
Hamlet (Kozintsev) 180
Hamlet. *See also Haider* (Bhardwaj)
   Arabic text 140
   Bhardwaj's Indian appropriation, *Haider* 136–8, 178
   Chinese-language production 131
   French adaptation 140
   intercultural relevance 134–5, 140
   Jatra production 134–5
Harbage, Alfred 70
Harewood, David 151
Haroon and the Sea of Stories (Rushdie), Tim Supple's production 160
Harrison, William 67
Hawkins, John 51, 59
Helfers, James P. 37

Hendricks, Margo 7, 73–4, 76, 102
Hennessey, Katherine 136, 138
Henry IV, Part 2 57, 72
Heywood, Thomas 72
historical perspectives
   colonial encounters in early modern literature 23–34
   global imaginings on the London stage 68–78
   racial and cultural milieu of early modern London 58–68
   racial and religious identity 48–55
   voyages of discovery and trade 35–48
Holderness, Graham 143
Holmberg, Eva Johanna 44
Howard, Deborah 42
Howard, Jean E. 71
Huang, Alexa (Alexa Alice Joubin) 131–2
Hulme, Peter 24, 29, 40, 96

India
   English literature as a field of academic study in 16
   imagining 'India' on the stage 157–9
   Indian themes in Shakespeare's plays 73–8
Indian boy (changeling) 1, 74–8, 168, 214 n.13
'In Praise of a Gentlewoman' (Gascoigne) 114
inter-culturalism
   Arab Shakespeares 138–47
   Hamlet, Arabic text 140
   multifarious forms and interpretations of Shakespeare plays 128

poetics and politics of
appropriation 127–38
intersectional struggle
Antony and Cleopatra
109–18
Cymbeline 119–24
King Lear 106–9
representations
postcolonially themed
criticism 105–24
'Shakespeare–Postcoloniality',
Johannesburg 1996
(conference) 101–4
Ireland, colonial perspective
40–1
'I See Kashmir from New Delhi
at Midnight' (Ali) 193
Islam 25, 50–1, 62, 69
Islamic culture, playing out of
fears and fantasies about 72
Islands (Brathwaite) 83, 90
Itinerary (Moryson) 70
Iyengar, Sujata 51

Jalaluddin Akbar 64
James, Heather 124
Jarrett-Macauley, Delia 151
Jatra (Bengali folk theatre) 134–5
'Jatra Shakespeare: Indigenous
Indian Theatre and
the Postcolonial Stage'
(Kapadia) 134
The Jew of Malta (Marlowe)
24, 72
Jews
expulsions of 42–3, 63–4
portrayal in English travel
writings 44–5
portrayal in *The Merchant
of Venice* 42, 45–6

Jiao Juyin 131
Jonson, Ben 68–9
Joubin, Alexa Alice. *See* Huang,
Alexa
Jowitt, Claire 37
Jules, Jenny 151

Kabir, Ananya J. 181
*Kamdeo Ka Apna, Vasant Ritu
Ka Sapna (The Love
God's Own, A Spring
Time Dream)* (Tanvir) 163
Kamps, Ivo 197 n.1
Kapadia, Parmita 5, 134
Karan, Amara (as Hero) 173
Kastan, David 32
Kaufmann, Miranda 68
Kemp, Will 32
Kernan, Alvin 53
Khan, Iqbal 109, 151–3
King Lear
Ong's multilingual
production 131–3
Visser's postcolonial reading
106–9
Kozintsev, Grigori 106, 140, 180

Lamming, George 16, 86
LEAR (Ong) 163
legacies of decolonization
81–94
Brathwaite's 'Caliban' 89–91
Césaire's *Une Tempête* 83–6
Lamming's *The Pleasures of
Exile* 86–8
Ngũgĩ's *Decolonizing the
Mind: the Politics of
Language in African
Literature* 91–2
Retamar's 'Caliban' 89

Leigh, Vivien 113
Lester, Adrian 151
Levant Company 59, 61
Lewin, Hugh 103
Little, Arthur 18, 114
Litvin, Margaret 128, 138, 140
Lives of the Romans (Plutarch) 78
Local Shakespeares (Orkin) 98
London
    early modern racial and cultural milieu 58–68
    global imaginings on the stage 68–78
Loomba, Ania 52–3, 75–6, 96

Macbeth
    Bhardwaj's appropriation 178
    depiction of international trade 64
    Jayaraj's adaptation, *Veeram* 16
MacDonald, Joyce Green 207 n.24
Madelaine, Richard 117
Malcolm X 84
Maley, Willy 119, 121, 123
Malone, Edmond 30
Maqbool (Bhardwaj) 178
Marlowe, Christopher 24, 69, 72
Massinger, Philip 24, 72
master–slave/servant relations
    in *A Midsummer Night's Dream* 77
    parallels between early modern England and modern day Delhi 169
    in *The Tempest* 86–7
Matar, Nabil 61, 72
Mau Mau rebellion 92–3

McIntosh, Yanna 114
Meow Meow 165
The Merchant of Venice
    location 42
    portrayal of Jews 42, 45–6
    racial conflict in 41–6
    relevance for postcolonial interpretation 24
    role of the mercantile economy 41, 43, 46
Metamorphoses (Ovid) 78
Middleton, Thomas 66
Midnight's Children (Rushdie), Tim Supple's production 160
A Midsummer Night's Dream 161, 167
    cultural and intersectional boundary crossing 157–8
    Eastern associations 64
    Emma Rice's adaptation 164–9
    Indian themes 73–8
    Palestinian productions 141–2
    possible reference to Elizabeth I 64
    Tim Supple's adaptation 159–64
Mikalachki, Jodi 123–4
Miller, Richard 84
miscegenation 52
Moberly, David 141
Moorish ambassador, portrait 61
Moryson, Fynes 70
Msamati, Lucian 151, 153–4, 156
Much Ado About Nothing 172, 173
    Iqbal Khan's adaptation 169–75

Mufti, Aamir 185
multi-racial Shakespeares in Britain 149–57
Muscovy Company 59
Mvula, Laura 109

Native Shakespeares (Dionne and Kapadia) 134
Nautanki 163
Nazki, Rashid 190
'Negritude' 84
Neill, Michael 43, 50, 52, 115
Newberry, John 64
Newman, Karen 53
Ngũgĩ Wa Thiong'o 16, 27, 83, 91–3
Northwest Passage 51
'"Nymphs and reapers heavily vanish": the Discursive Contexts of *The Tempest*' (Barker/Hulme) 29

'"Obscured by Dreams:" Race, Empire, and Shakespeare's *A Midsummer Night's Dream*' (Hendricks) 73–4
Omkara (Bhardwaj) 178
O (Nelson) 130
One Thousand and One Nights (Tim Supple's production) 160
Ong Keng Sen 131, 133–4, 163
Orientalism (Said) 1, 5, 14, 17, 26, 35, 91
and the paradigm shift in Shakespeare studies 94–9
Orkin, Martin 97–8, 102, 108, 121
Othello 156
Bhardwaj's adaptation 178
film version set in US high school 130
and the history of race and racism 97–8
Iago's racialized terminology 47
non-traditional casting in Iqbal Khan's RSC production 152–7
race, religion and identity 48–54
racial conflict in 47–8
relevance for postcolonial interpretation 24
and representations of otherness on the English stage 71–2
role of race in casting Iago 154, 156
and the visit of the Moorish ambassador 61
'Othello and the "Plain Face" of Racism' (Orkin) 97
otherness
allure 66–7
binary definitions 25
Othello and representations of on the English stage 71–2
in Shakespeare's works 71
Ovid 78
Oyelowo, David 151

The Palestinian Girl (Sobol) 121
Panja, Shormistha 185
Paradise on a River of Hell (Bazaz and Gaur) 181, 191–3
Peck, Linda Levy 66
Peele, George 24, 72

Peer, Basharat 181, 183, 185, 189–90, 193
Pericles 71
Platter, Thomas 59–61
The Pleasures of Exile (Lamming) 86–8
Plutarch 78
postcoloniality conference (1996), Johannesburg 101–5
'Postcoloniality of a Special Type' (Visser) 106
'Postcolonial Shakespeare: British Identity Formation and *Cymbeline*' (Maley) 119
postcolonial theory, concept 3
The principall Navigations, Voiages and Discoveries of the English nation (Hakluyt) 36–8
The Prison Notebooks (Gramsci) 1
proto-colonialism 1
Purchas, His Pilgrims (Purchas) 36, 38, 65
Purchas, Samuel 36, 38, 65
Putting History to the Question (Neill) 43, 50

Quarshie, Hugh 151, 155, 156
'Quoting the Playhouse in *The Tempest*' (Bruster) 31–2

Race, Gender, Renaissance Drama (Loomba) 96
racial perspectives
   historical perspective of racial and religious identity 48–55

Iago's racialized terminology in *Othello* 47
Othello and the history of race and racism 97–8
race, religion and identity in *Othello* 48–54
racial conflict in *The Tempest* 46–7
Raleigh, Walter 31, 59
Raman, Shankar 74–5
Renaissance Man 5, 17
The Renegado (Massinger) 24, 72
Retamar, Roberto Fernandez 27, 83
Rich, Barnabe 40
Richard III: An Arab Tragedy (Al-Bassam) 144–7
Riebeeck, Jan Van 107
Royster, Francesca T. 115–16
Rushdie, Salman 193

Al-Saber, Samer 141
Said, Edward 1, 3, 14, 118
Salve Deus Rex Judaeorum (Lanyer) 114
Sandys, George 44
Schechner, Richard 134
scholars of colour 18–19
Schouten, William Cornelison 51
Selimus (Greene) 72
Sen, Amrita 202 n.9
Serreau, Jean-Marie 84
Shades of Difference (Iyengar) 51
Shahani, Gitanjali
   Charry and 215 n.5
   and Singh 3
Shakespeare, Race and Performance: The Diverse Bard (Jarrett-Macauley) 11

Shakespeare Against Apartheid (Orkin) 108
'Shakespeare and Hanekon: *King Lear* and land' (Visser) 106
Shakespeare and the Jews (Shapiro) 63
Shakespeare in Production (Madelaine) 117
'Shakespeare–Postcoloniality', Johannesburg 1996 (conference) 101–4
Shakespeare studies, Said's *Orientalism* and the paradigm shift in 94–9
Shapiro, James 45, 63
Sharma, Madhav (as Leonato) 173
Sheikh, Nilima 181, 192–3
Simon, Josette 109–10, *111*, 114, 118, 151
Singh, Jyotsna G. 8, 53
Skura, Meredith 32–4
slave-trade related perspectives
  and England's imperial beginnings 67
  in Hakluyt's writings 37–8
  in John Hawkins' writings 59
  in *Othello* 47–9
  and racialism 51
  in *The Tempest* 47, 84, 86–7, 88–91, 93
Smith, Ian 53
Sobol, Joshua 121
South Africa. *See also* apartheid
  conference on Shakespeare and post-coloniality 101–4
  political background 102
  Truth and Reconciliation Commission 121–3
  and Visser's postcolonial reading of *King Lear* 106–9
Soweto 104
Speed, John 41
Spenser, Edmund 40
spice trade 64, 76–7
Spivak, Gayatri 94
Strachey, William 39
Supple, Tim 159
Survey of London (Stowe) 67
Syal, Meera 151, 169, 175
  as Beatrice *172*

Talawa Theatre Company 150
Tamburlaine (Marlowe) 24, 72
'The Taming of the Tigress: Fatima Rushdi and the First Performance of *Shrew* in Arabic' 141
Tanvir, Habib 163
Tara Arts 150–1
The Tempest
  borrowings from travel narratives 39
  Brathwaite's 'Caliban' 89–91
  Césaire's *Une Tempête* 83–6
  colonial implications 23–34
  'Dead Indian' 73
  Lamming's *The Pleasures of Exile* 86–8
  legacies of decolonization 81–94
  Ngũgĩ's *Decolonizing the Mind: the Politics of Language in African Literature* 91–2

Prospero's treatment of
   Caliban 2
 racial conflict in 46–7
 relevance for postcolonial
   interpretation 24
 Retamar's 'Caliban' 89
 topographical dualism 40
*Territory of Desire:
   Representing the Valley
   of Kashmir* (Kabir)
   181
*The Theatre of a City: The
   Places for London
   Comedy 1598–1642*
   (Howard) 71
*Theatre of the Empire of Great
   Britain* (Speed) 41
'"This thing of darkness I
   acknowledge mine":
   The Tempest and the
   discourse of colonialism'
   (Brown) 27
Thompson, Ayanna 152
Titus Andronicus 24, 72
tobacco 59
trade
   depiction of international
     trade in *Macbeth* 64
   trading companies in
     England and Europe 59
   voyages of discovery and
     35–48
Tragedy of Mariam (Cary) 115
travel and racial difference,
       early modern writings on
       47–8

*The Triumphs of Honor
   and Industry*
   (Middleton) 66
*The Triumphs of Honor and
   Vertue* (Middleton) 66
Troilus and Cressida 73
'A True Repertory of the
   Wracke, and Redemption
   of Sir Thomas Gates'
   (Strachey) 33, 39
Truth and Reconciliation
   Commission, South
   Africa 121–3

Ubuntu 123
Une Tempête (A Tempest)
   (Césaire) 83–6
Van Senden, Casper 62–3
Varma, Jatinder 150–1
Vasan, Anjana 151
Vaughan, Alden T. 39–41
Vaughan, Virginia Mason 33,
   39–41
Veeram (Jayaraj) 16
The Virtuous Octavia
   (Brandon) 114
Visser, Nicholas 106–9
Vitkus, Daniel 53, 72
voyages of discovery and trade
   35–48

Wallerstein, Immanuel 27
Walsingham, Francis 37
whiteness 3, 17–18, 96, 117,
   152, 155
world cinema 178

Printed in Dunstable, United Kingdom